T0300669

HEROD THE GREAT

Herod the Great

Jewish King in a Roman World

MARTIN GOODMAN

Yale
UNIVERSITY
PRESS
New Haven and London

Yale University Press books may be purchased in quantity for educational, business, or promotional use. For information, please e-mail sales.press@yale.edu (U.S. office) or sales@yaleup.co.uk (U.K. office).

Set in Janson Oldstyle type by Integrated Publishing Solutions.
Printed in the United States of America.

Library of Congress Control Number: 2023941995
ISBN 978-0-300-22841-0 (hardcover : alk. paper)

A catalogue record for this book is available from the British Library.

This paper meets the requirements of ANSI/NISO Z39.48-1992 (Permanence of Paper).

10 9 8 7 6 5 4 3 2 1

Frontispiece: Herod as pharaoh. The image of pharaoh in a woodblock created by Hans Holbein for the Froschauer Bible, first printed in 1531, used in 1546 to depict Herod. (Zurich, Zentralbibliothek, AW 14, p. xxv [*detail*])

ALSO BY MARTIN GOODMAN

A History of Judaism

Rome and Jerusalem: The Clash of Ancient Civilizations

Josephus's The Jewish War: A Biography

The Ruling Class of Judaea: The Origins of the Jewish Revolt Against Rome, A.D. 66–70

The Roman World, 44 B.C.–A.D. 180

Judaism in the Roman World: Collected Essays

Mission and Conversion: Proselytizing in the Religious History of the Roman Empire

State and Society in Roman Galilee, A.D. 132–212

Jews in a Graeco-Roman World (editor)

The Oxford Handbook of Jewish Studies (editor)

CONTENTS

MAPS

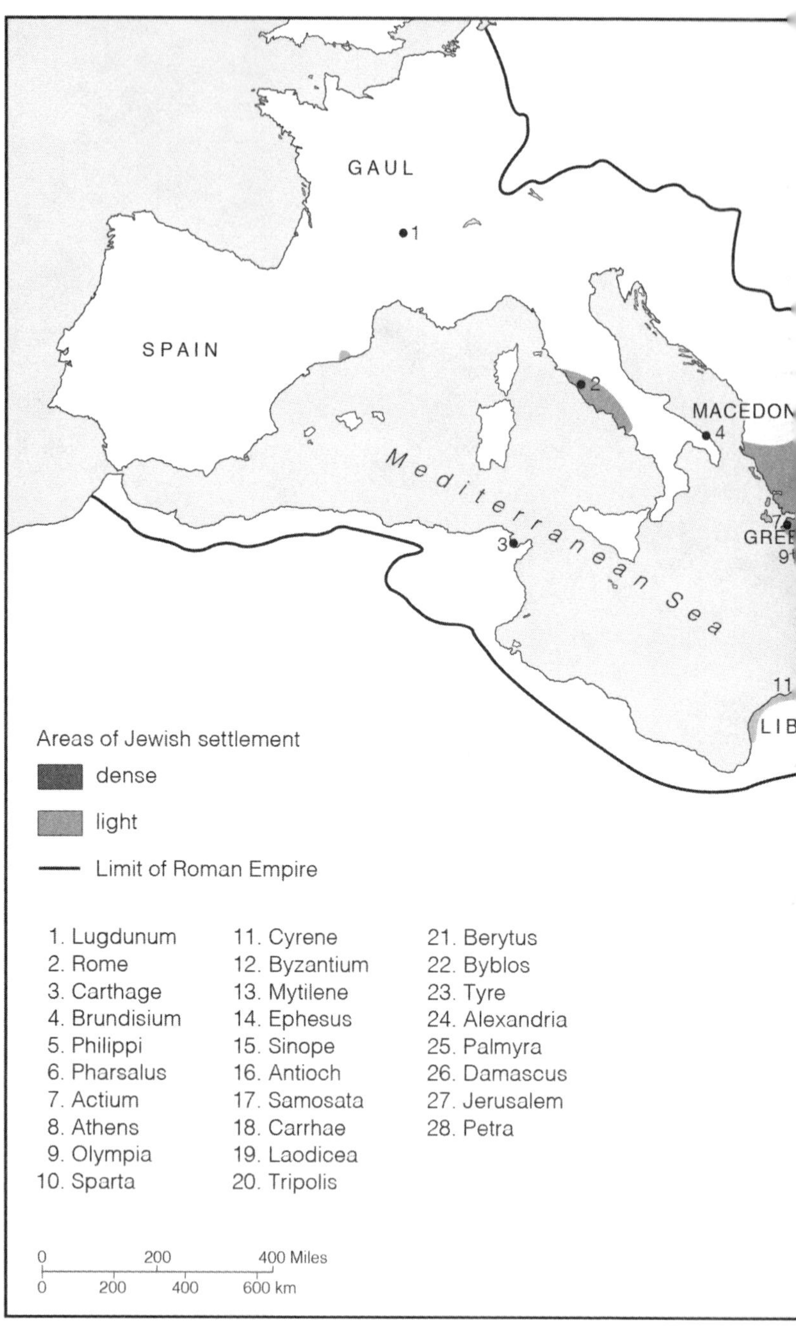

The Jewish world in the time of Herod. (Map drawn by Alison Wilkins)

Caspian Sea
Black Sea
15
BITHYNIA
PONTUS
ASIA MINOR
12
GALATIA
PHRYGIA
CAPPADOCIA
13
IONIA
14
LYCIA
CILICIA
COMMAGENE
MESOPOTAMIA
R.Tigris
PARTHIAN
EMPIRE
Cos
16
17
18
19
20
21
22
23
26
25
SYRIA
BABYLONIA
R. Euphrates
Cyprus
Crete
Persian Gulf
27
24
28
EGYPT
Red Sea
R. Nile

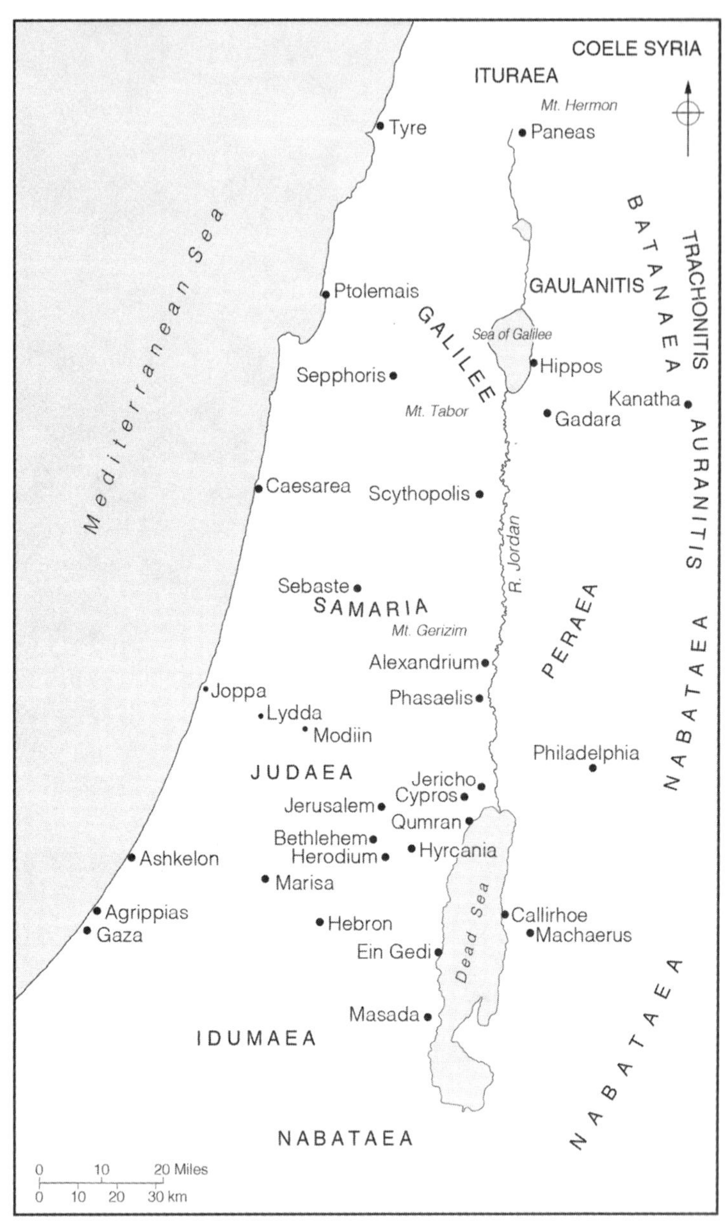

The kingdom of Herod in 4 BCE. (Map drawn by Alison Wilkins)

HEROD THE GREAT

PROLOGUE

A Jewish Life?

In December of 40 BCE Herod stood in the midst of the Senate in Rome—an exotic stranger examined with curiosity by a crowd of Roman aristocrats who debated his future in a language he did not understand. He had come as a suppliant, seeking aid in rescuing his country from the Parthian invaders who had occupied Jerusalem. His family had been left behind in desperate circumstances in a distant region of the world about which the senators knew and cared little. He had brought with him no troops, only a small coterie of companions, and no money. He had been in Rome for less than a week, and he had few acquaintances in the city and even fewer friends. But by the end of the day he had been proclaimed king of Judaea.[1]

The journey from Jerusalem to Rome had been perilous and exhausting. Herod had escaped his enemies by luck as he fled Jerusalem on horseback, accompanied only by a disorganized rabble. He had been forced to leave his womenfolk behind in the fortress of Masada, and he had been pursued by the dreadful news of the gruesome death of his beloved elder brother. Friends and allies in Nabataean Arabia on whose support he had thought he could rely had deserted him on the way. Only with difficulty had he made his way to the border with Egypt. He had nearly been stymied on arrival in the gleaming city of Alexandria by the great queen Cleopatra, who had expected him to stay with her at least until the safe sailing season in the spring. The voyage north from Egypt toward the southern coast of Asia Minor had indeed been beset by winter storms, and the ship reached the Aegean only after jettisoning cargo. Herod had acquired on credit a trireme on the island of Rhodes which enabled him to sail more rapidly to Brundisium (modern Brindisi), from which he followed the land route to Rome. At the age of thirty-three, he was making his first visit to Italy. He had no idea what would greet him on his arrival in the city which controlled the Mediterranean world, but he knew that he had to ingratiate himself with those few Roman leaders he had met during their tours of duty in the East if he were ever to return to his homeland.

On first sight the sprawl of brick buildings packed tight on the hills of Rome failed to impress him as he approached the city, passing between the elaborate family tombs that lined the Appian Way. Rome was to be transformed in Herod's lifetime, but for someone who had seen Alexandria and Antioch, with their regular street plans and magnificent monuments, Rome when Herod first visited did not look like the capital of an empire, despite the city's wealth and a rash of new public buildings. Yet all the world knew that Rome was where power lay. The serried ranks of hundreds of senators in their broad-striped white togas meeting in the somber surroundings of the Temple of Concord at the west end of the Forum presented an image of dignified entitlement by which strangers were expected to feel intimidated.

At least the senator who ushered him into the assembly was a friend; he had struck up an acquaintance with the man in Antioch a few years previously. Herod listened, only half comprehending, while this friend, Messalla Corvinus, praised him in eloquent Latin as a reliable ally of the Romans. Messalla reminded all present of the loyalty to Rome which had previously characterized Herod's father, Antipater. He called on the senators to recognize the contrast between Antipater's reliability and the double-dealing of the Hasmonaean high priest Antigonus, the king installed in Jerusalem by the Parthians, Rome's most powerful enemy. It was not difficult to arouse indignation against Antigonus. Many in Rome recalled the time in his youth when Antigonus was held captive in the city precisely to prevent him from interfering in the government of Judaea. Antigonus had more than once absconded to wreak mischief in his homeland, and the senators were incensed that he had spurned Roman authority so blatantly. Now he was declared an enemy of the Roman people.

Rejection of the legitimacy of Antigonus's rule was simple, but no amount of rhetoric would make a practical difference to his position in Judaea while he had the committed support of the Parthian forces which had brought him to power. The solution put before the Senate was bold. The Senate, assured that "it would be an advantage in their war with the Parthians that Herod should be king," endorsed unanimously a proposal by Mark Antony to offer Herod the throne.[2]

Enthusiasm for the proposal had been guaranteed by the status of the proposer. Mark Antony was the most powerful man in the Roman state. No one raised the obvious objection that it was a contravention of Roman custom to recognize a commoner as king over an allied nation rather than a scion of the current royal family. Unanimity was aided by the visible support of the young Octavian Caesar, the only politician in Rome in 40 BCE with the capacity to rival Antony. Only a few months earlier, war had threatened between the two men, but in October they had agreed on an accommodation which satisfied the immediate ambitions of each, and in November they had sealed their pact through the marriage of Antony to Octavian's sister. Now, as the Senate broke up after its meeting, Antony and Octavian flanked Herod as the new king, a powerful, athletic figure, distinctive in his Greek tunic among the crowd of robed senators, walked in formal procession behind the consuls and other magistrates from the Forum up to the Capitol to place there a copy of the decree which had just been passed and to attend a sacrifice to Jupiter Capitolinus. This dazzling first day of Herod's reign was rounded off with a feast provided in his honor by Mark Antony.

Everything had happened at extraordinary speed. Within a week Herod had left Italy and set off to take control of the kingdom so unexpectedly granted to him. Three years of arduous military operations followed before Herod was able to oust Antigonus and gain control of his capital, Jerusalem, but his reign was to last thirty-six years, until his death in 4 BCE. His rule brought him into close contact with many of the most powerful figures in the Roman world. It also transformed the landscape of the land of Israel.

Herod cared greatly about his reputation to posterity, so it is ironic that he is generally remembered not as a great monarch but as a murderous tyrant. With colossal ambition and vast expenditure he created a legacy which has survived up to the present day, including spectacular building projects on the grand scale, among them the monumental reconstruction of the Temple in Jerusalem with the vastly extended platform that still dominates the ancient city. Much is known about his achievements and travails, but posterity has found it harder to judge their significance. Should we marvel at his ability to establish himself as a great king despite his origins as an outsider? Should we admire the powerful personality which enabled him to impose his will on the world around him? Or should we sympathize with Herod as a victim—despite his bravado—of the political storms that overwhelmed the wider world during his reign and the intrigues of his dysfunctional family? How is it possible to empathize with a man who was so prone to the human frailties of jealousy and suspicion that later generations have portrayed him as a monster?

Above all, is it right to consider Herod's life a Jewish life? Modern visitors to Israel view the extant remains of his building program, from Caesarea to Masada and Herodium, as visible evidence of Jewish rule over the land two thousand years ago, but the buildings themselves lack any distinctively Jewish markers, and none, apart from the Temple and the patriarchal and matriarchal tombs in Hebron, has any obviously Jewish purpose. We have seen that the origins of Herod's rule lay not in Judaea but in Rome, where he celebrated his appointment to the throne by attending a sacrifice to Jupiter. How did the cities, palaces, pagan temples, and fortresses on which Herod expended so much of his wealth reflect his life as a Jewish king?[3]

Was he even Jewish? The Jewishness of Herod was questioned by some both in his lifetime and for centuries afterward. When in 1546 a printer in Zurich sought an illustration for an encounter between Herod and the aged Hasmonaean Hyrcanus to enhance a new translation from Hebrew into Yiddish of the standard history of Herod read by Jews in his time, the image he chose to copy from the Froschauer Bible portrayed Herod not as a Jewish king but as a pharaoh.

If, despite these later depictions, we can be certain (as we can) that Herod thought of himself as a Jew, we shall have to ask what sort of a Jew he considered himself to be, and how his Jewish identity shaped his tumultuous life close to the center of events during a revolution which reshaped not just Judaea but the whole Roman world.

* * *

Das xlvij. Cap.

Pharao heißt jnen das land Gosen eyngeben. Der hunger wirt so groß das die Egypter jr vych vnnd välder dem künig versetzend. Jsrael beschweert Joseph seiner begrebnuß halb.

A

D O kam Joseph vnd sagt Pharao an/vnd sprach: Mein vatter vnnd meine brüder/jr klein vnd groß vych / vnnd was sy habend / ist kommen auß dem land Canaan/vnd sihe/sy sind im land Go

Pharaoh greeting Joseph in the Froschauer Bible. (Zurich, Zentralbibliothek, AW 14, p. xxv [*detail*])

קויבן אונ׳ דארום. זא גיא אונ׳ זי׳ן אן דייבר שטאט אונ׳ רייין ד
דיך ביט מיא אן דיא שטרייטובן דער שטאט ירושלים. דיר צו
בויזט : אבר דער הורקנוס דער וואלט ביט הירן צ
צו אירן רידן אונ׳ ער גינג הורקנוס גען ירושלים :

וויא דער גיט וריס. אונ׳ אלט ואן דער קויבן הורקנוס צון צ
בבל קוימט גען ירושלים אויך דש בינגרן דיש קויבן הורודוס
דער אין הוך צו לישט טוירן ליס :

ווינא . אונ׳ ער גינג אויש דער הורודוס
צו גיגן אים. ער אונ׳ אלי זייני הערן מיט אים. אונ׳ ער האלזט א
אין אונ׳ ער קויסט אין אונ׳ ער בראלט אין צו זייבם הויז אונ׳
ער עירט אין זיר בור דען אויגן דיש בולקש אונ׳ ער מאלט צו
בור אים. איין פושט אלי טאג שטעטיגליך אונ׳ ער נענט אין ב
באטר בור דען אויגן דיש גאנבן בולק אבר אין הייאליכקייט ה
הט

The same image used in a Yiddish translation of *Sefer Yosippon* printed in 1546 to depict Herod greeting the former high priest Hyrcanus. (National Library of Israel, 8-91 A 549, p. 492 [*detail*])

Herod's non-Jewish contemporaries often displayed their busts on their coins, but Herod avoided public display of his image in Judaea, and no portrait of him survives from antiquity. Jews in later generations had to use their imaginations to depict the king in light of the literary tradition.

For most Jews in antiquity, the best a modern biographer can provide is an analysis of myths and legends, but in tracking the vicissitudes of Herod's Jewish life, we have the huge advantage that his long and tumultuous career is far better documented than that of any other Jew (Jesus apart) before the high Middle Ages. Much of this documentation is ultimately derived from the observations of a close adviser who was also a professional historian and biographer, Nicolaus of Damascus.[4]

Nicolaus was a Greek intellectual from a distinguished family in Damascus, in Syria. His own successful career as teacher, orator, and diplomat was recorded in a self-glorifying autobiography of which substantial fragments can still be read in excerpts preserved in Byzantium many centuries later by the scholar-emperor Constantine Porphyrogenitus. Nicolaus was a polymath. He composed philosophical and ethnographic works as well as tragedies and comedies. His greatest achievement was a universal history which covered all of world history in 144 books. Already sufficiently distinguished in his youth to be appointed tutor to the children of Antony and Cleopatra in Alexandria in the thirties BCE, in old age Nicolaus settled in Rome and became a friend of the emperor Augustus. Many of the years between his time in Alexandria and Rome were spent in Judaea at the court of Herod.

Nicolaus's origins in Damascus were probably what led him to focus the early part of his universal history on the empires of the ancient East. But Nicolaus was not himself a Jew, and it was his time in Herod's court that best explains his interest in the history of the Jews. No manuscripts of his great work survive, but we know that in at least two of the books (books 123 and 124) he presented a narrative of the reign of Herod, down to the king's death, full of circumstantial detail about events in court. As Herod's counselor and spokesman for at least the last ten years of the ruler's life, Nicolaus knew Herod very well. He had access to Herod's memoirs and he wrote as an insider within Herod's inner circle, with the raw immediacy of a contemporary observer and the passion of a participant in the destructive intrigues which marred Herod's last years.[5]

It is reasonable to wonder how objective such an account is likely to have been. Doubts were raised in antiquity by the Jewish historian Josephus, through whose own writings Nicolaus's history is preserved. Josephus, who was born four decades after the death of Herod, relied heavily on Nicolaus's *Universal History* for his narrative of Herod's rule, both in the first book of his account of the Jewish war against Rome, composed in the seventies CE, and in the much more extensive narrative he included in his monumental *Jewish Antiquities*, finished some two decades later, in 93. The *Antiquities*, which was intended primarily for a gentile Greek-speaking readership, covered in twenty books the history of the Jewish nation from the creation of the world down to his own time. That Josephus was able to devote no less than two and a half of these twenty books to the career of Herod, with numerous stories about his private life and political vicissitudes, was a direct result of the availability of the account composed by Nicolaus almost a century earlier.

For Josephus to rely on material lifted from previous writers was entirely legitimate according to the conventions of Greek historiography within which he wrote. Accusations of a lack of originality were not a concern, and no one expected the historian to indicate his source. But it was common to let loose occasional barbs about the deficiencies of earlier accounts, and Josephus asserted explicitly that Nicolaus produced a partisan picture: Josephus claimed that, since Nicolaus "lived in Herod's realm and was one of his associates, he wrote to please him and to be of service to him," and that he was "consistent in exclusively praising the king for his just acts, and zealously apologizing for his unlawful ones."[6]

The criticism was plausible, but it clearly did not prevent Josephus from relying heavily on Nicolaus's narrative of Herod's career, whatever he thought of his predecessor's judgment on Herod's morality. In any case, at least some of Nicolaus's account of Herod's life must have been written after the king's death, when Nicolaus was in Rome with the emperor Augustus as his new patron. No longer beholden to Herod or his family, he was free to write what he knew about the faults as well as the achievements of his former employer.[7]

Nicolaus could take for granted that his readers would be interested in Herod's travails because, by the time of his death, the king was a well-known personality both in Rome and across the Greek world. No one could have predicted such fame when he was born in an obscure corner of the southern Levant.

1

A World in Turmoil

Herod was born around 73 BCE, either in Idumaea or, more probably, in Jerusalem. He died in Jericho almost seventy years later. Born into a world already in turmoil, he witnessed and participated in its wholesale transformation.[1]

Herod's life began in the court of the Hasmonaean queen Shelomzion (in Greek, Salome), who ruled what was then an independent Jewish state. From infancy, he lived near the center of power: his father, Antipater, was one of Shelomzion's trusted ministers. But he was only ten years old when Jerusalem was besieged and captured by Roman forces, and it was in Rome that he was proclaimed king in 40 BCE. The last sixty years of his life were dominated by the power of Rome and the ambitions of individual Roman aristocrats. Thus, although his ability to navigate the rivalry of competing Hasmonaean descendants of Shelomzion provided the basis of Herod's rise to prominence as a young man, many of the most significant names which will crop up as his story unfolds will be Roman: Pompey and his rivals, Crassus and Julius Caesar; Cassius, one of Caesar's assassins; Mark Antony and Octavian. Of these, the most influential was to be Octavian, who in 27 BCE adopted the name Augustus and ruled supreme in the Roman world as emperor for the last quarter-century of Herod's life.

The profound impact of the political imbroglios of Roman senators from faraway Italy on the life of this Jewish youngster living on the eastern edge of the Mediterranean was the result of tectonic shifts in power during the century before Herod was born. The great Hellenistic empires established across the Near East by the successors of the Macedonian king Alexander the Great at the end of the fourth century BCE had by the time of Herod's birth almost crumbled away, under pressure from Parthia in the East and Rome in the West. By the start of the first century BCE the Seleucid kingdom, which had once governed from Anatolia (in modern Turkey) to Iran, was largely confined to warring rivals in Syria and Phoenicia (modern Lebanon). The Ptolemaic dynasty in Egypt had been so weakened by internal rivalries that Ptolemy XII Auletes, who succeeded to the throne in 80 BCE after the assassination of his predecessor by an uprising of his subjects in Alexandria, ruled only as a puppet of the Roman state.

There had been nothing accidental about the process of continual territorial acquisition by Rome. Roman imperialism was a product of the constitution of the Roman Republic, under which power was shared by competing aristocrats who were granted limited periods to make a name for themselves after election to a magistracy. In a society which granted prestige above all for victory in war, it was inevitable that opportunities for glory by foreign conquest would be pursued by ambitious politicians during their terms of office. As a result Rome, a small city-state on the plain of Latium near the west coast of Italy, had by 100 BCE conquered Greece and all of Asia Minor, and it was only a matter of time before Judaea also came under Roman control.[2]

When that moment came, around the time of Herod's birth, the success of Roman imperialism had begun to put unbearable strain on Rome itself. The political structures of the state, which had proved so effective in stimulating conquest in earlier centuries, would not suffice to keep in subjection a large part of the Mediterranean world. Armies needed to stay in the field for more than an annual campaign. Generals appointed in theory as temporary commanders could win prestige on these extended campaigns and accumulate wealth far exceeding that of the annual magistrates who presided over affairs at Rome. It had become clear in the decades before Herod's birth that it would be possible through ruthless determination for one of these generals to achieve total domination of the whole political system of Rome.[3]

In far-flung regions which had come under Roman sway by the early first century BCE, these Roman governors were already behaving like kings, holding the power of life and death over the inhabitants of the regions they conquered. In other regions Roman control was imposed at one remove by native rulers characterized as friends of Rome. The friendship was of course unequal: in Roman eyes, these allied kings depended for their authority on the approval of the Roman Senate just as much as did provincial governors sent out from Rome. In their search for influential political patrons, client kings were thus drawn inexorably into the maelstrom of fierce competition between senatorial factions which bedeviled Rome in the late republic.[4]

It was a tricky world for an outsider to navigate, and no one in Judaea at the time of Herod's birth would have had any idea of its complexity. It is thus unlikely that in the late 70s Shelomzion and her minister Antipater had even heard of the two ambitious generals, Pompey and Crassus, who had just recently come to the forefront of Roman politics through military campaigns in distant lands at the other end of the Mediterranean. Roman forces had yet to be seen in the southern Levant. Shelomzion ruled in Judaea over an independent Jewish state, which in the preceding decades had reached the height of its glory, benefiting from the collapse of Seleucid power to conquer neighboring territories. At the time of Herod's birth, Judaea was a regional superpower.

Shelomzion had inherited her realm from her husband, Alexander Jannaeus, a scion of the priestly Hasmonaean family which had come to power in Jerusalem through the revolt of the Maccabees in the 160s. The founding myth of the Hasmonaean dynasty portrayed the heroic struggle of Judas Maccabee as a rejection of the Hellenization to which previous high priests in Jerusalem had succumbed, yet by the end of the second century BCE, Hasmonaean rulers had embraced not only the Greek language and Greek customs but also a characteristically Hellenistic concern for military conquest as justification of royal rule. Thus Alexander Jannaeus styled himself king as well as high priest on his coins and behaved openly as a Hellenistic monarch, devoting almost his entire reign of twenty-seven years to continuous campaigns. By the time of his death in 76 BCE, the hill country west of the Jordan, all the adjoining territory along the Mediterranean coast (apart from Ashkelon, which remained independent), and the whole of Peraea (Transjordan) from north of the Sea of Galilee to the Dead Sea, lay in Hasmonaean hands.[5]

It was into the service of Alexander Jannaeus that Antipas, the grandfather of Herod, was recruited sometime in the early first century. Designated governor of Idumaea, his ancestral homeland, which had been incorporated into the Hasmonaean realm only a few decades earlier, Antipas avoided the dangerous court politics of Jerusalem by focusing on the administration of a region whose loyalty to the Jewish state could not be taken wholly for granted. There is no evidence that he was drawn into the family intrigues that surrounded his royal master, who, rumor had it, had become king only with the aid of Shelomzion: in 103 Shelomzion was said to have chosen Jannaeus as her spouse after the premature death of her first husband, Aristobulus, who was Jannaeus's brother. The extent of Shelomzion's power was demonstrated openly a quarter of a century later by her own accession to the throne after the death of Jannaeus himself.[6]

The reign of Shelomzion laid bare the extent to which the Jewish state was now administered on Hellenistic lines, despite the role of the Jerusalem Temple as its central institution. Wielding of political power in public by a queen was not a practice found in earlier Jewish tradition, which had excluded women from open display of political authority, but warrior queens had long been found in the Hellenistic world. The great Cleopatra VII, with whom Herod was compelled to negotiate in the early years of his reign, was only the last of a number of powerful women from the Ptolemaic dynasty who ruled Egypt in the second and first centuries BCE. Shelomzion was herself to rule for nine years.

Despite her anomalous position in the eyes of some Jews, Shelomzion was remembered favorably in later Jewish tradition, primarily because of her conservative religious policies. She was depicted by Josephus as a passive ruler, but this evaluation seems unwarranted even on the basis of Josephus's own account: she is said to have demonstrated impressive strength of will in controlling the ambitions of her younger son, Aristobulus, despite his denunciations of her on the grounds that it was unreasonable for a woman to reign while her sons were in the prime of life. If, unlike her late husband, she preferred to refrain from foreign expeditions, an obvious explanation may be her age: she was already in her mid-sixties when she succeeded to the throne. Her policy of buying peace with bribes when she feared that her realm might be overwhelmed by the chaotic politics of the wider Syria region was simple prudence.[7]

We do not know whether Herod met Shelomzion. If he did, he would have been very young, for he was around six years old when she died in 67 BCE. As far as we know, his grandfather Antipas retained his role as governor of Idumaea into Shelomzion's reign, but Antipas fades from the record, and presumably retired or died around this time. Jerusalem was still a small place, not yet adorned with many splendid public buildings, but the young boy must surely have been aware of the looming pale-limestone edifice of the royal palace on the western hill which provided the old queen with views of the Temple Mount, ensuring that her court dominated the city. Within the court his father, Antipater, was beginning to establish the connections that would bring him and, in due course, Herod himself to the center of power.

Prohibited by her sex from serving herself as high priest, Shelomzion insisted on bestowing the high priesthood on her older son, Hyrcanus, despite his lack of energy and the opposition of Aristobulus. The intense fraternal strife this engendered provided opportunities for advancement for Antipater, who plunged himself enthusiastically into court intrigue in support of Hyrcanus. Antipater was thus well placed to take a major role in the power struggle which erupted on the queen's death, when Hyrcanus inherited the throne under the terms of his mother's will, and Aristobulus marched on Judaea to depose him. After a battle near Jericho, at which many of his soldiers deserted, Hyrcanus withdrew into private life, leaving the kingdom and high priesthood to Aristobulus—until Antipater led a campaign to restore his patron to his legitimate position. It was Antipater who persuaded Aretas, the king of the Nabataeans, to march against Aristobulus on behalf of Hyrcanus.[8]

How aware of all this was young Herod? Uprooted from his home in Jerusalem and sent with his siblings for safekeeping to his mother's family in Petra, the Nabataean capital, he was surely old enough to appreciate something of the risks of his father's campaign and the dangers which would face the family until victory was achieved. We do not know how long he was kept out of harm's way in Petra as, despite military successes, the war dragged on for year after year: for a child in the prosperous rock-cut city, hidden from outsiders in a narrow gorge in the Wadi Arabah, Petra must have seemed a haven of peace.

That peace was not to last. It is likely that the whole family was back in Judaea two years later when Aristobulus, confined to a defensive position on the Temple Mount, took the fateful step of appealing for help from Roman forces. The Roman commanders approached by Aristobulus were involved in operations north of the Hasmonaean realm, annexing territory in Syria to Roman rule to satisfy Pompey's appetite for even more military glory. Large bribes offered to Pompey and his lieutenants, first by Aristobulus and then by Hyrcanus, served to stimulate the Roman's lust for conquest. Arriving in the region in person in spring 63, and deciding definitively against Aristobulus on the grounds of the perceived arrogance of his ambassadors, Pompey took personal charge of the siege of Aristobulus's forces on the Temple Mount, ostensibly on behalf of Hyrcanus and Antipater but ultimately in preparation for a triumphal procession through Rome to celebrate his great victory.[9]

No later tradition records where Herod was as the Temple Mount came under siege in the summer of 63. Was he in Jerusalem with his father or (perhaps more likely) staying with relatives in the safety of Idumaea as the walls of the Temple were battered by missiles in a battle that lasted three months, culminating in Pompey's bloody victory in the late autumn? Perhaps he heard only after the event about the siege engines and the crashing towers, or about the houses on fire, the mass slaughter, and the desperate suicide of those who hurled themselves down the precipices rather than accept their fate. But a boy of ten would surely have been old enough to appreciate with horror in the months and years after the war the extent of the destruction wrought by the Roman forces on the holy shrine and the simmering outrage among ordinary Jews over the desecration of the sanctuary by the Roman commander, who had shocked them by entering the Holy of Holies to examine whether the shrine was as empty as it was rumored to be.

Perhaps Herod was already building around himself a protective shell as he witnessed at close quarters the return of his father's friend Hyrcanus to the prestigious position of high priest at the same time as Pompey brought to an end the national independence of the Jewish state, denying to Hyrcanus the title of king and confining under Roman rule the state that had previously ruled over others. For Herod as he entered his teenage years regrets about national trauma were surely balanced by the personal ascendancy which the defeat of Aristobulus, led in chains in Rome in Pompey's triumphal procession in 61, afforded to his father as Hyrcanus's closest adviser. Hyrcanus's emasculated powers were bound to elicit challenges which Antipater could portray himself as uniquely qualified to meet.[10]

Chief among such challenges were attempts by the sons of Aristobulus to seize back control of Jerusalem. Mobilizing Hyrcanus when such threats from his nephews appeared was not easy: Hyrcanus was so feeble in his response to the capture of major fortresses east of Jerusalem by one of his nephews in 57 that the Roman governor of Syria, who had been forced to suppress the insurrection in person, temporarily stripped him of his secular power, confining him to his religious role as high priest and placing the country under the administration of five separate aristocratic councils. Antipater must have viewed this development with dismay, for it appeared to deprive him of the political role he had made his own. Herod, at age sixteen, could see his own prospects of political advancement shrink before they had even begun.[11]

Antipater did not despair. Deprived of one patron, his solution to his personal predicament was to make himself as invaluable to the Romans as he had long been to Hyrcanus. Thus, when, two years later, in 55, Judaea was invaded again by the same son of Aristobulus, Antipater was ready to aid the governor of Syria, not only by providing picked troops to support Roman forces in a major engagement near Mount Tabor in Galilee but also by negotiating with some of the Jewish supporters of the insurrection to persuade them to change sides before the battle. The lesson that Roman politicians might value such intervention on their behalf would not have been lost on Herod, now eighteen, as he prepared to enter political life.[12]

Finding a Roman patron was obviously the way ahead for a young man seeking advancement, but it was hard for a provincial in Jerusalem in the mid-fifties BCE to discern where power now lay in Rome—and therefore which Roman to court. The control of Rome by Pompey and Crassus had been complicated by their decision in 60, together with Julius Caesar, a younger senator who had already revealed ruthless ambition, to set aside their rivalry temporarily for a mutually beneficial alliance that would enable the three of them to monopolize political patronage. The alliance of these ambitious generals was informal and inherently unstable, but it was much resented by their fellow Roman aristocrats.

Negotiating to advantage this centralization of power within a triumvirate was not easy even for Roman senators, but it was much more problematic for politicians in distant Judaea. Pompey had not returned to the eastern Mediterranean since his campaign the previous decade, and he was in any case out of favor with the Jews, who blamed him for the desecration of the Temple. Caesar was making a name for himself through the conquest of distant Gaul, on the northwestern fringe of the Roman world, but he had never visited the Levant and was unknown to provincials like Antipater and Herod. Crassus, the most senior and wealthy of the three, might have seemed a more attractive proposition when he set off from Rome to Syria in 55 in search of glory through an invasion of the kingdom of Parthia on the eastern border of the sphere of Roman influence. But, intent on raising funds for the huge force of seven legions required for his campaign, Crassus stole the gold and other treasures from the Jerusalem Temple that Pompey had left untouched, and Jews did not mourn the humiliating disaster that ended in his death on June 9, 53, in a battle against the Parthians near the town of Carrhae, an event that left Pompey and Caesar to dominate the Roman world.[13]

Within a few years of the death of Crassus, Pompey was also dead, and Caesar had become the greatest patron of all. How did this come about, and how did the shifting sands of power within the Roman elite impinge on the young Herod when, in his early twenties, he erupted into the politics of Judaea in 47 at a time of crisis, and when he found himself within only a few years acclaimed king of Judaea?

2

Overcoming Obstacles

Herod's rise to prominence in Judaea in the early 40s BCE owed little to his origins beyond the political influence of Antipater in Hyrcanus's court. Herod's father was an Idumaean and his mother a Nabataean Arab. The right of a person of such a lineage to rule over Judaea was specifically questioned by the Hasmonean Antigonus in late 39, when he told the Romans that "it would be contrary to their own notion of right if they gave the kingship to Herod who was a commoner and an Idumaean, that is, a half-Jew, when they ought to offer it to those who were of the (royal) family, as was their custom."[1]

Antigonus's assertion that Idumaeans were only half-Jews was polemical, for the Romans he addressed had been charged with depriving him of his kingdom in favor of Herod in accordance with the Senate's decision the previous year—but the insult may have been prompted primarily by wordplay in Greek: *idumaios* (Idumaean) sounds very similar to *hemiioudaios* (half-

Jew). But it was true that Herod was an Idumaean: it was as an Idumaean that Josephus first introduced Herod's father, Antipater, into his narrative of Jewish history in his *Antiquities*. Josephus's account of events in his own lifetime, including the great war against Rome in which he had been embroiled in the sixties CE, made clear that Idumaeans retained a sense of their community as separate from Judaea for at least a century after Herod's death.[2]

Idumaea was rolling hill country south of Judaea whose eastern border dropped rapidly below sea level through arid territory to the Dead Sea. It was not in itself a bad place to live. As in Judaea, some areas were suitable for grain and olive production, but the land also offered vineyards for winemaking and grazing for goats and sheep, while the ancient city of Hebron was famed for pottery production and glassblowing. Herod's grandfather Antipas must have had access to considerable resources, for he was said to have "made friends of the neighboring Arabs and Gazaeans and Ascalonites, and completely won them over with large gifts." Herod's father was also said to have amassed a large fortune by the time he first intervened in Judaean politics on behalf of Hyrcanus in 67 BCE. Whether the family's fortune derived from landowning or industry or the long-distance trade route which ran through Idumaean territory from the coastal city of Ashkelon to Petra in Transjordan is not known, but they evidently belonged to the wealthy ruling elite of the region long before they became embroiled in the politics of Judaea.[3]

Behind Herod's defensiveness about his Idumaean origins lay less the story of his specific family than the complex history of relations between Idumaea and Judaea in earlier generations. Descended from the nomadic tribes known in the Hebrew Bible as Edom, who had settled east of the Jordan and south of the Dead Sea many centuries before Herod's birth, the Idumaeans had gradually moved westward into more fertile territory. By the second century BCE they were to be found occupying parts of southern Judaea and the northern Negev, clustered around the city of Marisa. When their territory was conquered by the Hasmonaeans toward the end of the century, the majority of the population converted to Judaism. Whether that conversion was voluntary was already in dispute in Herod's day. The Greek historian Strabo, a contemporary of Herod's, wrote that "the Idumaeans are Nabataeans, but owing to a sedition they were banished from [their territory], joined the Judaeans, and shared in the same customs with them." Josephus believed a different account, probably derived from Nicolaus, which asserted that the Idumaeans had converted under compulsion.[4]

Throughout Herod's lifetime some unconverted Idumaeans still worshipped the god Cos. At least one of Herod's Idumaean friends—his brother-in-law Costobar, whose religious affiliation (or that of his parents) is reflected by his name—did not think it right for the Idumaeans to adopt the customs of the Judaeans. But that the majority of the population did adopt Jewish customs is not in doubt. Two centuries after their conversion, when crowds of Idumaeans defended Jerusalem against Rome during the revolt of 66–70 CE, they referred to the city as their metropolis. Idumaeans proudly also proclaimed themselves Jews. It is likely that most Idumaeans during Herod's childhood looked to Jerusalem as their capital city, for there is no evidence that the Romans ever considered separating the region from Judaea. It was thus not by accident that Herod's father chose to give Jewish names to two of his children, Joseph and Salome. In later years Herod demonstrated his attachment to the land of his ancestors by building the grand precinct of perfectly laid ashlar blocks, still well preserved, which enclosed the cave of Machpelah in Hebron, as well as the finely worked marble cenotaphs of Abraham and Sarah and their descendants.[5]

More difficult to pin down is Herod's attitude toward his mother's family. His mother, Cyprus, was said by Josephus to have come from an illustrious family from Arabia, which in context must have been Nabataea, the kingdom to the east of Idumaea. In his account in the *Antiquities* of the beginning of Antipater's political career, Josephus implied that Antipater had found his Arabian wife in Idumaea; this is not impossible, but Josephus's parallel account in the *Jewish War* stated specifically that the marriage of his son to Cyprus had won Antipas the friendship of the king of Arabia. Wherever Cyprus met her future spouse, it can be surmised that she was probably connected to the Nabataean royal family.[6]

The Nabataeans, like the Idumaeans, originated as semi-nomads, but by the first century BCE they had settled in Peraea, an area with urban centers such as Kanatha and Petra, and advanced agricultural techniques which enabled them to cultivate marginal land by careful conservation of scarce water supplies. Their prosperity, which increased markedly in Herod's lifetime and reached a peak in the generation following his death, was based on control of the international trade routes that passed through or near Petra and took advantage of the increasing unification of the Levant and Mediterranean under Roman hegemony. Their spoken language was probably an early form of Arabic, but their inscriptions were written in a distinctive form of the international language of trade, Aramaic. Herod would have communicated with his Nabataean relatives either in Aramaic or in Greek.[7]

We have seen that the family link to Nabataea was sufficiently strong for Antipater to send his small children, including Herod, to Petra, the capital city of the Nabataean king, for safekeeping, presumably with their mother's family, when he embarked with the Nabataean king Aretas in 67 on his campaign to evict Aristobulus from Jerusalem and install his patron Hyrcanus. What impression this visit made on Herod as a young child, age only six, under what must have been traumatic conditions is hard to gauge, but his frequent interventions in Nabataean affairs later in his life, once he had come to power in Judaea, suggest that he felt he had a stake, through his mother, in Nabataean society.[8]

On the other hand, no ancient source hints that Herod ever presented himself as Nabataean, and we are told nothing about contact with his mother's relatives after his childhood. Cyprus assimilated into her husband's social milieu and focused her ambitions on promoting the interests of her children.[9]

The contrast between the outsider status in Judaea of his family and Herod's eventual life as its king was noted in antiquity, but we should not imagine him starting life at the bottom of the social heap—as we have seen, both his grandfather and his father held powerful positions within the Hasmonaean court. That said, Herod's origins gave him no reason to anticipate ruling Judaea in his own right. An anecdote about Herod as a boy preserved by Josephus (presumably, if it was genuine, treasured, like all such anecdotes, because in hindsight it turned out to be true) concerned a prophetic utterance by a man called Manaemus, who claimed divinely inspired knowledge of the future. Passing by Herod on the way to the house of his teacher, Manaemus greeted him as "king of the Jews." When Herod, who thought he was being teased, reminded Manaemus that he was only a private citizen, Manaemus laughed gently and patted him on the rump, saying that he would indeed be king and rule happily, although his reign would become evil when he forgot piety and justice. At the time, Herod was said to have paid no attention to such predictions. The idea that he might become a king was beyond his imagination.[10]

The teacher to whose house Herod was going would have taught either reading, writing, and arithmetic (if the boy was between seven and eleven), or grammar (if he was between eleven and fifteen). So far as is known, Herod spent his schooldays entirely in Jerusalem. Up to his mid-teens, he probably received an elite Greek education in the city, where Greek was in use alongside Aramaic and Hebrew. Later in life he is known to have sought instruction in rhetoric, history, and philosophy, but he is unlikely to have had an opportunity to progress beyond secondary education in his youth—Nicolaus wrote that Herod took up study of these subjects in the intervals of a public career, at a time when he was already a person of authority.[11]

Herod would have spoken Aramaic and may possibly also have known some Hebrew. We do not know whether he gained any deep learning in the Jewish literary tradition encapsulated in the Bible, but he must have acquired a knowledge of the basic history of the Jewish people and the cultic worship performed by the priests in the Temple. However, nothing suggests that he had any desire to become expert in such matters: there is no sign that he was interested in the philosophies of religious enthusiasts such as the Pharisees, whose ideas had been influential with some Hasmonaean rulers, including Shelomzion. When he turned in later life to the study of history, it was presumably Greek history, since he was told by Nicolaus that the subject was "proper for a statesman, and useful also for a king."[12]

Jerusalem was not an exciting place for a teenager to amuse himself when Herod was growing up there. It offered no theatrical or athletic performances for the public to enjoy—these were innovations introduced later by Herod himself. But doubtless the young men hung around together; this must have been when Herod gained his love of hunting and horsemanship, at which he excelled. Physical exercise was closely related to military training, and Herod was proud of his expertise in wielding both javelin and bow. Josephus several times noted his concern later in life with his physical appearance, his pride in his powerful physique and his hair, which was carefully groomed in his mid-twenties and dyed discreetly after he reached his sixties. But we cannot know whether this care reflected his real attitude toward such matters or astute attention to his public image. At some point he may have fallen in love with a boy named Hippicus, about whom nothing else is known; he commemorated

Hippicus much later by erecting a magnificent tower on the wall of Jerusalem in the name of his friend, "lost in war after valiant fight." Homosexual passions between young men, admired in Greek social circles, would be looked on askance by many pious Jews, but the naming of the tower is evidence at least that Herod was unabashed about the depth of his friendship.[13]

Herod's most important education during his teenage years came from his father: he learned much about practical politics as Antipater steered Hyrcanus through the storms battering Judaea throughout the 50s. The family was close-knit, and Herod shared this political education with his elder brother, Phasael. His relationship with Phasael and with his younger siblings—two brothers (Joseph and Pheroras) and a sister, Salome—were to be important throughout his life. So too was his relationship with the wider family of his father, who in some cases confirmed their friendships through marriages: Salome was married while still young to her uncle Joseph, Antipater's brother.

Herod himself was in due course to be married within the family first to a niece (a daughter of his brother) and then to a first cousin (the daughter of his father's brother), but his first marriage, in his mid-twenties, was to Doris, an aristocratic native of Jerusalem. The marriage, the first known to have been contracted by anyone in Herod's family with a member of the Jewish elite, was presumably set up by Antipater on behalf of his son. The match suggests that Herod was already being groomed by his father for a prominent role in the Judaean state. The first impetus to Herod's public career came not from these links to Jerusalem aristocracy, however, but from momentous events in Rome, where the tensions inherent in the competitive ethos of senatorial politics exploded into civil war.[14]

We have seen that the death of Crassus in 53 left Pompey and Caesar dominating the Roman state, but they had always been uneasy allies, and in 49 their mutual suspicions descended into civil strife, which was to last long after the deaths of both men. For nearly two decades the Roman world was caught up in a conflict which involved the levy of more troops around the shores of the Mediterranean than at any time until the wars of Napoleon in the early nineteenth century CE. Massive militarization sucked huge resources of manpower and wealth out of all the regions under Roman sway, impelled not by ideology or patriotism but by the competing ambitions of individual Roman aristocrats.

These civil wars were not inevitable: when earlier politicians had used troops assigned for foreign conquest to march on Rome and impose major reforms on the state, they had then retired to private life. But when Caesar, after nearly a decade of victorious campaigns in Gaul—which had the advantage of adding vast sums to his private coffers—crossed the river Rubicon in the north of Italy and marched on Rome with his legions, he sought monarchic rule. Stopping only briefly in Rome to take money from the state treasury, he waged campaigns against Pompey and his supporters in Spain and Greece, and in August 48 BCE won a decisive victory after a pitched battle at Pharsalus in Thessaly. Pompey fled to Egypt, where he was stabbed to death on September 28. The contemporary Jewish author of the Psalms of Solomon celebrated the demise of the arrogant sinner who had brought battering rams against the walls of the Temple in Jerusalem fifteen years earlier. The author, calling on God for vengeance, reported, "I did not wait long until God showed me his insolence pierced on the mountains of Egypt, more despised than the smallest thing on earth and sea. His body was carried about on the waves in much shame, and there was no-one to bury (him)."[15]

Antipater and Hyrcanus were quick to demonstrate their support for the victor. Soon after Pompey's death, Antipater persuaded the Jews in Onias, a district in northern Egypt, to come over to Caesar's side in his campaign against King Ptolemy. In return Caesar allowed Hyrcanus to retain his position as high priest in Jerusalem and rewarded Antipater with that of procurator of Judaea. Quite how the procuratorship, an administrative role as agent of Rome with particular responsibility for financial matters, related to the power which continued to be exercised by Hyrcanus is unclear, but the post was evidently substantial: Caesar sent orders to Rome to engrave the honors granted to Antipater on the Capitol "as a memorial of his own justice and of Antipater's valour." The new appointment enabled Antipater to launch his two oldest sons into public life. Phasael became governor of Jerusalem. Herod was entrusted with the government of Galilee.[16]

It was precisely then, the first time when Herod is known to have entered public life, that his father was granted Roman citizenship by Julius Caesar. The grant of citizenship was mentioned by Josephus in passing, as a reward from Caesar to Antipater for his military efforts on Caesar's behalf in the Egyptian Delta. The grant was said to have been conjoined with exemption from taxation. Individual grants of citizenship by magistrates on behalf of the Roman state to provincials considered worthy of the privilege were very rare in the eastern provinces in the mid-first century. They functioned as a means of personal recognition for favors received. Essentially symbolic in practice, since the new citizens lived too far from Rome to participate in the elections and public assemblies which might influence the course of Roman politics, such grants marked out a new provincial elite.[17]

Thus, from the start, Herod's public career was a product of Roman patronage. In the seven years between his father's acquisition of Roman citizenship and his own appointment as king of Judaea, Herod's career was devoted to winning the personal confidence and friendship of Roman politicians at a time of unprecedented instability. Success required a demonstration of competence and charm. It could also require flagrant bribery and an unscrupulous willingness to change sides.

These qualities were employed to great effect by Antipater, who had backed the losing side in the civil war between Pompey and Caesar. His claim to have suddenly become a warm supporter of Caesar, demonstrating his new loyalties after the defeat of Pompey at Pharsalus by energetically devoting himself to Caesar's cause, was, unsurprisingly, challenged by his political opponents in the Hasmonaean ruling family, including Antigonus, the son of Hyrcanus's brother Aristobulus. Antigonus is said to have accused Antipater and Hyrcanus of having helped Caesar in Egypt solely out of fear that they would otherwise suffer for their previous friendship with Pompey. The accusation may well have been fully justified, but Antipater successfully countered the charge when summoned to Caesar by stripping off his clothes and displaying the scars from the wounds he had suffered fighting for his new friend.[18]

Herod, hard at work bringing Galilee under firm control, was still too junior to be invited to meet the great Julius Caesar himself, but his energetic clearance of Galilean bandits who had been attacking the neighboring borderlands of Syria brought him to the attention of the governor of Syria, Sextus Caesar, a distant relative of Julius. Protection by Sextus proved vital when Herod's actions in Galilee nearly brought his public career to an abrupt end almost before it had started.[19]

Herod was in his mid-twenties when he was appointed to the command in Galilee. In Herod's time this was not an unusual age for an ambitious politician to take on such military and administrative responsibilities, but his youth was explicitly stressed by Josephus in both his narratives, and youth and inexperience may provide the most plausible explanation for his ordering the summary execution of some bandits he captured rather than bringing them before a court for trial. Such energetic ruthlessness was popular with the local settled population, but there was an outcry from the mothers of the men he had executed without due legal process. Summoned by Hyrcanus to face trial in Jerusalem on charges of murder brought by leading Jews who resented the influence of Antipater and his sons on Hyrcanus and his regime, Herod elected to respond with defiance. He arrived before the high priest's court looking strikingly unrepentant. Abjuring the black mourning attire expected for a defendant, he appeared instead clothed in purple with his hair carefully coiffed. Ominously, he was accompanied by a military posse. The Roman governor of Syria, Sextus, ordered Hyrcanus to acquit Herod of the charge, threatening dire consequences if his wishes were ignored. The court was too intimidated to convict, and the trial was suspended.[20]

Defiance had proved conspicuously successful. Leaving Jerusalem to join Sextus in Damascus, Herod was rewarded for his loyalty to Caesar's cause by the addition of Samaria and Coele Syria (an enclave of Syria north of Mount Hermon) to the territories under his administration. His position within Caesar's party was evidently secure. From now on, he knew that he would not need to rely on Hyrcanus as long as he could appeal directly to a Roman patron. It was clear that real power lay in the authority and military might of the Roman governor of Syria. Thus when Herod's opponents in Jerusalem persuaded Hyrcanus to issue a second summons to trial, Herod felt sufficiently independent of his Hasmonaean patron to march on Jerusalem with an army, threatening to wreak revenge for the insult. Prevented from violence by the interventions of Antipater and Phasael, he returned to his command in Galilee without attacking, yet secure in the knowledge that he had demonstrated that his power was not to be constrained by the jurisdiction of the Jewish court.[21]

Sextus was said to have granted Herod his rule over Samaria and Coele Syria in return for a bribe, but Herod responded with firm support for the Caesarean party: when Sextus was assassinated by Caecilius Bassus, one of Pompey's sympathizers, and Caesar's generals launched an offensive against Bassus in the autumn of 45, Herod and Phasael were sent by Antipater to join forces with the Caesarians. Devotion to Caesar's cause may have been mere prudence while Caesar lived, but it became problematic when, on March 15, 44, Julius Caesar was also assassinated, and the civil war which broke out after his murder brought to Syria one of the leaders of the self-styled liberators who had hacked him to death, Gaius Cassius Longinus (known to posterity as Cassius).[22]

The assassination had been brought on by fear of Caesar's ambition, which soared after 46 with the reality of unchallenged power. In 44 he was one of the two consuls who were appointed each year to govern Rome, but this was not enough to satisfy his aspirations. He had already been elected to the post of *dictator* for life, with a priesthood established in Rome to worship him as a god, and rumors that he might next accept a royal crown prompted a conspiracy among many of his fellow senators, who stabbed him to death in the Senate. The conspiracy was led by Cassius and Marcus Brutus, two supporters of Pompey against Caesar who had been granted clemency by the man they now murdered.

Caesar's death plunged the Mediterranean world back into chaos for more than a decade. When Brutus and Cassius proclaimed *libertas*, "freedom," on the coins they minted, they had in mind a return to the traditional politics of Rome, in which senators like themselves enjoyed equal opportunity to seek and bestow patronage as they rose through the ranks. But they proved fatally mistaken in their evaluation of what they had achieved. The ambition and loyalty to Caesar's memory of Marcus Lepidus, Caesar's lieutenant in his role as dictator, and of Mark Antony, who had been Caesar's fellow consul for the year, and above all the single-minded and ruthless determination of Caesar's young great-nephew and heir, Marcus Octavius, saw to it that there was no return to the old system of aristocratic competition.

Octavius, adopted posthumously by Caesar, liked to be addressed as Caesar Octavianus (hence "Octavian"). He was to propel himself by 31 BCE to a power as absolute as anything Caesar had sought, and starting in 27 he would be known as the emperor Augustus. His rise to sole power could not have been anticipated by anyone in March 44: the future emperor was serving as a junior officer in an unimportant military operation on the eastern Adriatic coast when he received, along with the shocking news of Caesar's death, the information that he had been adopted by his great-uncle in his will and named chief heir to Caesar's enormous fortune.

Octavian could certainly expect his wealth and the name of Caesar to open up a glittering career in Roman politics, but with no senatorial or military experience it would typically have been some years before he began to make his mark. He was not prepared to wait. Already calling himself Caesar, he raised two legions as he traversed Italy on the way to Rome by recruiting some of Caesar's veterans with the promise of pay from his inheritance. His search for advancement was unconstrained by loyalty to Caesar's memory. His troops were equally self-serving. In the coming months, he used these forces first to win the status of a Roman magistrate by fighting against Caesar's friend Antony in support of Caesar's murderers Brutus and Cassius; then, when the two consuls for 43 were killed in the campaign, to march on Rome to demand the consulship for himself; and finally, in November 43, to swap sides and agree as consul to cooperate with Antony and Lepidus in a triumvirate granted absolute power by the Roman people "for settling the state." Their primary task was to avenge the death of Caesar by marching against the liberators, Brutus and Cassius.[23]

The two assassins were already preparing their defenses in the eastern Mediterranean, and soon these faraway events would have a direct impact on Judaea, as Cassius set about raising money to build up his forces against the impending attack. Antipater, Phasael, and Herod now needed urgently to demonstrate where their loyalties lay. Cassius was no stranger to Syria; he had held a senior administrative position in the province when Crassus embarked from there on his ill-fated Parthian campaign in 53, and he had governed the territory from 53 to 51 after Crassus was killed. Antipater had been in contact with him then, persuading him in around 52 to invade Judaea to suppress supporters of Aristobulus who threatened the security of Hyrcanus's tenure of the high priesthood. But the two men are not known to have established a bond of friendship: when the Jews were instructed by Cassius in 43 to come up with the huge sum of seven hundred talents to pay for the troops he was raising, Antipater undertook to collect the money only out of fear, according to Josephus, distributing the task among his associates. (Of course the reliability of this explanation for Antipater's cooperation with Cassius may be questionable since it came only after Cassius was dead.)[24]

The associates to whom Antipater distributed the task included his two sons. Herod was assigned responsibility for extracting one-seventh of the total sum from the inhabitants of Galilee. The crisis presented an opportunity: Cassius was a new Roman to impress. The first to bring his quota, Herod rapidly established himself as a close friend, and when Antony and Octavian declared war on Cassius and Brutus as expected, Herod was rewarded by Cassius with reappointment to the position of governor of Coele Syria that he had held under Sextus Caesar. Cassius also provided Herod with an army, both cavalry and infantry, presumably to maintain order in a notoriously unruly region. Herod had already demonstrated his military competence in the suppression of bandits in Galilee. There was even a rumor that Cassius promised to appoint Herod king of Judaea after the war that "had just then begun with Antony and the young Caesar," although nothing came of the promise, and it is not clear why Cassius should have wanted to court trouble by promoting Herod above his father and elder brother, both of whom were also active on his behalf.[25]

It had been a meteoric rise to political prominence, but everything Herod had achieved in the first five years of his public career was thrown into disarray when his father, Antipater, was assassinated in the summer of 43 by Malichus, a rival politician in the entourage of Hyrcanus in Jerusalem. At a dinner hosted by Hyrcanus at which they were fellow guests, Malichus suborned the wine steward to put poison into Antipater's wine. Antipater died shortly after leaving the banquet.

Malichus's motives for killing Antipater are obscure—he is said to have had broad popular support in Judaea, and he may have wished ultimately to supplant Hyrcanus and take the throne of Judaea for himself—but there is nothing obscure about his fate at the hands of Herod. With the assistance of Cassius, Herod took rapid revenge. According to one account, Malichus had acted out of concern over Herod's increasing power as much as Antipater's, and Herod may have been spurred on by a guilty suspicion that his father's death might have been caused to some extent by his own ambition. He pretended to Malichus, who feigned regret for Antipater's death, that he wished to be his friend, and invited him to a dinner in the city of Tyre. When Malichus accepted the invitation, he was intercepted on the seashore on his way to the dinner by military tribunes (junior officers in the Roman army), who had been dispatched by Cassius at Herod's request, and stabbed to death.[26]

The loss of his devoted father was a crushing blow, but Herod was now thirty years old and well entrenched in his own right, thanks to Cassius, as a major figure in the administration of a large area of the Levant in the interests of Rome. And although there remained, even after the death of Malichus, other rivals eager to supplant the power of Herod and Phasael in the court of Hyrcanus, the brothers had no difficulty in maintaining their influence as long as they had the strong support of Cassius as Rome's representative.

But Cassius was not to last long: in the late autumn of 42 he left Syria to face the forces of Antony and Octavian, and died in Macedonia at the Battle of Philippi. Herod and Phasael were now vulnerable. With Judaea in turmoil in the chaotic months before Philippi, Herod had been fully taken up with a series of military engagements against Malichus's brother, who tried to seize power from Hyrcanus, and against Marion, ruler of Tyre, who took advantage of the absence of effective control from Rome to seize portions of Galilean territory. At the same time, he was briefly too incapacitated by illness even to come to the aid of his brother when Phasael was attacked by one of Malichus's supporters. We do not know what made him ill, but if his illness prevented him from supporting Cassius at the Battle at Philippi, he could count himself fortunate. Nonetheless, there could be no doubt that once again, he and Phasael found themselves, on the death of Cassius, backers of the losing side in Rome's civil conflict. The new Roman patron of the eastern Mediterranean was Mark Antony.[27]

Fortunately for Herod, Antony had been friendly with his father some fifteen years earlier. Antony, like Cassius, had served in the eastern provinces in the fifties BCE, as a cavalry commander under the governor of Syria. In 57 he had come to know well both Antipater and his sons because his Roman forces had fought alongside Antipater's picked troops in a fierce battle outside Jerusalem against Hyrcanus's nephew Alexander. Herod had been only sixteen when the friendship of Antony with his father was forged, but Antony had not forgotten Antipater and the hospitality he had been shown. He was inclined to look upon Antipater's sons with a benevolent eye.[28]

In the aftermath of Philippi, such personal favor was indispensable for Herod's retention of a political role in Judaea. His rivals knew well that his enthusiastic support for Cassius made it impossible for Herod to claim any principled adherence to the cause of Julius Caesar, whose personal patronage had been so vital to his rise to prominence five years earlier. Soon after Philippi, a delegation of leading Jews traveled to see Antony in Bithynia to accuse Herod and Phasael of usurping power from Hyrcanus. But their embassy was only one of many provincial delegations eager to establish contact with the victors, and Herod managed to prevent their getting a hearing.[29]

Antony's interests lay less in arbitration between rivals within local provincial elites than in establishing sufficient control over the eastern Mediterranean to be able himself to rival his fellow triumvirs in Italy and the West, in particular Octavian. Herod and Phasael were able a year later to brush aside accusations of excessive exercise of power brought by another delegation of a hundred influential Jews, when they came to accuse them before Antony in Daphne, a suburb of Antioch in Syria. The brothers appealed to the explicit backing given them by Hyrcanus and reminded Antony of the hospitality he had received from their father some sixteen years earlier. And Herod had in any case begun to establish his own personal connections with a wider network of leading Romans who could bestow patronage when it mattered: his advocate at Daphne was Messalla Corvinus, who was to speak for him in Rome in 40, a fine orator and patron of literature who, like Herod, had attached himself to Antony after supporting Cassius. Both Herod and his brother were appointed by Antony to serve as tetrarchs (subordinate rulers) of Judaean territory under the increasingly nominal leadership of Hyrcanus.[30]

Herod must have felt that he had once more ensured his own security through a mix of bravado, competence, and diplomacy. The Roman state had entrusted to Antony the complete control over the eastern Mediterranean that both Pompey and Caesar had once wielded, and Herod had every reason to suppose that his friendship with Antony was all he needed to ensure his future. Was he even aware of the chaos being engineered by Antony's brother and wife in Italy in their fruitless efforts to undermine Octavian, or the looming threat of further civil war in the early months of 40, when Octavian defeated the two and consolidated his own position? So many Roman battles over the previous decade had taken place in the East that it must have been tempting for Herod and Phasael to ignore the tensions in the West.

Antony had no such luxury. He had spent the year 41 preparing an offensive against Parthia, hoping to win glory by avenging the defeat suffered by Crassus a decade earlier, but he got no farther than Palmyra in the Syrian desert, and in the spring of 40 he could see that his position in Rome was being undermined. He was forced to hurry west to confront Octavian. His departure left all the eastern provinces dangerously exposed to Parthian forces, and taking advantage of the Romans' disarray, the Parthians invaded their territory and overran the Levant, exacting vengeance for the aggression of Crassus. The forces Antony had left in Syria were not strong enough to protect the border. The provincials who had clustered around Antony to seek his patronage found themselves deserted.

Herod and Phasael were particularly vulnerable, as Hyrcanus's nephew Antigonus tried yet again to remove them and their retinue from power. Antigonus's bribes persuaded the Parthian forces to march south from northern Syria to Palestine. A detachment reached the walls of Jerusalem, where Herod and Phasael were defending the city as it came under siege during the pilgrimage festival of Shavuot. Josephus reports that "while Phasael guarded the wall, Herod with a company attacked the enemy in the suburbs and after a stout fight routed many tens of thousands," but the heroic narrative may tell us only that the Parthians faced some resistance. If so, it did not last long. Hyrcanus and Phasael were tricked into going on an embassy to Parthian headquarters in Galilee, where they were imprisoned. Hyrcanus was mutilated, rendering him unfit to serve as high priest in the Temple, and shortly afterward exiled to Babylonia. Soon Phasael was dead: according to one account, he dashed his head against a rock because he was restricted by chains from killing himself by any other means, but other stories about his death reported that he had been poisoned by doctors sent by Antigonus or that he had died while fighting against the Parthians.[31]

Left behind in Jerusalem without the support and guidance of his beloved older brother, Herod escaped southward toward the palace fortress of Masada. The flight from Jerusalem was a family affair, with his youngest brother, Pheroras, and his future wife, Mariamme, to whom he had been betrothed two years previously, in the caravan. Also in the caravan were Herod's mother, Cyprus, and Mariamme's mother, Alexandra, Hyrcanus's daughter. The journey was chaotic. Cyprus came close to death when a wagon overturned, and at one point Herod is said to have contemplated suicide. Constantly harassed on the way by the forces of Antigonus and the Parthians, Herod gained only a brief respite through a victory in a fierce and bloody battle seven miles south of Jerusalem; he would later build a palace at the site, the Herodium, in commemoration. In desperate straits, and uncertain how best to deal with the large crowd that had followed him out of Jerusalem in the forlorn hope that he would protect them, Herod turned to another brother, Joseph. Joseph met Herod and his company in Idumaea and advised him to disperse his followers: only the women were to be kept in Masada, with plentiful provisions and a guard of eight hundred soldiers under his command for their protection. Leaving the women of the family safely with Joseph on Masada, Herod traveled toward his childhood refuge in Petra, in Nabataean territory, where, unaware of the death of Phasael, he hoped to raise funds for his older brother's ransom from Malchus, the Nabataean king.[32]

Malchus had ascended the throne some twenty years earlier, soon after Herod left Petra as a boy. He had ties of friendship with Herod's father, from whom either he or his father had borrowed extensively. Herod's expectations of financial assistance were thus well founded, but he discovered to his horror that in his current predicament, "the Arabs were no longer his friends." Malchus ordered Herod to quit his territory, claiming to be acting under constraint from the Parthians—although in fact, according to Josephus, he and his advisers were more interested in embezzling the money deposited with them by Antipater. Informed by messengers that he was not welcome in Petra, Herod is said to have given the messengers "the reply which his feelings dictated." By the time further messengers arrived with a report that Malchus had changed his mind and would be happy to receive Herod, it was too late. Herod had now reached the border of Egypt and was on the way to Rome.[33]

The decision, despite the arrival of autumn and the end of the sailing season, to set off across the Mediterranean to seek help from his friend Antony was an act of desperation. With Antigonus installed by the Parthians in Jerusalem as king and high priest, Herod had nowhere else to turn: his patron Hyrcanus was in captivity, and Phasael, the brother alongside whom he had fought and schemed, was dead. Antony would surely eventually return to the East and restore Roman control, and he needed to be apprised of the extent of the crisis he had left behind. The journey had to be risked despite the dangers. Disaster nearly struck when Herod was beset by storms, and on reaching the island of Rhodes he had to commission the building of a new ship, but eventually he made landfall in Brundisium.[34]

In one respect the timing of Herod's arrival was fortunate: a few months earlier the tensions between Antony and Octavian had been resolved in a very public pact concluded at a summit between the triumvirs in Brundisium in October. When Herod made his way across Italy to meet Antony in Rome, he could reasonably anticipate finding his patron freer to turn his attention to matters beyond the political infighting that had drawn him away from his eastern command than would have been the case earlier in the year. On the other hand, Herod could expect little more than to be received with pity and perhaps an offer of support in retrieving the position of tetrarch to which Antony had appointed him a year and a half earlier.

We can only guess what prompted Antony's decision to propose to the Senate that Herod should instead be made not tetrarch but king. We should not discount the possibility that, as was later claimed on Herod's behalf, he was motivated by admiration of Herod's energy—demonstrated not least by the journey he had just undertaken—and fond memories of the hospitality he had received from Antipater long ago. The rumor that he hoped to benefit from Herod's promise of a sum of money if he became king may have been no more than hostile speculation. The real reason may have been simple pragmatism: Antony was keen to use his eastern command to win glory and prestige but would clearly face a major task in ejecting the Parthian invaders before he could embark on an offensive. The unequivocal support of a reliable and competent native of the region would be invaluable in the forthcoming campaign. Herod had shown admirable competence in the ruthless administration of Galilee, and no rival candidate was available to help to return Judaea to the Roman sphere of influence.

Josephus notes that the decision of the Senate came as a surprise to Herod. This assertion, which presumably came from Nicolaus, is plausible, even if it may have suited Herod to claim that he had not sought the throne—Josephus states explicitly that he had not come to Rome to claim the kingship for himself, "for he did not believe that the Romans would offer it to him, since it was their custom to give it to one of the reigning family." With Hyrcanus in exile in Parthia, Herod had hoped to gain Roman recognition of the claims of Hyrcanus's grandson,

Jonathan Aristobulus. But Jonathan was still a young teenager and unknown to the senators, and the Senate could not judge how effective he would be in championing Roman interests, even with Herod as his minister. In less than seven days after his arrival in Rome, Herod found himself, against all precedent, appointed king of Judaea.[35]

As we have seen, Herod was presented to the Senate by the same Messalla who had been his advocate in front of Antony at Daphne a year earlier. The speech in Daphne had presumably been given in Greek, but the speech in the Senate must have been in Latin. Messalla, who became a patron of the Latin poets Tibullus and Ovid, would have had no difficulty finding the words to make his case. It is doubtful, however, how much Latin Herod understood; he would have had to trust the good sense and goodwill of the friend speaking on his behalf.[36]

The pomp and circumstance of the ceremony in Rome designated Herod a king, but his kingdom still lay outside his reach, in the hands of Antigonus and the Parthians. Lacking the troops and money required to gain control of his realm through his own efforts, he relied on the willingness of Roman commanders to put their forces at his disposal. His patron Antony remained in Italy, negotiating the division of power with his fellow triumvirs, and did not leave Rome until October 39. For nearly a year Herod had to rely on the half-hearted help of Antony's henchmen in Syria, knowing that the reconquest of Judaea was not for them a priority. Judaea was too far south in the Levant to be strategically significant for Rome. Focused on the campaign to evict Parthian forces from Syria in the north, Antony's subordinates showed no interest in diverting resources to aid Herod, preferring (it was said) to accept bribes from Antigonus.[37]

But by the winter of 39 Antony was in Athens, taking charge again of the Parthian campaign, and Herod now had a real hope of the military assistance he would require to conquer Judaea, starting with the rescue of the members of his family who had been besieged in the fortress of Masada by Antigonus since the previous year. Herod seems to have considered the creation of a new network of close family to provide support as a priority now that Antipater and Phasael were both dead. His brother Joseph was designated his partner in rule, and sent that winter with two thousand infantry and four hundred cavalry to their home region of Idumaea to prevent any movement in favor of Antigonus, while Herod himself went to Samaria as a base for the subjugation of Galilee. Herod placed his youngest brother, Pheroras, in charge of the commissariat for the troops. Early in the following year he entrusted Joseph with the delicate negotiations required to ensure that the Roman general Machaeras, who had been instructed by Antony to support Herod's campaign, did not succumb to the temptation to accept the bribes freely offered by Antigonus.[38]

Herod had learned all too painfully that the patronage of powerful Romans like Antony needed to be constantly earned, and he decided to relinquish his personal control of operations in Judaea temporarily in order to demonstrate his support for his friend by assisting him in his campaign against the Parthians in Commagene (in southeast Turkey). He succeeded in impressing Antony with his initiative and military skills as well as his loyalty by fending off Parthian cavalry which ambushed his troops while he was leading them by a perilous route from Antioch to assist in the siege of Samosata, but events back home in Judaea, where he had handed over control to Joseph, proved disastrous. Contrary to Herod's instructions, Joseph marched toward Jericho with five Roman cohorts sent to him by Machaeras. His intention was to carry off the corn crop, which was at its ripest in midsummer, but his inexperienced troops were cut to pieces by the forces of Antigonus under the command of his lieutenant Pappus, who ordered Joseph's head to be cut off. Pheroras tried to redeem the severed head for the huge sum of fifty talents, but it is not clear whether the offer was accepted.[39]

On his return to Judaea, then, Herod was intent on revenge as well as conquest. After the rapid subjugation of Galilee, which included the capture of brigands whose hiding places in caves proved accessible to attackers only through an innovative technique of letting down soldiers in large cages lowered by ropes from the top of the cliffs, he was soon embarked on an expedition to Jericho to take vengeance on Antigonus and Pappus for Joseph's death. In fierce fighting Pappus was killed, and Herod was wounded in the side by a javelin. The wound was slight, and he took comfort as he recuperated by celebrating two miraculous escapes from mortal danger, first when the roof of a house collapsed on him and some other diners; then when he was confronted by enemy soldiers who had taken refuge from a storm in an inner room of a house where he was taking a bath: despite coming across him while they were armed and he was naked and defenseless, his enemies were too intent on running away to do him any harm. It was hard not to interpret his salvation from such perils as evidence of divine protection, and Herod chose to celebrate his survival with a savage act of vengeance for Joseph, cutting off the head from the corpse of Pappus and sending it to Pheroras.[40]

The campaign had taken more than two years of intermittent warfare, but by the spring of 37 Herod was camped outside Jerusalem, preparing to attack the city from the north. The besieging force combined Herod's soldiers with a much larger army led by Sosius, the Roman governor of Syria. Sosius had a mandate from the Senate and Antony to depose Antigonus, who had been declared an enemy of Rome. The siege was hampered by the need for food to be brought from a distance because the area around the city had been deliberately denuded of supplies, but eventually siege engines and catapults battered down the walls, confining the defenders to the Upper City, the western hill, and the inner precincts of the Temple.[41]

Herod's major concern during the fighting seems to have

been less the eventual conquest of the city, which was more or less guaranteed by the substantial Roman forces on his side, than the avoidance of blame by his future subjects for any damage inflicted on the buildings, especially on the Temple. Restraining Sosius's troops from the slaughter and looting Roman soldiers expected as a reward for victory was not easy. Both the soldiers and Sosius himself had to be bought off. Even so, some of the Temple porticoes were burned during the fighting, although he could lay the blame at the feet of Antigonus and his supporters. By July the fighting was over. With Jerusalem in his hands, Herod could begin to establish his rule.[42]

Antigonus decided to surrender to Sosius, rather than Herod. He was well aware of the revenge Herod had taken on Pappus for the death of Joseph, and expected a similar fate, given his own role in the death of Phasael. Sosius in turn sent him as a captive to Antony. Standard Roman practice was to keep captured kings as hostages in Rome. Sosius may have expected to include his defeated enemy in the triumphal procession through the streets of Rome for his victory over Judaea—which, in the event, he was not to celebrate until September 34, three years later. But Herod was unwilling to allow such a powerful rival to survive and bribed Antony to put him to death. Herod feared, according to Josephus, that if Antigonus were taken by Antony to Rome as a prisoner, "he might plead the justice of his cause before the Senate and show that he was descended from kings while Herod was a commoner."[43]

Herod's concern was fully justified: he had been nominated king by the Roman state, and he had gained physical control of his kingdom with the aid of Roman forces, but the Romans could always change their minds, and his rule lacked legitimacy in the eyes of his Jewish subjects. Before the siege of Jerusalem, some Jews from Jericho and elsewhere in Judaea had come over to his side out of hatred of Antigonus or a vague enthusiasm for change, but he had not come to power through a groundswell of popular support. He was hated by the partisans of Antigonus, whom he had supplanted, and he was resented by his former rivals in Hyrcanus's regime.[44]

Herod knew all too well that his hold on power was tenuous. Over the previous thirty years, ever since he had first become aware of the political world in which his father operated, armies had marched into Judaea to seek a change of regime on at least nine occasions. Deciding that it would have been the height of folly to assume that his own rule was more secure, he had forty-five of Antigonus's leading supporters executed. Within a few years of his conquest of Jerusalem, all but one of the members of the court which had been convened by Hyrcanus in 47 to try Herod for the summary execution of the bandits in Galilee were put to death.[45]

Ultimately, Herod's rule continued to rely, as it had done in the previous ten years, on the friendships he cultivated with powerful Romans, and in 37 he was wholly dependent specifically on the whims of Mark Antony. Over the following years he wooed Antony's support by such unsubtle methods as giving the name Antonia to the strengthened fortress that protected the Temple in Jerusalem. But for the first years of his reign Herod's relationship with Antony was frequently imperiled by his complex relations with three women: Cleopatra, queen of Egypt, who was Antony's lover; Alexandra, the Hasmonaean daughter of the former high priest Hyrcanus in whose service both Herod and his father had risen to prominence; and, above all, Mariamme, Alexandra's daughter and, from 37, Herod's wife.[46]

Herod was betrothed to Mariamme around the year 42, when she was still a child, probably about twelve. Her father, Alexander, and paternal grandfather, Aristobulus II, had both been killed by supporters of Pompey in 49, and she seems to have been left in the care of her mother, Alexandra, and her maternal grandfather, Hyrcanus. For Antipater and Herod, the advantage in 42 of consolidating their influence by linking their family to the ruling dynasty was obvious, even though it required Herod to put aside his wife Doris, whom he had married only a few years earlier and with whom he had a young son, Antipater. On the bride's side, Hyrcanus could see Antipater and his sons increasingly using their Roman contacts to exercise independent authority, and he promised Mariamme in marriage to Herod to encourage them to remain loyal to him and his family. A year later, in 41, he was citing the betrothal to Antony as a demonstration of his confidence in Herod's abilities and trustworthiness.[47]

The marriage itself did not take place until 37, but we have seen that already by 40 Mariamme and her mother were included in the family group sequestered in Masada for safekeeping while Herod traveled to Rome to seek help in the recapture of Jerusalem. With Hyrcanus in exile in Parthia, and her brother Jonathan Aristobulus even younger than she, Mariamme had no other way of staying safe as Judaea was overwhelmed by war. By the time the marriage itself took place, Mariamme was about seventeen. The only adult family member able to look after her interests in relation to her new husband was her mother. It was a task Alexandra was to perform with great energy.[48]

Herod was uncomfortably aware of his need to present himself to his Jewish subjects as linked to a source of legitimate authority within Jewish society by marriage to a Hasmonaean princess. During the siege of Jerusalem he took time off to go to Samaria to celebrate the wedding before returning to Jerusalem for the final assault; the two were thus already married by the time he finally gained control of his kingdom. Initially Herod seems to have felt that a combination of this marriage and the purge he had carried out of Antigonus's supporters had effectively neutralized any Hasmonaean opposition that remained. The following year he felt sufficiently secure to welcome his former patron Hyrcanus back to Judaea from his Parthian exile as a friend and father-in-law rather than as a potential rival for power.[49]

But he retained his suspicion of the ambitions and resentment of those who longed for a return to rule by the Hasmonaean dynasty. Herod knew that his usurpation of power might well be resented by Mariamme's mother, who would naturally consider her son Jonathan Aristobulus entitled to inherit the authority wielded in Jerusalem by his Hasmonaean ancestors for a century and a quarter. Herod's fears of the ambitions of Alexandra and her descendants were to haunt his rule almost to his last days.

Hyrcanus had exercised his nominal rule over Judaea primarily as high priest in the Temple. Antigonus had occupied the same position when Hyrcanus was deposed and dispatched to Parthia, but this was not a role open to Herod, who was not a priest. Nor could it be offered again to the ineffectual Hyrcanus, since Antigonus had mutilated him, cutting off an ear specifically to render him ineligible for the office, which could be held only by a priest without a physical blemish. When Herod decided to sidestep rival power bases by inviting an obscure Babylonian Jew of impeccable priestly lineage to become high priest, passing over Jonathan Aristobulus on the grounds that he was too young to hold the post, Alexandra responded with fury. She lobbied Antony to insist that the position go to her son, calling on the support of Antony's paramour, Cleopatra of Egypt.[50]

Alexandra's pressure succeeded in forcing Herod in 35 to appoint the seventeen-year-old Jonathan to the high priesthood. The acclamations from the wider Jewish population which greeted the youth in the Temple at the festival of Tabernacles that year demonstrated all too clearly the danger Herod could face if he allowed the young man such a prominent public role. The sight of Jonathan approaching the altar wearing the high priestly vestments evoked a mass outpouring of emotion from the crowd in the Temple precincts, an effusion that combined good wishes and prayers with grief that this handsome young priest was not also in control of the political fortunes of Judaea as his ancestors had been. Soon after the episode in the Temple, Jonathan was drowned while swimming in the palace complex at Jericho. Herod's story was that the death was a dreadful accident—the boy's friends had been larking around and held him underwater for too long. Claiming to be grief stricken, Herod put on a show of deep mourning. But Herod was widely disbelieved, not least by Alexandra. With help from Cleopatra, Alexandra engineered a summons for Herod to account to Antony for the death of her son. By the time a nervous Herod presented himself to Antony in Laodicea in Syria to answer the charge, it was early the following year, the spring of 34.[51]

Through a combination of bribes and smooth words Herod contrived to persuade his Roman patron not to interfere with the internal affairs of Judaea, but the episode permanently damaged his relationship not only with his mother-in-law but also with his wife. Both Mariamme and her mother were thought to be willing to use her great beauty to political advantage in gaining the support of Antony. Herod was deeply in love with her, but his quite rational mistrust of her ambitions was exacerbated by the antagonism his own blood relations felt toward her, particularly his mother and his sister Salome, who resented Mariamme's sense of entitlement, derived from her Hasmonaean pedigree.[52]

The establishment of trust between the couple was not helped when it emerged that Herod had left secret instructions before he went to see Antony that if he failed to return, Mariamme was to be put to death to avoid her falling into Antony's lecherous hands. The instructions were left with Herod's uncle Joseph, who was to take care of his kingdom during his absence. Joseph was married, none too happily, to Herod's sister Salome. When Herod discovered that Joseph had revealed these instructions to Mariamme, he sprang to the conclusion, prompted by Salome, that Joseph and Mariamme must have had an affair, and had Joseph executed. The accusation may well have been unjustified; there is no record of an inquiry or trial. It is hard to know how Herod expected Mariamme to react to his plans for her demise if he failed to return. She is reported to have complained, not unreasonably, that "it was not the act of a lover to command that if anything serious should happen to him [Herod] at the hands of Antony, I should be put to death too, though not guilty of anything."[53]

Herod had been aware since his meeting with Antony at Daphne in 41 that any approach to his Roman patron had to allow for Antony's susceptibility to the whims of Cleopatra, by whom he had first been seduced in the late summer of that year when she came to greet him in Cilicia, making her appearance dressed as Aphrodite and conveyed on a golden barge. Ancient biographers of Antony asserted that he was so captivated by the Egyptian queen that he neglected even the most pressing political crises in Italy and on the Mesopotamian frontier. Even if this was an exaggeration, Antony's insistence on treating Cleopatra as his wife, publicly acknowledging his paternity of the children the queen bore him in 40 and 36, would have signaled to Herod the need to please Cleopatra if he were to maintain the goodwill of her Roman lover.

It would not be easy. The queen was evidently impressed at first by Herod's reputation for military competence—she tried to detain him in Alexandria when he was on his way to Rome in 40, giving him a magnificent reception in the hope of persuading him to take command of a campaign on her behalf—but once he was installed as ruler of Judaea after the capture of Jerusalem in 37, he found himself caught up in her intrigues and territorial ambitions.[54]

These intrigues related to Alexandra, who (as we have seen) was affronted that her son Jonathan Aristobulus had been passed over by Herod for the high priesthood and wrote to Cleopatra to ask her to intervene with Antony on Jonathan's behalf. Why Cleopatra chose to take up Alexandra's cause is not clear. Apparently Antony's interest in the request was piqued only when he was shown a picture of Jonathan, who was exceptionally handsome. The matter might have come to an end once Alexandra got her way and Jonathan was appointed high priest, but the affair left Herod suspicious that Cleopatra was plotting to deprive him of his kingdom. When it emerged that Cleopatra had tried to persuade Alexandra to slip away clandestinely from Judaea to Egypt with Jonathan in tow, Herod seems to have become convinced that the Egyptian queen was helping Alexandra out of hatred toward himself.[55]

The suspicion must have been reinforced after Jonathan Aristobulus drowned, for it was Cleopatra who pushed Antony into summoning Herod to see him to explain the young man's demise, which Alexandra was convinced had been murder. Herod is said to have believed that Cleopatra never ceased doing her best to make Antony his enemy. If so, she did not succeed. At their meeting in Laodicea, as Herod later reported in a letter to his supporters in Judaea, Antony, won over by gifts, told Cleopatra that it was improper to demand a king to give an account of how he exercised his power and that she should not meddle in Herod's affairs.[56]

If Cleopatra was inclined to interfere in Judaea, one reason would have been geography. The kingdom of the Ptolemies over which Cleopatra ruled had stretched at its height, in the third century BCE, far beyond its base in Egypt, encompassing much of the southern Levant, including Judaea. Cleopatra saw her influence over Antony as an opportunity to reinstate that earlier glory. Expansion of Ptolemaic territory was not obviously in the interests of Rome, and Antony initially resisted her demands. But by 36 he was beginning to soften, with the result that, although her request that all of Judaea and Arabia be removed from their independent royal rulers and transferred to her dominion was not granted in full, she did receive control of parts of Judaean and Nabataean territory and of some cities on the coasts of Phoenicia and Palestine.[57]

In 34 Antony went farther and transferred to Cleopatra the lucrative balsam groves around Jericho, which lay within the borders of Herod's current kingdom. Herod of course had no choice but to acquiesce to this loss of sovereignty, since the transfer was mandated by Antony on behalf of the same Roman state that had granted him his kingdom in the first place. However, he managed to persuade Cleopatra, during a visit to him in Judaea in 34, to lease the balsam plantations to him. He also took on the lease of the parts of Nabataea she had acquired, thus in practice enlarging the area under his control, albeit at the considerable annual cost of two hundred talents payable to the queen.[58]

Quite how Herod contrived to engineer this unusual lease arrangement is unclear. Josephus reported that Cleopatra tried to entice Herod into a sexual relationship during her visit, either out of passion or as a trap, but Herod evaded her advances and plotted with his friends to have her killed. The report is not inconceivable, but in light of the vicious propaganda about Cleopatra which pervaded Roman society after her eventual downfall, it is probable that this story, like many other stories about intended but unfulfilled projects, was invented at a later date. Certainly there was nothing hostile about Herod's public behavior: at the end of Cleopatra's visit to his court he escorted her back to Egypt, showered her with gifts, and in due course paid her the rental on the lease for the land given her by Antony.[59]

Whatever Cleopatra's personal feelings toward Herod, in the end her territorial ambitions were to smooth his own perilous navigation in the sea of Roman politics when the war clouds gathered two years later. After the failure of his offensive against Parthia in 36, Antony had lost the enthusiasm for military conquest which had brought him prestige in Rome, and in 32 Octavian took to portraying his rival as an incompetent drunkard, slave to the Egyptian queen. In a decisive battle in September 31, Octavian's general and close friend Marcus Vipsanius Agrippa defeated Antony's forces at Actium in Greece. Antony and Cleopatra fled to Alexandria with what remained of their navy. As Antony's friend, Herod could reasonably have been expected to fight alongside his patron in his hour of need, and indeed Antony's biographer Plutarch, a contemporary of Josephus, listed Herod the Jew among the subject kings who fought by Antony's side. But in fact, although Herod prepared auxiliary troops for Antony and sent him money and wheat, he had the good fortune to be absent from the Battle of Actium itself.[60]

Herod's absence was due to his engagement, on instruction from Antony (who was himself responding to the urgings of Cleopatra), in a war against the Nabataean king Malchus, who had defaulted on the tribute he owed to the Egyptian queen. Herod's relations with Malchus had been cold since Malchus had failed to provide assistance when Herod was in need a decade earlier. Cleopatra was said to have have been motivated by a hope that the two kings would weaken each other, ensuring that neither side emerged victorious. When Herod's troops unwisely relaxed in the flush of victory after fierce engagements against a large Nabataean force on the Auranitus plain, they were subjected to a surprise attack by one of Cleopatra's generals. Deprived of his army's camp and demoralized by his losses, Herod was reduced to sporadic raids into Nabataean territory, and then reduced still further in the spring of 31 by an earthquake in Judaea of unprecedented severity in which house collapses killed a considerable proportion of the population. The histories do not say whether any of Herod's own family were included among the dead, and the army itself had been camped out in the open and escaped physically unscathed, but many of his soldiers would have lost relatives, and their morale must have been shattered by the disaster. Herod sued for peace, but his envoys were killed by the Nabataeans, who saw an opportunity to make inroads into Judaea. Herod changed tack and went on the offensive. Crossing the river Jordan, he won a series of bloody engagements near Philadelphia (modern Amman). But the campaign took some months, and, crucially, by the time Herod's final victory over Malchus was achieved, it was too late to join Antony in the campaign against Octavian which ended at Actium at the beginning of September.[61]

Despite his absence from the battle, after Actium Herod once again found himself on the losing side in the Roman civil conflict and forced to justify his actions to the victor. He had met Octavian when he was in Rome in 40, and on that occasion Octavian had supported his appointment as king of Judaea, partly in recognition of the support Herod's father, Antipater, had given his own adoptive father, Julius Caesar, in Egypt after the death of Pompey. But Herod's stay in Rome had been brief, and the two men had not met in the nine years since. Other friends of Antony, including the Messalla who had pleaded Herod's case in 42, had prudently gone over to Octavian before the final showdown at Actium—indeed Messalla, who had been appointed by Octavian as consul for 31 in place of Antony after Antony was declared an enemy of the Roman people, fought alongside Octavian in the fateful battle. Not so Herod. As Josephus noted, "His situation seemed desperate both to Herod himself and to the enemies and friends around him as well, since it appeared unlikely that he would remain unpunished for the great friendship which he had formed with Antony."[62]

Trepidation was natural, but Herod was only one of many local rulers who had supported Antony while he was the representative of Rome, and it would be impractical for Octavian to impose regime changes across the entire eastern half of the empire over which he now reigned supreme. In the *Jewish War*, Josephus claimed that Octavian felt his victory over Antony to be incomplete while Herod remained Antony's ally, but this assertion is not to be found in his later account in the *Jewish An-*

tiquities and may not be based on any early source. At any rate, with Octavian preparing to march from Asia Minor to Egypt to complete the destruction of Antony's forces, Herod took the initiative and sought an audience in Rhodes in spring 30. He left his kingdom in the hands of his youngest brother, Pheroras. Pheroras had not previously been assigned any responsibilities since his supporting role in the campaign before the siege of Jerusalem in 37, but by now he was well into his thirties, and Herod must have considered him sufficiently mature.[63]

Presenting himself to Octavian "without a diadem, a commoner in dress and demeanor, but with the proud spirit of a king," Herod acknowledged that he had been made a king by Antony and that he had given Antony all the support he could, although he claimed (less plausibly) to have done his best to counter the baleful influence exerted over Antony by Cleopatra and even to have sought her death. (This latter claim may be the origin of the rumor about Herod's unfulfilled murderous intentions during Cleopatra's visit to Judaea four years earlier.) He urged Octavian to examine "not whose friend, but what sort of friend, I have been." He could, of course, have gone back farther into his personal history and added observations about his friendship with Cassius until that proved impolitic after Philippi, but some things were best left unsaid.[64]

The speech as reported by Josephus is doubtless embroidered, but whatever was said proved successful. Octavian restored to Herod his ruler's diadem, "urging him to show himself no less a friend to him than he had formerly been to Antony." It helped that Herod had already been useful to Octavian in his preparation for the impending assault against Antony and Cleopatra in Egypt. Some gladiators who had been training to fight for Antony had missed the battle in Actium and tried to join him in Egypt after it was lost but were intercepted by Herod before they could cross the Egyptian border. Herod also supported Octavian by provisioning his army as it marched south from

Syria. A few months after their meeting in Rhodes, Herod received Octavian at Ptolemais "with all royal attendance . . . and an abundance of provisions," ensuring there was no lack of either wine or water as the troops crossed the desert. Finally, he lavished the huge sum of eight hundred talents on presents for his new Roman patron.[65]

The high value of Herod's support for Octavian sprang from the geographical importance of Judaea as the net closed in on Antony in Alexandria. Antony himself seems to have been well aware of Herod's importance at this juncture, and he sent to Judaea one of his most trusted advisers, a Spartan called Alexas, with a brief to dissuade Herod from changing sides. The project was derailed when Alexas himself tried to defect to Octavian, but the attempt demonstrated both Antony's awareness that Herod was otherwise likely to desert his erstwhile friends (despite Herod's protestations to Octavian about the loyalty he had so long shown to Antony) and that Antony and Cleopatra had come to realize how valuable Herod's support could be in their current predicament. For the royal couple themselves, it was all too late: by mid-August 30, Alexandria was in Octavian's hands and both Antony and Cleopatra had killed themselves. Octavian was the undisputed ruler of the Roman world.[66]

The visit to Rhodes and Octavian's journey south through Herod's kingdom seem to have established a strong bond between Herod and Octavian, a bond that was to last, with only one brief upset, for the rest of Herod's life. By the time Herod was hastening to meet Octavian in Egypt in the early autumn of 30 to congratulate him following the suicides of Antony and Cleopatra, the two men are said to have been able to converse as old friends. Among the favors bestowed on Herod was a gift of the four hundred Gauls who had been Cleopatra's bodyguard. A few months later Herod escorted Octavian for hundreds of miles on his way north from Egypt to Antioch in Syria before returning to his own kingdom in Judaea.[67]

In the interval between the defeat of his patron Antony at Actium and his successful visit to Octavian in Rhodes the following spring, Herod was plagued by insecurity. Without Antony's support and constantly concerned that his right to rule Judaea might be called into question by anyone who could claim greater legitimacy through Hasmonaean descent, he had his old patron Hyrcanus put to death. Herod's action was not wholly irrational, in that for much of his youth he had witnessed Judaea mired in conflict as different members of the Hasmonaean family persuaded foreign powers to provide military aid in their struggles to control Jerusalem, but even in antiquity the execution of Hyrcanus was seen as hard to justify. Herod had known the old man since childhood, when Hyrcanus as high priest and ethnarch had entrusted power to Antipater, and as a young man Herod himself had entered Judaean politics through Hyrcanus's patronage. The two men had been close: Hyrcanus had protected Herod when enemies tried to undermine him in the eyes of Antony after Philippi, and he had trusted Herod sufficiently to return to Jerusalem from Parthia just five years previously in order to be with his family. Notoriously lacking in energy and competence even in the prime of life, Hyrcanus was hardly likely to seek power for himself in old age. The charge, according to Herod's memoirs, was that Hyrcanus had been lured by Alexandra into treasonous correspondence with the Nabataean king Malchus. It was said that Hyrcanus had received letters from Malchus which showed that the old man planned to take refuge in the Nabataean court with his daughter in order to plot against Herod from outside his kingdom. More skeptical sources, according to Josephus, alleged that the charges had been trumped up and that Malchus had sent only greetings and a present when he wrote to Hyrcanus, who was an old friend.[68]

The execution of Hyrcanus smacked of panic—and it proved counterproductive. By 29, more than a year later, Herod was secure in the political backing of Octavian, and Hyrcanus could have constituted no threat even if he had wished to cause trouble. But it was too late for Herod to hope for forgiveness from Hyrcanus's granddaughter Mariamme, and the angry accusation that he had killed her grandfather was part of her response when Herod now accused her too of treason and had her put on trial.

The precise cause and course of the trial of Mariamme are now impossible to reconstruct. We do not know how much Herod was influenced by the feud between his wife and his mother and sister, who hated Mariamme for mocking their low birth. Herod's suspicion of treason was mixed up with sexual jealousy, and the charges brought against her may have included adultery. According to Josephus's narrative in the *Jewish Antiquities*, Herod rashly left the same secret instructions about Mariamme when he went to see Octavian on Rhodes as he did when he had visited Antony some four years previously, with identical disastrous results when she learned about them. Matters were said to have come to a head when Mariamme refused to have sex with him one afternoon when he "lay down to rest and out of the great fondness which he always had for her called for Mariamme. And she came but she did not lie down in spite of his urging." Instead Mariamme contemptuously took him to task for having killed both her grandfather and her brother. Herod's sister Salome took the opportunity to stir up his paranoia about Mariamme's hostility by suborning his butler to say that Mariamme had given him a drug to give to Herod, claiming it was a love potion for the king. The butler confessed that he did not know what was in the love potion, but Herod was all too ready to assume that it must have been poison.[69]

In a state of rage, Herod summoned his wife to a trial before a council of his closest friends, bringing "an elaborately framed accusation against her concerning the love-potions and drugs which she was said to have prepared." Herod himself was "intemperate in speech and too angry to judge." The rest of the council, realizing the state he was in, condemned her to death.

Alexandra, who had fought so fiercely for her children for so long, abandoned her daughter at the last to save her own skin, berating her for wicked ingratitude to her husband. Salome and her friends argued against suggestions that Mariamme might be locked away in a fortress, pointing to the popular disturbances which could break out if she were allowed to live, and Mariamme was taken away to execution.[70]

Whatever his plans to have her killed if he did not return, Herod was distraught when she died. The marriage may have been doomed from the start. We have seen that Mariamme was still a child when she was promised to Herod by Hyrcanus. It is improbable that her views on the match were sought, and, in light of Herod's undistinguished origins, it is unlikely that she would have been enthusiastic if she had been asked. That the marriage would be full of tension could have been predicted. Harder to anticipate was her strength of character and the passion her beauty evoked in Herod, as demonstrated by his descent into wild grief after he had put her to death. We are told that she was a woman of surpassing beauty and dignity of bearing; we are also told that she could be unreasonable and quarrelsome, but this may well reflect the characterization of her personality by Herod after she was executed, or the stereotyping of a powerful woman by Nicolaus or Josephus. What is certain is that her relationship with her husband was tempestuous. She is said to have assumed that Herod's devotion to her would prevent him from harming her despite the "excessive freedom of speech" with which she berated him, but she turned out to be mistaken.[71]

Ruthlessness in the face of all potential opposition had been a feature of Herod's rise to power, but he collapsed in the months after Mariamme's death in 29, losing all interest in the administration of his kingdom as he mourned his dead wife, calling out for her as if she were alive. It is unclear how much the physical ailments that afflicted him were the product of remorse and passion, or of overindulgence in banquets and other distractions through which he sought comfort as he shut himself away in the city, Samaria, where he had married her eight years earlier. An inflammation in his head which led to a temporary loss of reason and brought him close to death coincided with a nationwide plague that killed many in Judaea, including a number of his close friends.[72]

With Judaea in turmoil and Herod incapacitated by grief, Mariamme's mother saw an opportunity to seize Jerusalem by gaining control of the fortresses which dominated the city and of the Temple. She argued to the commanders of these fortresses that she should be entrusted with their care on behalf of Herod and her grandsons, born to Herod and Mariamme. She was, after all, the closest remaining relative to the boys, Alexander and Aristobulus, who were both still under ten years old. But the commanders, who included Herod's cousin Achiab, were unimpressed and informed Herod, who recovered sufficiently to have her put to death. By 27, with the discovery and execution soon after the death of Mariamme of a group of supporters of the Hasmonaean dynasty called the Sons of Baba, who had been in hiding in Idumaea since the defeat of Antigonus in Jerusalem ten years earlier, "none was left alive of the family of Hyrcanus, and the kingdom was wholly in Herod's power, there being no one of high rank to stand in the way of his unlawful acts."[73]

Herod was free to create a kingdom to celebrate his rule. The timing was opportune, for in the same year Octavian, exhibiting the unscrupulous determination with which he had brought down his rivals, made clear to all his intention to rule Rome indefinitely as an autocrat. Expected to disband the legions raised during the civil wars, Octavian had instead retained command of a large standing army whose loyalty could be ensured by dispersal around the empire to discourage coordinated coups by the generals he appointed. All political patronage now flowed from him. In a carefully staged ceremony in the Senate on January 13, 27, he declared that the republic had been restored and that senators could now compete freely for magistracies and military commands—an act of beneficence celebrated by the Senate and people of Rome by the bestowal on Octavian of ceremonial honors and titles, including the name "Augustus"—but everyone knew that political advancement now depended ultimately on the emperor's whim.

The new system was inherently precarious: Roman aristocrats, previously tempted into politics by the hope of glory, now knew that the greatest prizes were beyond their reach, and many might reasonably prefer to enjoy a life of leisure. Others might overstep the mark by seeking too much power for themselves. It would take time, and experimentation, for Augustus to devise the best system of checks and balances to ensure both competence and loyalty in the government of the far-flung provinces of the empire. Integral to the new system from the start, as a way to check the ambition of senators and prevent the emergence of rivals, was the installation in parts of the empire of native rulers, personally appointed by Augustus, whose jurisdiction was recognized by Rome in return for their loyalty to his regime. The use of such provincial monarchs, who would pose no threat in the realm of Roman politics precisely because they were not members of the senatorial elite, was novel and deliberate. Collaboration was encouraged by treating these kings as Romans, the social equal of the emperor himself, and by arranging for the education of their sons in Rome. Prime among the beneficiaries of this new world order was Herod of Judaea.[74]

3

A Roman Kingdom

By 27 BCE and in his mid-forties, Herod's power was secure, but in his personal life he was more fragile than he had ever been. Rejected by the woman he loved so passionately, he had executed her in a frustrated fury only to regret bitterly what he had done. We have seen that for a while he lost all interest in administering his kingdom, but when drinking and carousing failed to solve his personal crisis, he flung his energies into hugely expensive infrastructure projects to remake his kingdom in his own image. He built himself a sumptuous new palace in Jerusalem filled with marble and gold, rebuilt and refurbished fortresses, erected numerous new public buildings both in his own realm and abroad, and threw money into the construction of new cities. Lavish expenditure on such projects was unconstrained even by a terrible famine, which began with a drought in around 25 and the failure of the harvest in two successive years. Herod was reduced to chopping up the silver and gold ornaments in his palace to buy grain from Egypt to feed the people, but work on the most ambitious of his many building projects, the rebuilding on a massive scale of the Temple in Jerusalem, seems to have begun just as the famine was coming to an end.[1]

Such grandiose plans were possible only because Herod could be confident that he had the backing of his Roman patron Augustus, who was himself embarked on a spending spree in the city of Rome to mark a new golden age of peace after the disaster of the civil wars, and was able to draw on the resources of the whole empire.

Herod's meetings with Octavian (called, starting in 27 BCE, Augustus) were sporadic after their time together in the year following the Battle of Actium. They met again ten years later when Augustus came to Syria in 20, and Herod was in Rome some three years after that, when he came to the city to fetch his sons by Mariamme and bring them home; he may have timed his visit deliberately to coincide with the celebration in 17 of the Secular Games, a special festival intended by Augustus as a symbolic proclamation of the achievements of the new regime after decades of chaos and the restoration of the traditional values which had made Rome great. Herod returned to Rome five years later, in 12, when he brought his sons back in order to accuse them of treacherous conspiracy before the emperor, but that may have been the last time he saw Augustus in person—the evidence for a final visit to Rome after 10 is thin.[2]

Friendship with Augustus was for Herod a guarantee not only of a secure grip on power but of opportunities to increase his wealth. Herod made substantial gifts to his patron, such as a donation during his visit to Rome in 12 of three hundred talents for the spectacles and doles provided by the emperor to the Roman populace, but gifts like these were outstripped by the ability of the emperor to enrich his friends, as Augustus was to demonstrate at the end of Herod's life: the emperor chose to return to Herod's family a substantial proportion of the money and goods Herod had assigned to him in his will, giving two hundred and fifty thousand pieces of coined silver each to Herod's unmarried daughters and fifteen hundred talents to his sons; he is said to have kept out of sentiment just a few of the precious vessels in the bequest, "not so much because of their great value as because they were regarded by him as mementoes of the king."[3]

Maintaining such a friendship from a distance, with only infrequent meetings over the years for which letters and embassies could only partly compensate, depended on a network of friends in common. As we shall see, Herod cultivated links with the emperor's close family—in his will, he left a substantial sum to Augustus's wife, Livia—and Herod's close family, including his sister Salome, established similar ties in their own right with the imperial court. Within wider Roman society, Herod struck up a friendship with a man called Pollio (probably Gaius Asinius Pollio, who had been consul in the year 40), and his sons by Mariamme stayed with Pollio when they were sent to Rome for their education. Messalla Corvinus, who had twice spoken on Herod's behalf, became a major public figure in Rome in the twenties BCE, celebrating a triumph in 27 for the suppression of a revolt in Gallia Aquitania. But the main friend whose support was to prove invaluable to Herod in his relations with Augustus was the emperor's closest supporter and confidant, Marcus Vipsanius Agrippa, and Agrippa became a major figure in Herod's life.[4]

Agrippa had risen to prominence in Rome by his exceptional military genius in loyal service to his friend Octavian. He had known Octavian from childhood and helped him raise the private army which launched Octavian's meteoric career in the months after Caesar's death. Octavian was not a skilled general and relied heavily on Agrippa in the thirties BCE for his victories in foreign campaigns and in the civil war, including the decisive victory at Actium. As Octavian, now called Augustus, consolidated his regime during the following decade, Agrippa reaped the reward, including marriage in 21 to Augustus's daughter Julia. When Agrippa died unexpectedly in 12, Augustus in his funeral oration said his son-in-law had been, in effect, his equal: "It was established by law that into whatever province the common affairs of the Romans might take you, no one in those provinces should have greater power than you. You rose to the greatest height through my esteem and your own virtues, and in accordance with the unanimous sentiment of all men."[5]

We do not know when Herod and Agrippa first met. Agrippa was urban praetor (one rank below consul) when Herod came to Rome in 40 for the dramatic meeting of the Senate at which he was appointed king of Judaea, but Herod stayed only briefly in the city, and there is no record of a meeting. Their friendship seems to have started only in 23 or 22, when Agrippa had been formally recognized by Augustus as his most senior colleague, with overarching responsibility for the whole eastern half of the empire. Agrippa was spending the winter in Mytilene, on the island of Lesbos, and Herod sailed to Lesbos to pay his respects. The two men seem to have established a close bond very rapidly. Already after this first meeting it could be said that "as for the two men who ruled the mighty Roman empire—Caesar and, next to him, Agrippa, to whom he was devoted—there was no-one after Agrippa whom Caesar held in greater esteem than Herod, while Agrippa gave Herod the first place in his friendship after Caesar." When Herod began work on his new palace in the Upper City in Jerusalem, the two splendid reception halls in the palace were named "Caesareum" after Augustus and "Agrippeum" after Agrippa.[6]

Agrippa was in Rome to assist in the Secular Games in 17 and may have seen Herod during his trip to the city around that time, but the next recorded meeting of the two men was in 15, when Agrippa visited Herod in Jerusalem. Herod pulled out all the stops to entertain his guest with sumptuous feasts and a guided tour of his newly founded cities and fortresses, as well as of the rebuilt Temple in Jerusalem—still partially a building site—where Agrippa, duly impressed, arranged for a great public sacrifice of one hundred oxen and feasted the populace.[7]

In 15, Agrippa left for Asia Minor before the winter set in, but Herod contrived to spend a considerable time with him in the following year, ostensibly sailing to participate in an expedition to reinstate the legitimate king in the Bosporus region (in modern Turkey), though it is likely that Herod's main interest lay in the opportunity afforded by the campaign to accompany Agrippa during the mission itself (which did not prove onerous) and on the return overland through Paphlagonia, Cappadocia, and Phrygia to the west coast of the province of Asia. Herod was not subtle in orchestrating ways to impress onlookers with the closeness of his friendship with the great man: on one occasion he is said to have reacted to Agrippa's willingness to accede to a request by embracing him "in grateful acknowledgement of his friendly attitude," eliciting to his delight an equally friendly response from Agrippa, who "behaved like an equal, putting his arms around Herod and embracing him in turn." The story was told, of course, precisely because the friends were anything but equal, but such physical demonstrations of friendship mattered, particularly when they could be witnessed by others. A year later, when Herod wished to reinforce the many letters of recommendation he had already sent Augustus in favor of his eldest son, Antipater, he took the young man with him to meet Agrippa in Mytilene. Agrippa's stint in the East was coming to an end after ten years, and Herod wanted him to take Antipater with him on his return to Rome and introduce him to the emperor.[8]

In Judaea, Herod publicized his special relationship with Agrippa by renaming the maritime town of Anthedon (close to Gaza) Agrippias, or Agrippeion. "So great was his affection for this same friend Agrippa" (as Josephus put it) that he engraved

Agrippa's name on the gate of the Temple in Jerusalem. So Agrippa's death around the end of March 12, at about the age of fifty and after only a short illness, must have been a terrible shock. Herod's grandson, the son of Aristobulus, was named Marcus Julius Agrippa (known as Agrippa I and himself king of Judaea nearly half a century after Herod's death). It is uncertain whether this was intended to honor Herod's friend in his lifetime or after his sudden death, but it ensured that the impact of Marcus Vipsanius Agrippa on Herod and his family would be remembered for at least the following century, since Agrippa I gave his son the same name.[9]

Herod cemented his direct links to Augustus by sending his own offspring to live in Rome—from around 23 to 17, his Hasmonean sons Alexander and Aristobulus; in 13, his eldest son (by Doris), Antipater; and, at some point before 7, his younger sons Archelaus, Antipas, and Philip. Other links between the imperial family in Rome and the Herodian family in Jerusalem were established through the women in each court. Thus Salome was close to Augustus's wife, Livia, although there is no record of where or when the two women met, and it is possible that their friendship was forged entirely through correspondence—letters were regularly transported efficiently across the Mediterranean world under the peaceful regime imposed by Augustus, albeit not always at speed. The significance of such links was not lost on the historian Strabo, a contemporary observer of the Roman world writing sometime after 6 CE, who noted that Augustus honored both the sons of Herod and Herod's sister Salome and her daughter Berenice.[10]

For Augustus and his relations, a major attraction of these exotic foreigners was simply the title of king. It would be hard to exaggerate the glamour of monarchy in Roman politics after Julius Caesar had been assassinated because it was believed he wanted a crown for himself. After Caesar, no Roman, even one as powerful as Augustus, could hope to be called king, but all

Romans continued to care deeply about royal titles. In the record of his achievements inscribed on monuments throughout the empire after his death, Augustus boasted about the nine kings or children of kings who were led as captives in his triumphs. Conversely, we shall see that in 4 BCE Augustus ignored the provision in Herod's final will that his son Archelaus should be appointed king of Judaea, pointedly giving him instead the lesser title of ethnarch until Archelaus could demonstrate that he deserved to be called a king. When Herod's younger son Antipas, younger brother of Archelaus, many years later petitioned the emperor Gaius Caligula for the title of king in place of tetrarch, the punishment for his arrogance was exile to the south of France.[11]

Evidently Romans, who only dimly recalled their own kings from five centuries earlier, found it exciting to consort with royalty. This was particularly true when royalty behaved just like ordinary people. We are told that the kings who were friends and allies of Augustus "would often leave their kingdoms and show him the attentions usual in dependents, clad in the toga and without the emblems of royalty." There was something exhilarating about power as a personal right inherent in the whole notion of kingship, which Roman society had rejected in the adoption of republican politics, with its messy complications of elections and shared authority.[12]

Apparently Augustus and his family came to be fond of Herod's household. Everything that Josephus recorded about the emperor's interventions with Herod in his relations with his sons suggests that Augustus cared about the young men, who had spent many years living with his own family, and we shall see that he did his best to save them from their father's wrath when Herod began to suspect them of treason.

Despite his royal title, Herod had been granted his kingdom by Rome, and had no inherited justification for his rule over Jews or anyone else. The boundaries of his kingdom were entirely at the whim of whoever controlled the decisions of the Roman state. There was thus no limit to the territory which might be handed over to him. At the height of his rule, when the great building projects in Caesarea and elsewhere were nearing completion, Josephus claimed (doubtless relaying a claim by Nicolaus) that "Caesar himself and Agrippa often remarked that the extent of Herod's realm was not equal to his magnanimity, for he deserved to be king of all Syria and of Egypt." And in practice, although his realm never reached that far, the borders of Herod's kingdom did indeed expand a great deal in the thirty-six years of his reign.[13]

When Herod was first named king by the Senate in 40, the territory assigned to him included Peraea (Transjordan), Galilee, and Ituraea (to the north of Galilee). In 36, Antony handed over Ituraea to Cleopatra, and in 34 Herod also lost the Jericho balsam plantations to Cleopatra, although he was able to lease them back. In 30, after Cleopatra's death, he reincorporated the region into his realm. At the same time he was also granted by Octavian rule over important cities beyond these areas, including Gadara, Hippos, Samaria, Gaza, Anthedon (later called Agrippias), Joppa, and Straton's Tower, extending his power in Peraea and Samaria as well as on the Mediterranean coast. Some years later, his realm was extended by a grant from Augustus of the basalt steppes of Trachonitis, Batanaea, and Auranitis to the east of the Sea of Galilee, and in 20 he was granted further territory north of Galilee on the death of the Iturean Zenodorus, who had originally leased it from Cleopatra but had allowed it to be overrun by bandits.[14]

Roman notions of the area to be ruled by a king of Judaea, then, were elastic. When a Roman governor was assigned a province it was often unclear where its geographical frontiers lay, and the regions which had been assigned by Rome to the Hasmonaean Hyrcanus in the nearly quarter of a century after the conquest of Jerusalem by Pompey had also varied considerably: in 63 Hyrcanus had been deprived by Pompey of all the coastal towns, of all the non-Jewish towns in Peraea, and of Scythopolis and Samaria, and in 56 he had been stripped for a while of all political authority and confined to his functions as high priest in Jerusalem. In 47, Julius Caesar had restored to Hyrcanus control over at least some of the territory "which the Jews had possessed from ancient times since they made a treaty of friendship with the Romans," and memories of the even wider regional power wielded from Jerusalem a few decades earlier by Shelomzion, Hyrcanus's mother, may have encouraged an assumption that Herod, as ruler over Judaea, should exercise authority over a similarly extensive realm.[15]

In any case it is likely that the Roman Senate in its deliberations in 40 lacked any clear notion how much of the territory assigned to Hyrcanus a few years earlier they intended to give Herod in his capacity as king of Judaea—not least because the whole region was currently in the hands of the Parthians—although we can be fairly sure that they would have assumed that he would rule over an area larger than Judaea itself. The boundaries of the areas allocated to his kingdom may have shifted even before the conquest of Jerusalem: the historian Appian recorded as one of the actions of Mark Antony in 39 the appointment of Herod as king in Idumaea and Samaria, and it is possible that these territories, which lay adjacent to Judaea to the south and the north, were only specifically added a year after his original appointment. If so, Herod would have been particularly pleased: he had a special interest in his home region of Idumaea, where family ties facilitated the imposition of control; and as governor of Samaria on behalf of Hyrcanus for a brief period while Julius Caesar was still alive, he had established political contacts there which would provide him with a secure base during his successful assault on Jerusalem two years later.[16]

The overriding concern for Rome in the allocation of territory to Herod was his ability to ensure secure government in the interest of Rome. It was up to Herod to devise means to control subjects of markedly heterogenous cultural backgrounds. The Jews of Judaea had established close bonds with the inhabitants of Idumaea and Galilee in the previous century when these regions had been conquered by the Hasmonaeans, but they had a long history of prickly relations with the Samaritans. The inhabitants of Peraea were mostly gentiles with no affinity to Jews or Jewish culture. Most lived in village communities dependent on agriculture, but some, particularly in the northern reaches east of the Sea of Galilee and in the foothills of Mount Hermon, found banditry more profitable. The gentile cities of the coastal plain and Peraea boasted a high degree of urban Greek culture and (especially since being freed from Hasmonaean rule by Pompey) a strong desire for political autonomy. Herod wooed Jews not least by presenting himself as their spokesman even outside Judaea (see below, Chapter 4), and he suppressed bandit areas with ruthless force, but his approach to the Greek cities within his realm was more complex and brought him onto a wider stage in the politics of the eastern Mediterranean.

The Greek city most vocal in its opposition to Herod's rule was Gadara (southeast of the Sea of Galilee), which had been declared independent by Pompey in 63 but then given to Herod by Octavian in 30 after more than three decades of autonomy. The city brought complaints against Herod to Agrippa around 23, when he was in Lesbos, and again to Augustus in 20, during the emperor's visit to Syria, but without success. Resentment flowed deep and surfaced again on Herod's death, when Gadara was one of a number of cities, along with Gaza and Hippos, finally granted independence by Augustus. Nicolaus noted in his autobiography his own unwillingness, presumably as a native of the neighboring city of Damascus, to argue on behalf of his patron, Herod's son Archelaus, against this bid for autonomy. On the numerous coins issued by Gadara down to the mid-third century CE, the city's era was always calculated from Pompey's grant of independence. The twenty-six years of Herod's rule were evidently viewed by later inhabitants of the city as a temporary aberration.[17]

Gaining the trust of the inhabitants of these bastions of Greek culture within his realm was clearly not going to be easy when they were so intent on independence, and Herod does not seem to have made much effort to win them over. The Gadarenes accused him of plundering their temples. Instead of trying to placate the hostile citizens of the existing Greek cities of his realm, Herod preferred to burnish his reputation as an enthusiast for Greek culture by the wide distribution of largesse to Greek cities and cultural institutions outside his own territory. Josephus wrote with considerable awe an extended panegyric of Herod's generosity:

> He provided gymnasia for Tripolis, Damascus, and Ptolemais, a wall for Byblus, halls, arcades, temples, and public squares for Berytus and Tyre; and then theatres for Sidon and Damascus, an aqueduct for the coastal city of Laodicea, and for the people of Ascalon baths, grand fountains, and colonnades of remarkable quality and size; and elsewhere he made dedications of parks and green spaces. Many cities received grants of land from him, just as if they were part of his own kingdom; others, like Cos, were endowed with a regular income to perpetuate the annual appointment of a magistrate to oversee the gymnasium, so that this office should never lapse. He supplied corn to all who needed it. Time and again he contributed funds for shipbuilding at Rhodes, and when the temple of Apollo there was burnt down he rebuilt a better temple at his own expense. Need I mention more? His donations to the people of Lycia or Samos, for example, or his generous subsidies to meet individual needs throughout the whole of Ionia? And then the plethora of his offerings in Athens, Sparta, Nicopolis, Pergamum in Mysia? That avenue in Syrian Antioch, once an off-putting expanse of mud—was it not Herod

> who paved all two and a quarter miles of it with flags of dressed marble, and, for shelter from the rain, furnished it with an arcade along its entire length?[18]

The peak of his benefactions to iconic Greek culture outside his realm was Herod's grant to rescue the Olympic Games from decay, "a gift not only to Greece at large but to the whole world." It is significant that this gift, which endowed the Olympics with revenue "for all time," was intended to "preserve the unfading memory of his term as president [of the games]," and that this term happened to coincide with one of his visits to Rome. The image of the king as a cultured philhellene was intended for a Roman audience as much as for the inhabitants of the Greek cities themselves: surviving inscriptions from the Acropolis in Athens which attest to the "good works and goodwill toward the city" of King Herod describe him as a "friend of Romans" and a "friend of the emperor."[19]

It was also with an eye on Rome that Herod cultivated relations with other client rulers who owed their status to the whim of their Roman overlords. Appian included a reference to Herod's appointment as king of Judaea in his account of Rome's civil wars, in his list of kings from Darius in Pontus to Amyntas in Pisidia and Polemon in Cilicia whose rule had been established by Antony "here and there as he pleased." The origin of these kings' rule meant that they had many interests in common as they negotiated with Rome, and in Herod's time Augustus was said specifically to have encouraged links of friendship and intermarriage among dependent kingdoms. Augustus would have much approved when, around 16, Herod married his son Alexander to the daughter of Archelaus of Cappadocia (in modern Turkey).[20]

Augustus was much less impressed by the frequent and difficult engagements with the royal house of Nabataea which were thrust upon Herod by the constraints of geography. There had been a history of mutual interference between the two contiguous realms since Hasmonaean times, and toward the end of Herod's life, in 9, a miscalculation about Nabataea for a while cost him the friendship of the emperor and threw his own rule into jeopardy.

After thirty years of reliance on Roman support, by 9 Herod may have been lulled into a false sense of security about his ability to rely on approval from the emperor for whatever actions he took in the environs of his kingdom. Herod may even have thought that Augustus would not be averse to transferring Nabataea into his hands in its entirety, just as other regions bordering Judaea had been transferred to him in the twenties. After all, when he had defeated the Nabataean king Malchus in 31 after his campaign to extract the tribute owed to Cleopatra, his success "so broke the spirit of the people of Arabia [i.e., the Nabataeans]" that "the nation chose him for its leader." A Nabataean recorded a dedication in the thirties BCE of a statue of "King Herod, master" at the entrance to the temple of Ba'al Shamin in the Nabataean cult site of Si'a. And, according to Josephus, based presumably on information from Nicolaus, who was deeply involved in the political arguments in Rome about relations between Judaea and Nabataea during Herod's last years, even as late as 7 Augustus did indeed consider giving Arabia to Herod—he is said to have changed his mind only on the grounds of Herod's age and domestic problems. So what caused the crisis which had so traumatized Herod two years earlier?[21]

Herod's opponent Malchus had died soon after his defeat in 31, and the new Nabataean king, Obodas III, rapidly established more cordial relations with his neighbor in Judaea. In time the relationship became sufficiently close for Herod to make him a substantial loan of sixty talents. Herod was able to soothe the tension which arose between the two kingdoms when Augustus in around 23 transferred to Herod a region to the northeast of Galilee that had earlier been sold to the Nabataeans by the Ituraean Zenodorus, whose entire territory was handed over to Herod by Augustus three years later. But the relaxation of tension between the two kingdoms for some twenty years after 31 owed less to any change in policy by Herod than to the character of Obodas, who is described as "inactive and sluggish by nature." The same characteristics provoked a crisis toward the end of Obodas's rule. The king's lethargy facilitated the machinations of his chief minister, Syllaeus, who was energetic, handsome, and ambitious, and who had his own connections in the court of Augustus in Rome, having played an important (albeit not conspicuously successful) role in the Roman expedition into Arabia Felix (modern Yemen) in 26–25. His foray into Judaean politics nearly provoked a permanent rift between Herod and Augustus.[22]

The affair began around 15, when Syllaeus, who evidently considered himself a natural ally of Herod, made a proposal to Herod to marry his sister Salome, noting that "the connection would not be unprofitable to Herod through his association with the government of Arabia, which was even now virtually in his hands, and by rights should be more so." We do not know how much Herod was influenced by his own Nabataean heritage through his mother, but he took the proposal sufficiently seriously to discuss it with Salome. She was much in favor, but the marriage plans broke down when Herod required Syllaeus to be "initiated into the customs of the Jews," probably by circumcision, before the wedding. Syllaeus declined on the grounds that "if he did submit, he would be stoned to death by the Arabs."[23]

It was after this rebuff to his plans to bring the governments of the two kingdoms closer together that Syllaeus began in around 9 to stir up trouble on the border between Nabataean and Herodian territory by allowing brigands to use the Nabataean kingdom as a base to pillage Judaea and Peraea. Herod mounted a punitive expedition to eliminate the brigands and recover the loan due for repayment by Obodas. Herod later claimed that the expedition had been authorized on behalf of the Roman government by Saturninus, the governor of Syria. This may well have been true, but since Josephus's account was derived from Nicolaus, who was commissioned by Herod after the event to justify his actions to Augustus and to denigrate the claims of Syllaeus, it is possible that his authority was less than explicit. What is certain is the furious reaction of Augustus when he gained the impression from Syllaeus that Herod had marched an army into the Nabataean kingdom without authority from Rome. There could hardly be a clearer example of Augustus's assumption that an allied king like Herod could take such military action only when explicitly permitted by the Roman state.[24]

Syllaeus was already present in the imperial court and able to make a dramatic plea to the emperor. Dressed in black, he grossly exaggerated the plight of his country. Those of Herod's friends who were present were caught unprepared by Augustus's response to Herod's unauthorized deployment of an army outside his own territory. Augustus wrote angrily to Herod that whereas he had formerly treated him as a friend, now he would treat him as a subject. Isolated in Judaea, Herod was plunged into despair and fear. Augustus refused to receive the envoys he sent to plead in his defense. It took a second embassy, led by Nicolaus, even to get a hearing from the emperor. And if the account given by Josephus, undoubtedly derived from Nicolaus himself, is to be believed, it took a wholesale attack by Nicolaus on the probity of Syllaeus before Herod was rehabilitated. The crisis precipitated by Syllaeus exposed in public the fragility of Herod's power when the goodwill of the emperor was withdrawn.[25]

Herod was all too aware throughout his career of the constant need to impress his patron. Fine words and gifts were all very well, but it was a matter for regret that Augustus provided so few opportunities for a client king to fight alongside Roman forces in support of a Roman campaign on the eastern frontier, as he had once thrown himself with enthusiasm into support of Mark Antony in his Parthian campaign. Herod does not seem to have taken a personal role in warfare again for some twenty years after the Nabataean war at the time of Actium. After the failure of the Roman expedition into Arabia Felix in 26–25, from which Herod was fortunately absent, though he sent a force of five hundred picked men from his bodyguard, Augustus decided that such expansionary wars were not worth the risk of defeat. Similarly, a diplomatic accord agreed by Augustus with Parthia in 20 brought an end to hostilities on that frontier.[26]

But when granted an opportunity to prove his enthusiasm in military operations on behalf of Rome, Herod did not hesitate. He had sailed in the spring of 14 on his own initiative, with what must have been a new navy, to the Black Sea in order to help Agrippa in an expedition against rebellious tribes in the Bosporus, eventually catching up with the Roman force at Sinope, on the north shore of modern Turkey. Building a navy was a fine demonstration to Agrippa (and thus, indirectly, to Augustus) of the benefits of the large new harbor, named after the emperor, that Herod had just completed in Caesarea Maritima on the Judaean coast. Herod was nearly sixty, but he was very fit and proud of his martial skills, and he may have been longing for the opportunity to demonstrate his prowess after nearly two decades without combat. It must have been all the more disappointing that, although the campaign proved sufficiently major for a triumphal procession through the streets of Rome to be voted to Agrippa to celebrate his victory, there is no record of Herod having taken part in the fighting, which was probably over by the time he arrived.

Disappointment was mitigated by diplomacy. The return journey to the Aegean by land enabled Herod to be seen basking in the company of Agrippa by the rulers of the countries through which they passed, including Archelaus of Cappadocia, whose daughter Glaphyra had only recently married his son.[27]

* * *

Herod was determined that his kingdom would be not only magnificent but also Roman, as befitted a close friend of the ruler of the Roman world. By the end of his reign the landscape of his realm had been transformed by the foundation of the new cities of Sebaste, Caesarea, and Agrippias to celebrate his Roman patrons. These new cities and his capital, Jerusalem, were adorned with buildings in modern styles imported from Rome.

Among the buildings which advertised Herod as a Roman was the ostentatious palace he built for himself in Jerusalem. The palace was described in rueful recollection by Josephus a few years after it had been destroyed in the sack of the city in 70 CE, a century after it had been erected for Herod's use:

> It was simply the ultimate in magnificence and every form of luxurious appointment. The entire site was enclosed by a forty-five–foot wall studded at regular intervals with ornamental towers, containing inside huge banqueting halls and guest rooms offering 100 beds. There was an indescribable variety of stone used for the interiors—stones rarely found elsewhere were here collected and applied in abundance. There were ceilings marvellous for the length of their beams and the splendour of their ornamentation. There were innumerable rooms of infinitely various design, but all richly furnished with most of their contents in silver or gold. Outside there was a whole series of interconnecting circular cloisters, each with pillars of different design, and all their open spaces laid to lawn. There were groves of various trees crossed by long walks with deep canals along their edges. Throughout the garden there were artificial ponds spouting water through a profusion of decorative bronze fittings, and around the watercourses there were numerous dovecotes for tame pigeons.

With its lavish interior decoration, extensive gardens, sculptures, and dovecotes, the palace was an exceptionally luxurious version of the Italian townhouse of Herod's day.[28]

So too in the private palaces Herod built for himself in Jericho, where the unique climate of the rift valley provided refuge from the winter cold, and in the fortified sites of Masada, Machaerus, and Herodium, where Herod could enjoy luxury away from the bustle of the city, Herod's architects incorporated Roman alongside Alexandrian styles in painting and stuccowork and made use of contemporary Roman construction techniques such as the diamond-shaped masonry of *opus reticulatum*, and the squared blocks of stone in parallel courses of *opus quadratum* and concrete vaulting. Imaginative use was made of the landscapes as the setting for architectural elements as in contemporary Italy, and in the private dining room in his new palace at Herodium, the walls were decorated with frescoes of Nilotic landscapes and banquets in the Italian style, while the royal apartments housed installations with separate cold, warm, and hot rooms for luxurious bathing in Roman fashion.[29]

Embrace of Roman customs entailed more than physical settings. Herod also dined in the Roman style, with diners reclining on benches placed in a horseshoe shape to enable conversation. Herod liked female company and does not seem to have favored the drinking culture and male bonding of Greek symposia, preferring men and women to dine together in his court—it was over dinner that Salome and Syllaeus had become acquainted, and their mutual attraction was noted by their fellow diners. Meals included luxury foodstuffs imported from across the Mediterranean. The storerooms of Masada contained celebrated Italian wines (Massic, Amineum, Vulsum, Caecubum, Tarantinum) as well as the Philonian wine brought over especially from Italy in 19 with the Latin inscription "for King Herod the Jew" on the jar handles, and many wines from the Aegean. There were fish sauces, some imported from as far away as Spain. A Roman visitor would have felt at home, although the allocation of important domestic roles to beautiful eunuchs would have seemed exotic: eunuchs were not a common feature of

Herod's third palace in Jericho, rendered much more luxurious by Herod than the earlier Hasmonaean buildings on the site. Herod spent much time in Jericho in the winter months, and it was here that he died in 4 BCE. (Photo: Zev Radovan / Alamy Stock Photo)

the imperial court in Rome in Herod's time, although Herod's gift in 10 of eunuchs to his son's father-in-law, Archelaus of Cappadocia, suggests that some others in the Roman world shared his taste for their company.[30]

Within this sophisticated court Herod aped aspects of the household of Augustus in Rome as much as he did the royal courts of the Hasmonaeans and other dynasts of the Hellenistic East: just as Augustus's slaves and freedmen carried out important roles in the government of the empire, so the eunuch who served as keeper of Herod's bedchamber was said to have been charged with taking care of the most important matters of state. The court was both Herod's home and the headquarters of his administration, with his family—siblings, wives, and offspring, and their relatives by marriage—at its center, along with old acquaintances from Idumaea and an inner circle of friends who maintained Herod's confidence as advisers and spokesmen.[31]

Many of these denizens of the court were non-Jews, employed at least in part as cultural luminaries to help Herod maintain a façade of civilized conversation at symposia and dinners. A few individuals originated from the city of Rome itself, but most came from the Greek cities of the eastern Mediterranean, and conversation at court was usually conducted in Greek. Nicolaus, who came from Damascus in Syria, claimed in his autobiography to have worked hard to provide the king with a general education in rhetoric, history, and philosophy. The sophisticated veneer brought concrete political benefits. Herod doubtless benefited, for instance, from the assistance of such courtiers when, like his Roman friends Augustus and Agrippa, he wrote memoirs which attempted to justify his more dubious political actions.[32]

Some of these advisers stayed by the king's side for decades. Ptolemy, the longest lasting—he was already providing help to Herod in 40, when he met him in Pamphylia (in southern Turkey) on the way to the fateful meeting of the Senate—was still at his side at his deathbed thirty-six years later. Overseer of the king's finances, and described in 10 as "the most honoured of his friends" when he played a pivotal role in the suppression of unrest, Ptolemy fell out of favor for a while in 7 but must have been reinstated by the time of Herod's last illness, since it was to him that Herod entrusted his seal and his will as he lay dying, and we know that Ptolemy received from Herod a tract of land in Samaria as a reward for his long service.[33]

Not all Herod's Greek friends were equally loyal or useful. Most notorious was a Spartan adventurer called Eurycles, an adroit politician whose command of a contingent in support of Octavian at Actium had proved sufficient to win him rule over Sparta. Arriving in Judaea some twenty years after Actium, and driven by a craving for money when, as Josephus put it, "Greece could no longer meet his extravagant requirements," Eurycles would contrive in his brief visit to extort money from almost every side in the strife within Herod's family that he himself fomented in the king's declining years. Herod's welcome of this dangerous guest "out of regard for his country" is testimony both to the continuing cultural prestige of Sparta in the early Roman Empire, based on idealized conceptions of Sparta's heroic past, and to Herod's desire for recognition in the wider Greek world, which, as we have seen, led to his patronage of the Olympic Games.[34]

Herod was entirely open about his desire to import contemporary Greek and Roman cultural norms into Judaea. Although this could be achieved within the private domain of his court without provoking open opposition, it was a different matter when he tried to introduce distinctively Roman public entertainment to his subjects in Jerusalem in honor of Octavian in around 27:

> He established athletic contests every fifth year in honour of Caesar, and he built a theatre in Jerusalem, and after that a

> very large amphitheatre in the plain, both being spectacularly lavish but foreign to Jewish custom. . . . Athletes and other classes of contestants were invited from every land, being attracted by the hope of winning the prizes offered and by the glory of victory. . . . He also offered considerable gifts to drivers of four-horse and two-horse chariots and to those mounted on race-horses. . . . There was also a supply of wild beasts, a great many lions and other animals having been brought together for him, such as were of extraordinary strength or very rare kinds. When the practice began of involving them in combat against one another or setting condemned men to fight against them, foreigners were astonished at the expense and at the same time entertained by the dangerous spectacle, but to the natives it meant an open break with the customs held in honour by them. For it seemed glaring impiety to change their established ways for foreign practices.

It is striking that athletics, chariot racing, and music competitions, all familiar features of festivals in the Greek world, aroused far less opposition from the Jewish audience than the distinctively Roman wild beast fights and gladiatorial shows, for which others in the eastern part of the Roman Empire were only gradually developing a taste at this date. Faced with this unenthusiastic response from his Jewish subjects, Herod did not persist with the quadrennial games in Jerusalem as planned, but the festival of dedication when the new city of Caesarea was completed around 12 was still Roman in content, with "a great number of gladiators and wild beasts and also horse races and the very lavish shows that are to be seen at Rome and in various other places."[35]

Caesarea was not the first city in honor of his new Roman patron with which Herod adorned his kingdom. In 27, just after Octavian adopted the name Augustus, Herod had begun the transformation of the ancient site of Samaria (northwest of modern Nablus) into the new city of Sebaste, with a gentile population made up of his veteran soldiers: "Sebastos," meaning "revered," is the Greek translation of the Latin name "Augustus." Herod is said to have selected for the settlement "those who had fought as his allies in war and many of the neighboring populations," making the new city "a source of security to himself" and apportioning to it "the nearby territory, which was the best in the country." Josephus's assertion that Herod "made it splendid in order to leave to posterity a monument of the humanity that arose from his love of beauty" reads like an echo of a speech by the king himself.[36]

A few years later, between 25 and 20, Herod began work at a coastal site called Straton's Tower on the new city of Caesarea, of which the jewel was an artificial circular harbor, which Herod named Sebastos. Built with contemporary Roman technology for constructing huge blocks underwater by using a hydraulic cement of sand and lime that hardens when immersed, the harbor celebrated Augustus not only by name but through its design. The magnificent tower at its entrance was designated the Drusion in honor of Augustus's stepson Drusus. The harbor was carefully aligned to a great temple dedicated to Rome and Augustus that stood on a promontory above the sea in the center of the city, "visible a great way off to those sailing into the harbour." It housed a colossal statue of the emperor, "not inferior to the Olympian Zeus, which served as its model."[37]

Herod had been quick off the mark in establishing worship of his Roman patron within his realm. Provincials tried to make sense in religious terms of the new political order by incorporating their new master into their existing systems of polytheistic worship when they started to erect temples to Rome and Augustus in the twenties BCE. But in much of the empire this ruler cult was slow to take root, not least because no one could be certain whether the ruler would be pleased, and Herod did not know in 27, when there was no precedent to guide him, how Augustus would react when his plans for the new city of

Herod's artificial harbor in Caesarea Maritima is still visible. The temple of Rome and Augustus stood on a promontory on the shore just above the harbor. (Photo: Duby Tal / Albatross / Alamy Stock Photo)

Sebaste included a temple dedicated to his worship. Constructed over the remains of the palace of the kings of Samaria and a Hellenistic fortress, the temple of Rome and Augustus and its large forecourt were the central focus of the city. Presumably Augustus did not complain, since a few years later, after the emperor's visit to Syria in 20, Herod erected to Augustus in the city of Paneion (modern Banias) in the north of his territory another "very beautiful temple of white stone," for which he selected a location in the mountains at the source of the river Jordan just below a beautiful cave. It seemed that Herod had found the ultimate way to demonstrate his enthusiasm for the new regime.[38]

The religious scruples of his Jewish subjects precluded the erection of a similar temple in his capital city of Jerusalem, but he found an ingenious way to adapt the Jerusalem Temple to

Remains of the temple of Rome and Augustus, built by Herod as the central focus of the new city of Sebaste in Samaria. (Photo: GRANGER—Historical Picture Archive / Alamy Stock Photo)

demonstrate his enthusiasm for Rome and its new master. Greatly enlarged with a peristyle court on an artificial platform, the remodeled Temple of the Jews made use of the most modern Roman engineering techniques, with arches to support the platform and porticoes with marble columns erected around the edges of the precinct. In other parts of the Roman world, polytheists incorporated the emperor into the pantheon of divinities to whom they offered sacrifices. This was not possible for the Jews, because the Jewish God was jealous and forbade his devotees to worship other gods. Herod therefore instituted a novel practice that Jews should make regular sacrifices not to the emperor himself but to their own God on behalf of the emperor.[39]

Herod's plan for the Jerusalem Temple seems to have received enthusiastic support from Augustus. The imperial cult elsewhere in the eastern provinces of the empire was funded by the local provincials, but the loyal sacrifices instituted by Herod in Jerusalem received financial aid from the emperor himself. As the Jewish philosopher Philo specifically recorded some sixty years after Herod had undertaken the work, Augustus "adorned [the] temple through the costliness of his dedications, and ordered that for all time continuous sacrifices of whole burnt offerings should be carried out every day at his own expense as a tribute to the most high God," specifying that "these daily offerings were to be of two lambs and a bull." We have seen that Augustus's friend and son-in-law Marcus Agrippa sacrificed a hecatomb during his visit to Jerusalem in 15 BCE, when, as Philo put it, "his discourse to those of his friends who were there with him consisted of nothing else but praise of the sanctuary." We are told by Philo that "throughout the days which he [Agrippa] spent in the city out of courtesy to Herod, he resorted to the precinct, delighting himself with the spectacle of the ornate structure and of the sacrifices, of the ritual observed in the services, and of the majestic aspect of the High Priest when arrayed in the sacred vestments and conducting the holy rites."[40]

We have seen that Agrippa's support was commemorated by the engraving of his name on the gate of the Temple. Augustus's presence was signified more symbolically by Herod's erection, "as a votive offering and at great cost," of a golden eagle above the Temple gate. For some Jews, this was a provocation. The eagle was pulled down from the Temple's façade just before Herod's death in 4 by Jews who saw it as a religious affront. Herod responded angrily that they had themselves committed sacrilege.[41]

What, apart from Herod's willingness to risk such opposition to the image despite his care to respect Jewish sensibilities elsewhere in the remodeled Temple, suggests that Herod considered the eagle a tribute to his Roman patron? The eagle was not a standard representation of Rome in this period, but plans to include eagle imagery in the symbolic depiction of the emperor may have been under way by the time Herod completed his major works in the Jerusalem Temple in 12. The eagle in the Jerusalem Temple may indeed have constituted the earliest deployment of what became an important element of imperial iconography.

According to one account, an eagle was released from Augustus's pyre on his demise in 14 CE. The eagle demonstrated that the emperor had gone to heaven to join the gods. Augustus was determined to ensure that, in the same way that he had begun his meteoric career by advertising his status as son of the divine Julius, he should be recognized by his fellow Romans as divine after death. The eagle was a counterpart to the celebrated comet which had followed the death of Caesar, and easier to arrange.

We do not know when Augustus began to make plans for his funeral, including this piece of theater, but the erection of his monumental mausoleum in Rome in 28 BCE suggests that he had begun making plans by then. In 23, when he believed himself close to death, he must have had some contingency funeral arrangements in place. If the release of an eagle from his funeral pyre was included among these plans at this date—just as work was beginning on the transformation of the Temple in Jerusalem—it would have made sense for Herod to adopt the eagle image to honor his imperial patron in the Temple where Jews were to pray to their God on his behalf.[42]

The rebuilt Jerusalem Temple fit comfortably into the Augustan program for the foundation or rebuilding of sanctuaries in Rome which would ensure the restored favor of the gods after the disasters of the late republic. Herod's reported claim, on announcing his plan to rebuild the Temple, that he would "by this act of piety make full return to God for the gift of this kingdom," was one aspect of his rule as a Roman king.[43]

How could Herod afford to pour so much money into the erection of temples, cities, and palaces, particularly when so many of his building projects were undertaken simultaneously and coincided with munificent gifts to communities and individuals outside his kingdom? Herod is explicitly said to have paid for the rebuilding of the Jerusalem Temple out of his own pocket, even though, as we have seen, he had found himself in severe financial difficulties as a result of drought and famine only a year or so before the rebuilding was begun. How did he find the funds?[44]

Herod's finances evidently puzzled some in antiquity. Josephus asserted that because Herod was involved in expenses greater than his means, he was regularly compelled to use harsh measures toward some subjects in order to finance his generosity to others. He preserved a rumor that Herod secretly looted gold and other valuables from the tomb of David, despite noting that this alleged tomb robbing was nowhere to be found in the account of Nicolaus about the monument to David erected by Herod at the site.[45]

Precise details about Herod's complex finances are impossible to unravel, but despite the considerable fortune he may have inherited from his Idumaean family, most of the wealth at his disposal during his reign came from the revenue opportunities bestowed by the Roman state. Some of his income was raised by taxation, which was sufficiently onerous for some of his subjects to demand after his death that yearly payments be lightened and sales taxes removed, but much was also derived from the exploitation of royal lands, customs duties, and tax farming contracts outside his kingdom. Herod inherited royal estates from his Hasmonaean predecessors, and, according to the complaints of a Jewish embassy to Rome after his death, he had a practice of confiscating the property of his political opponents.[46]

Among Herod's most lucrative properties were the balsam groves of Jericho and En Gedi that he had been compelled to transfer to Cleopatra for a few years in the thirties. In his later years other sources of income included interest on his extensive loans to the Nabataeans, rental on lands used by the Nabataeans for grazing, and a slew of tax concessions outside his kingdom (in Lycia and Cilicia, both in modern Turkey, and in Syria). In 12 Augustus entrusted to him the exploitation of the copper mines of Cyprus, with the right to half the income in return for a single payment to the coffers of the Roman state of three hundred talents. Precisely what was entailed in Herod's appointment by Augustus in 20, at the height of his building program in Judaea, as procurator (financial administrator) of "all Syria" (or, in another version, as "an associate of the procurators of Syria"), is not known, but we can be certain that the post was intended to generate an income for Augustus's protégé. Romans in the imperial period took for granted that officials would be enriched by administrative posts in the provinces, by legal means or otherwise. So long as their appointments were thought to have had the approval of the emperor, few expected to face consequences unless they were guilty of the most egregious corruption.[47]

In the long term Augustus's investment in Herod's energy and commitment were to pay off handsomely. Among Herod's most impressive achievements were the encouragement of international trade from across the Mediterranean into the southern Levant through the creation at Caesarea of the largest harbor in the eastern Roman Empire after Alexandria in Egypt, and the encouragement of international tourism to Jerusalem through the rebuilding of the Temple. Much of the wealth thus generated went eventually to the Roman state, which had facilitated its acquisition. By far the main beneficiary of Herod's death under the terms of his will was Augustus: Herod left to the emperor a substantial fortune of ten million pieces of coined silver, "besides vessels of gold and of silver and some very valuable garments." From the point of view of the Roman emperor, the Jewish king had used well the investment by his patron and friend. The kingdom of Herod in Judaea was a jewel in the crown of Augustus's Roman revolution.[48]

4

Ruling as a Jew

How Jewish in the eyes of his fellow Jews and of Romans was the king who had been granted his realm by Rome and ruled on Rome's behalf? Despite the desperate slur of the Hasmonaean Antigonus in his plea to the Romans that Herod was only half-Jewish because his father was an Idumaean, Romans thought of him as Herod the Jew. His younger contemporary Strabo described Herod as a native of Judaea. We have seen that he was identified in Latin as "King Herod the Jew" on the wine jugs shipped from Italy to Masada in 19 BCE. In Herod's eyes, at least, the identification was correct. Herod was so proud of his Jewish identity that Nicolaus was said to have invented, specifically to please the king, a genealogy of Herod's family claiming it was descended from elite Jews who had come to Judaea from Babylon, presumably in the time of Cyrus in the sixth century BCE. But what did it mean to be Jewish in the Roman world in Herod's time? And more specifically, what did his Jewishness mean to Herod?[1]

Neither Herod nor anyone else in the Roman world considered being both Jewish and Roman in itself a problem. Multiple identities were common—provincials thought of themselves as Roman even while continuing to identify as Greeks or Gauls. There was no reason for Herod to consider the idiosyncrasies of Judaean customs a bar to dual identity, particularly when the emperor had shown such favor to the Jews' central shrine in Jerusalem. It was true that Jews followed ancestral practices which other people found bizarre, but so too did other inhabitants of the Roman world. Such local idiosyncrasies provided material that antiquarians like the elder Pliny catalogued with curiosity rather than deplored. The time would come when the Jews would be represented in state propaganda as an external enemy of Rome, but this was long after Herod's death, when Vespasian and Titus used their victory against Judaea in 70 CE as justification for their seizure of power in Rome. We should avoid retrojecting to Herod's day the agonizing about Jewish identity that afflicted such Jews as the historian Josephus in the aftermath of Titus's destruction of the Temple, and which has preoccupied many Jews in the diaspora in more recent times. Herod would have seen no such cause for concern: he could parade his Jewishness with pride.[2]

To live as a Jew meant no more than to follow the traditional customs of the inhabitants of Judaea. By the first century BCE, this was a lifestyle into which outsiders could opt as proselytes, but for Herod, who was born a Jew and spent his childhood in Judaea in the vicinity of the Jewish high priest and his entourage, a Jewish lifestyle would have come naturally. We can assume, for instance, that Herod was circumcised as a baby and that he had his sons circumcised since we know that he insisted that men who wished to marry his female relatives undergo the operation. We can assume also that Herod was at least believed to have paid some attention to Jewish food taboos: a quip attributed to Augustus that it would be better to be Herod's pig than his son would have fallen flat if it were well known that Herod habitually ate pork, and it is probably significant that no pig bones were identified among the food remains in the Herodian levels in the palace at Masada. And although we cannot know how regularly and conscientiously Herod abstained from work or travel on the Sabbath, we can probably assume that he occasionally observed the Sabbath in some way since the Roman satirist Persius almost certainly had in mind the Sabbath when he described as "Herod's day" the time when "the lamps . . . have spat forth their thick clouds of smoke, when the floppy tunnies' tails are curled around the dishes of red ware, and the white jars are swollen out with wine."[3]

Harder to evaluate is what a Jewish lifestyle meant to Herod. Was he motivated by piety, a desire to keep the requirements of the Torah, or did he simply wish to fit in with his Judaean compatriots when he was with them? It is likely that Herod's apparent avoidance of figurative art in most of the wall paintings and mosaics in his residences reflected current taboos in Judaean society—in place of the depiction of humans and animals in mythical scenes that was standard in contemporary villas in Italy, Herod's artists generally confined their repertoire in public rooms to geometric patterns, olive branches, fig leaves, vine leaves, and pomegranates. But sophisticated animal and human figures were included in the design of wall paintings in the private bathhouse and dining room at Herodium, so perhaps he omitted such iconography elsewhere in his palaces less as a reflection of his own tastes than to avoid offending Jewish visitors. Avoidance of offence was not a straightforward matter: views about the permissibility of figural art varied among Jews. The Torah forbade the creation of images, but in later periods Jews embraced figural art with enthusiasm, provided that the images were not worshipped, and there was much debate about the best way to fulfill the commandment.[4]

In fact, widespread debate about the interpretation of the

Torah more generally could be found throughout the Jewish world. Despite a common core of agreement among Jews that piety required worship of the God of Abraham, Isaac, and Jacob (whose actions in the world were recorded in the sacred histories and to whom sacrifices and oblations were offered in the Jerusalem Temple) and a general acceptance that Jews were required to obey the commandments accepted by Israel in the covenant sealed through Moses on Mount Sinai, much less agreement existed about what these requirements meant in practice. Most of the sacred texts that came to constitute the Hebrew Bible had been accepted by the majority of Jews as authoritative a century before Herod was born, and the teachings enshrined within these texts were expounded in regular public meetings in synagogues. But precisely how the sacred texts should be interpreted was still disputed, not least in the light of practices and ideas within Jewish society which, through force of custom, had often come to be treated as normative.[5]

The issues debated covered a wide range. Jews in Herod's day disagreed on the observance of purity laws and the Sabbath restrictions, on the correct computation of the calendar on which the cycle of the festivals depended, and on the validity and desirability of oaths and vows. Demons and angels were generally assumed to exist, but how they operated in the world and how much they intervened in human affairs were matters for speculation. Widespread belief in the ability of prophets to foretell the future coexisted with assertions that prophecy through divine inspiration had come to an end with previous generations. Jews argued about whether there would be life after death and, if so, what it would be like. Many speculated about the end times, although they disagreed about the nature of the eschatological future or when it would happen. The belief that a messiah would come to destroy the enemies of Israel was common, but there was no agreement about whether the messiah would be a Davidic king or a priestly figure, whether he would be a human or a supernatural being, or what he would do. Some Jews identified with distinct philosophical groups, such as the Pharisees, Sadducees, and Essenes, or with communities like the sectarians whose scrolls, hidden in caves near the Dead Sea, came to light in the middle of the twentieth century.

Where did Herod stand in these debates? Despite later Christian traditions about his role at the birth of Jesus and the location of his mausoleum near Bethlehem, we have no idea whether he was interested in contemporary speculation about the end of days or the nature of the messiah. Nor do we have reason to believe that he had strong views on the religious importance of frequent immersion in water, as other Jews did in his time, although it may be significant that many of the elaborate bathing pools installed in his palaces were constructed to be sufficiently large and deep to function also as ritual baths. We can be more certain that he took seriously the oaths of loyalty he demanded from his subjects, but we do not know whether this attitude reflected his own views about the sanctity of oaths or a political calculation based on the high valuation of oaths by the Jews under his rule.[6]

We can be certain also that Herod shared with many of his Jewish contemporaries a faith that some pious people had been granted insight into the future by God: we are told that when he was at the height of his power as king, he summoned to him the Essene Manaemus, who had earlier predicted his ascension to the throne, in order to quiz him about how long he would reign. The answer from Manaemus—that he could not be precise, but he could say that Herod had twenty or thirty years more to rule—was evidently considered satisfactory, since it marked the start of Herod's special favor toward the Essenes. An aside from Josephus, who tells the story, that he has reported these things, "however incredible they may seem," to demonstrate the exceptional insight vouchsafed to Essenes, suggests that Herod's credulity in such matters was not common among Josephus's non-Jewish readers.[7]

The Jewish God, unlike the gods in the polytheistic Roman world, was well known to be jealous and to forbid the worship of other divinities. If Herod was fully committed to conforming to the Torah he would have been well aware that he should not have attended the sacrifices to Jupiter Capitolinus in Rome with which he began his reign. We do not know how Herod felt about that episode in retrospect. But it is noteworthy that no other similar episode occurs in the histories and that, although Josephus describes Herod defending to a Jewish audience his lavish spending on building and repairing many pagan temples on the grounds of political expediency, he does not show him excusing himself for pagan worship. On the contrary, Herod presented himself to his Jewish subjects as devoted to the Jewish God, most strikingly in the monumental rebuilding of the Temple.

Herod was right to consider Jerusalem and its Temple as the heart of Judaea. In contrast to the mixed population of Jews and gentiles in surrounding regions, Judaea was inhabited only by people who thought of themselves as Jews. The country lacked many natural resources, but the Judaean hills produced adequate wine, olives, and grain to support—when the rain fell in its due season—a substantial population. Most Judaeans lived in villages scattered around the hill country. Jerusalem was the only major conurbation. Jews looked to Jerusalem as the hub of government, commerce, entertainment, and culture. Within the city, the Temple was the only site not just for religious devotions through sacrifices and libations but also for mass meetings of all kinds. It is therefore not entirely surprising that at least one contemporary, the Greek historian and geographer Strabo, apparently categorized Herod simply as a Jewish successor to the Hasmonaeans who had presided in the Jerusalem Temple: he was "a native of the country who had slunk into the priesthood." The most important task of a ruler of Judaea was to control the country's central shrine.[8]

Strabo may well have thought that rulers of Judaea also served as high priests in Jerusalem, since political leaders in Greek cities and in Rome routinely fulfilled priestly roles in civic cults. The restriction of priestly status within Jewish society to a kinship group strictly defined through paternal descent was a peculiarity which does not seem to have been widely appreciated by outsiders. But Herod himself was acutely aware that he would never be able to exercise the direct authority over the Temple enjoyed by his predecessors and that selection of a high priest who would pose no political threat would be crucial.

Despite the long history of the Jerusalem cult, no recent precedent could be found to solve this problem in 37, when Herod conquered Jerusalem and deposed Antigonus as high priest as well as king. Most of his fellow Jews would have assumed that a legitimate high priest had to, like Antigonus, belong to the Hasmonaean dynasty. Hasmonaeans had fulfilled this role for over a century; the obvious candidate for the post of high priest was Jonathan Aristobulus, the younger brother of Herod's recent bride, Mariamme. But in 40 Herod had assumed with good reason that the Romans might back Jonathan as king, and providing so public a platform for a potential rival would have been rash.[9]

Herod tried initially to circumvent the problem by appointing a high priest who had no independent political clout, selecting for the post Ananel, a long-term friend who came from a priestly family in the Babylonian diaspora. He passed over Jonathan by arguing that at the age of fifteen he was too young to be high priest. Whether Herod was able to cite either custom or law in support of the implied minimum-age requirement is unknown. But we have seen that Jonathan's mother, Alexandra, lobbied the king so intensively that he was impelled to confer the post on the youth in the following year, instigating demonstrations as disastrous as Herod had feared and possibly prompting him to stage the "accidental" drowning of the young man in a Jericho swimming pool. No male Hasmonaeans eligible for the high priesthood now survived, since the aged Hyrcanus, who had first presided in the Temple some four decades earlier, was disqualified because of his physical mutilation. For the rest of his reign Herod looked to other priestly families for suitable candidates to represent the Jewish nation before God in his chosen sanctuary.[10]

In effect, since all the high priests he selected owed their position to his patronage, Herod gave himself the means to provide appropriate prestige for a loyal new Judaean elite of impeccably priestly ancestry to replace the Hasmonaean aristocracy he had supplanted. Thus, although on the demise of Jonathan, the previous high priest, Ananel, was again entrusted with the office, assumptions that the high priesthood would be held for life and inherited within the same family were brought to an end. Herod deposed incumbents and appointed successors to the post as he thought fit. At least seven men served in the Temple in this capacity during his reign. Most of the new high priests came, like Ananel, from diaspora families. In around 24 he conferred the office on Simon son of Boethus, whose family originated from Alexandria, on account of his exceptionally beautiful daughter, another Mariamme, later Herod's third wife. Josephus considered Herod's conferral of the post on Simon a reasonable way for the king to acquire this second Mariamme as his wife by increasing the prestige of his future father-in-law; Simon was otherwise insufficiently illustrious to be related to the royal family but "too important to be treated with contempt."[11]

If Herod's subjects had any doubts that he intended to rule Judaea as a Jewish king, they were dispelled by the identification with his fellow Jews exhibited in his ambitious rebuilding of the Temple in which these high priests were to officiate. Ac-

The site of Herod's Temple in Jerusalem from the south. Excavation has uncovered remains of the monumental flight of steps which led up through great gates and broad stepped tunnels built under Herod's Royal Portico to the platform on which the Temple stood and on which the Dome of the Rock now stands. (Photo: Duby Tal / Albatross / Alamy Stock Photo)

cording to a speech to a Jewish crowd put into Herod's mouth by Josephus in his account of the start of this project, Herod claimed to have brought the nation of the Jews to a state of prosperity it had never known, and to be remedying, out of piety, the failure of "our fathers" to make the Temple they built after their return from Babylon under the Persians as impressive as the Temple of Solomon. In another speech, near the end of his life, he is said to have contrasted his achievement with those of the Hasmonaeans, who "had been unable to do anything so great for the honour of God in the hundred and twenty-five years of their rule." The contrast was justified and telling. By the time of Herod's death he had transformed the ancient shrine into a monument to his rule and his devotion to the Jewish God. The remaining traces, still visible on and around the Temple Mount, continue to inspire those who visit the site today.[12]

We are fortunate to have a picture of Herod's Temple from someone who saw it in its glory, although Josephus's description was composed some years after the Temple's destruction, and he may have occasionally erred in detail either through faulty memory or because of alterations to the building in the decades after Herod's death. In Josephus's account, the high central section of the main sanctuary, constructed from huge blocks of hard white stone, was visible from afar. Its entrance doors were adorned with embroidered curtains, with floral designs in purple dye. The doors were framed by a golden vine with bunches of grapes that caught the eye as much for its expensive materials (probably gold leaf) as for its size and artistry. Surrounding the sanctuary was a square compound erected on a huge artificial platform supported by arches built up along the side of the natural rock. The sanctuary itself was reserved for priests. The rest of the compound was divided by balustrades and steps to mark the areas into which gentiles or women were not permitted to pass.

Along the inside edges of the compound, which was supported by a large wall—itself, according to Josephus, "the most impressive piece of work ever heard of by man"—stood a series of porticoes. In the portico which ran along the eastern wall, looking toward the great door of the sanctuary, Herod added the trophies he had himself taken from the Nabataeans, presumably in his campaign against Malchus, to the existing dedications of war spoils. The eastern corner of the northern wall was dominated by the fortifications of the citadel, which were strengthened by Herod in the early years of his reign, during the lifetime of Antony, after whom it had been renamed. From the western wall, the city lay opposite the Temple "like a theatre" on the other side of a deep ravine. One of four gates led by a viaduct to the royal palace. Most magnificent of all was the Royal Portico of polished stone which ran the entire length of the south wall: three stories high, with 162 Corinthian columns, each so wide that it took three men to encircle it with arms outstretched. The columns were set out in four rows to form three aisles, of which the middle aisle was twice the height of the others. The whole edifice towered above a valley so deep that the view to its depths from the roof could induce vertigo.[13]

Construction work on the Temple was carried out with exceptional care. To avoid sacrilege within the sacred precincts, priests were trained as masons and carpenters. The inner sanctuary was rebuilt in a year and a half. Herod celebrated the completion of this first phase of the renovation with a sacrifice of three hundred oxen, ensuring by unsubtle means that his role in the project was publicly acknowledged: "It so happened that the day on which the work on the Temple was completed coincided with that of the king's accession, which they were accustomed to celebrate, and because of the double occasion the festival was a very glorious one indeed."[14]

Herod could not have emphasized more clearly to his Jewish subjects his wish to be identified as a Jewish king, dedicated like the Jewish kings of the distant past to preserving the divine protection which ensured the welfare of the nation. Unable to emulate his more recent Hasmonaean predecessors by venturing himself into the sanctuary, he kept a close eye on the priests he appointed to preside over the Temple cult, incorporating, it was said, into the Temple design a secret underground passage from the Antonia fortress to the eastern gate of the inner sacred court for his special use. It is not known whether the passage was ever used, but the Antonia was only one of the vantage points, along with the royal palace to the west of the Temple Mount and the Royal Portico on the southern edge of the Temple compound, designed to provide the king with physical oversight of the national shrine.[15]

In the Antonia, Herod kept custody of the vestments which adorned the high priest when he annually ventured alone into the Holy of Holies to represent Israel before God on the Day of Atonement. A charisma seems to have settled on any priest who had once entered the sanctum wearing these shining robes of gold, purple, scarlet, linen-white, and blue. On his breast he would wear the glittering ephod, a cuirass with two round golden brooches set with huge sardonyxes and twelve precious stones attached to the front in glistening rows: sardius, topaz, emerald; ruby, jasper, sapphire; agate, amethyst, jacinth; onyx, beryl, chrysolite. Herod had learned in his childhood the deadly attraction of the power which accrued to the high priest's role when Hyrcanus and Aristobulus had fought each other for the position. This very practical way of ensuring that only his nominee would be able to appear in such glorious apparel was Herod's innovation. It was exceptionally effective. The high priest who presided over the Temple which Herod had rebuilt with such magnificence was beholden entirely to the king.[16]

Such loyalty brought its own problems. Reassurances from the high priest and his entourage encouraged Herod to press ahead with his plans for the Temple on the assumption that all his Jewish subjects would applaud his efforts. The redesign of the Temple precincts took place during the high priesthood of Herod's father-in-law Simon son of Boethus. It was Simon who must have authorized the installation of the golden eagle above one of the gates in honor of Augustus, enabling Herod to remain until the last months of his life in willful ignorance of the strength of hostility within a segment of the Jewish populace to such blatant disregard of religious norms. It was only after Herod had removed Simon from his office in the year 5 as punishment for his daughter's alleged complicity in treason, appointing in his place a new high priest who proved less competent in establishing his authority, that violent demonstrations against the eagle image erupted.

The erection of the eagle seems to have been an aberration in Herod's attempts to treat the religious taboos of his Jewish subjects with tact, for in other respects he made considerable efforts to avoid human and animal depictions both in the Temple and in his wider dealings with those regions of his kingdom in which Jews were the majority population. The coins minted during his reign generally avoided types that might offend Jewish sensibilities: with the exception of one coinage issue which depicted (perhaps significantly) an eagle, his moneyers eschewed representations of living things (including a portrait of the king himself) or unambiguously pagan cult symbols. They relied instead on a repertoire of images which mostly continued the iconography of the coinage minted by the Hasmonaeans earlier in the first century BCE.[17]

Herod was certainly aware that sculptures of living beings could cause serious offence. One cause of the disturbances at the games he celebrated in Jerusalem in honor of Octavian around 27 was the belief of many of those present that the Roman trophies placed around the theater were images of men, and it was "against their national custom" to bring these into the city. The protests were assuaged only when the trophies were stripped to reveal—to general laughter—that underneath them was bare wood. Herod did not attempt to disguise his spending on pagan temples and statues and sculptured forms in the manner of the Greeks, but he claimed that he had departed in these ways from Jewish custom only outside Jewish territory, and only by command and order of the Romans, and that within Judaea his largesse had been directed only to the Jewish God.[18]

Evidently Herod cared greatly that his Jewish subjects should think of him not just as a specifically Jewish king but as a Jewish king devoted to piety. After the death of the first Mariamme, he ceased to link his fortunes to the house of the Hasmonaeans and claimed instead to be outstripping their achievements in the footsteps of the glorious kings of the house of David. Around the year 10 he erected a memorial of hugely expensive white marble at the entrance to David's tomb in Jerusalem. He is said by Josephus to have made explicit comparisons between his own rebuilt Temple and that of David's son Solomon, whose coffin was believed to be housed within the same tomb. Later stories reported by Josephus, alleging that Herod was motivated by a desire to loot treasure from the tombs of these kings, were probably calumnies invented after Herod's death.[19]

In some ways Herod's claim to piety was advantaged by the accident of birth which precluded his serving as a priest. Unlike the Hasmonaean rulers, who had needed to take a stance because of their role as high priests on numerous disputes concerning the correct conduct of the Temple rites, such as the precise purity rules to be applied for worshippers and the dates when the festival sacrifices should be offered, Herod could stay above the religious fray. He did not need to be drawn in when religious pressure groups like the Pharisees, Sadducees, and Essenes clamored for their own interpretations of the Torah to be followed in the national shrine. Thus, although Sadducees had played an important role in Jewish society in the time of Alexander Jannaeus, and some Sadducees were prominent in the religious politics of Judaea a few decades after Herod's death, we have no record of a confirmed Sadducee taking a public role during Herod's reign. Herod is said explicitly to have had a high opinion of the Essenes, but the reason for his enthusiasm was also said to lie not in their religious worldview or an interest in their monastic way of life but in the expertise of the prophet Manaemus. Similar personal reasons were alleged for Herod's toleration of the Pharisees: he was purportedly grateful for the advice given to the inhabitants of Jerusalem by Pollion the Pharisee and his disciple Samaias to admit him to the city during the siege in 37, even though the reported argument of these Pharisees—that eventual submission to Herod was in any case inevitable as divine punishment of the inhabitants for their sins—was hardly flattering to the new king.[20]

Herod's favor toward the Essenes and Pharisees became an issue on the two occasions when he tried to consolidate his authority by demanding that his Jewish subjects take an oath of loyalty—once just to him, with "a sworn declaration that they would maintain a friendly attitude to his rule," and once both to himself and to the emperor. Loyalty oaths were not unusual in the Roman world and (at least in the latter case) may well have been prompted by the imperial regime, but the Essenes and some Pharisees objected on grounds of conscience and were permitted to abstain. Josephus, presumably echoing Nicolaus, did not understand why the Pharisees showed hostility toward Herod by refusing to take the oath after they had been "able to help the king greatly because of their foresight." But their refusal made sense in the context of the debate within Judaism in Herod's day over the best way to avoid the danger of sacrilege by making an oath which might later have to be broken for unanticipated reasons. The Essenes, who declined to take oaths of any kind apart from the great oath they took on initiation into the group, found it easier to persuade Herod to allow them to evade the loyalty oath than the Pharisees, who were prepared to take an oath only if they could be certain they would not have to break it. On the face of it, the scruples of the Pharisees made the oath all the more desirable from the point of view of the king, and the Pharisees who refused—more than six thousand—were excused only after the payment of a fine.[21]

Herod's toleration of such religious enthusiasts did not prevent an attempted coup over religious concerns. The flashpoint was the mass demonstration which greeted the games in Jerusalem in honor of Octavian in around 27. The protests were defused, as we have seen, by the revelation that the trophies on display were made of wood, but ten conspirators, unconvinced, concocted a plan to assassinate the king while he was in the theater. Betrayed by a spy before they came near Herod, they were tortured and put to death. The names and backgrounds of the plotters are not recorded, but they were said to have acted "not for the sake of gain or because of their own feelings but, what was more important, on behalf of their communal customs, which all now had the duty either to preserve or to die for." Popular support for their cause became apparent from the fate of the spy. He was openly killed and dismembered by his enemies, and no member of the public was willing to give up the identity of his killers to the authorities until the truth was extorted through torture.[22]

If further opposition on religious grounds remained suppressed until the great outburst which greeted the news of Herod's death two decades later, credit should probably be given not so much to Herod's propaganda as to the effectiveness of his police state. We are told, presumably with some exaggeration, that "no meeting of citizens was permitted, nor were walking together or being together permitted, and all their [the citizens'] movements were observed." Much use was made of spies, including (it was said) Herod himself, who "would often put on the dress of a private citizen and mingle with the crowds by night" to get an idea of how people felt about his rule. Many complainers were taken, "either openly or secretly," to the fortress of Hyrcania, where they were put to death.[23]

As in all successful repressive regimes, the real extent of discontent is hard to gauge, but it seems that in the later part of his reign at least, Hyrcania and other fortresses, such as Herodium, Alexandrium, Machaerus, and Masada, which had either been built entirely by Herod or adapted from prior use by the Hasmonaeans, were used more for the king's security from his own subjects than as protection against external attack on the

An aerial view of Masada, showing Herod's palace on the northern tip of the rock and the Dead Sea to the left. The palace was designed for the king's comfort, but its location was selected for security. (Photo: akg-images / Bible Land Pictures / Jerusalem; photo by Z. Radovan)

realm. Similarly, Herod's prime reason for maintaining the bodyguard of Thracians, Germans, and Gauls which eventually accompanied his bier in battle array would have been his need for protection against his own people.[24]

It is unlikely that in designating Herod king not just of Judaea but of the Jews, Mark Antony specifically intended the Senate to provide his protégé with a role in protecting the interests of Jewish communities living throughout the wider Roman Empire and beyond. Nor is there any reason to think that Herod envisaged himself in such a role in the early years of his reign. But by the twenties BCE, when he was secure in his power in Judaea and his ambition soared, he seems on occasion to have succumbed to the temptation to portray himself as a patron of Jews wherever they lived. The temptation was especially strong when he could wield such patronage before a Roman audience, demonstrating the reach of his influence not only to other Jews but also to the Romans on whom his own power depended.[25]

Many parts of the eastern Roman empire had become home to Jews over the previous few centuries, as had the city of Rome. The diaspora had grown in part as a response to overpopulation in the homeland, and in part through the resettlement of captives in war. These Jews' preservation of distinctive national customs in communities clustered around synagogues rendered them particularly visible in the cities where they settled. Half a century after Herod's death, the philosopher Philo recorded Jews living in Egypt, Phoenicia, Syria, Pamphylia, Cilicia, Asia, Bithynia, Pontus, Thessaly, Boeotia, Macedonia, Aetolia, Attica, Argos, Corinth, the Peloponnese, Euboea, Cyprus, and Crete. All these Jewish communities were well established by Herod's time, as were others in Cyrene (modern Libya) and elsewhere. The Jewish population in Rome had expanded greatly from the mid-first century BCE following the deportation to the city of numerous slaves after the capture of Jerusalem by Pompey in 63. When freed, these slaves became a distinctive group within the urban plebs. The Roman orator Cicero implied in 59 that they could prove a powerful voice in influencing the court during the prosecution of his client Flaccus on a charge of having stolen from the Jews of Asia the sums they had collected for transmission to the Temple in Jerusalem.[26]

Both Romans and Jews considered the fortunes of all these Jewish communities interlinked. Many years after Herod's death, his great-grandson Agrippa II reportedly declared, just before the outbreak of the great Judaean revolt in 66 CE, that the fate of the diaspora Jews scattered throughout the world was intimately bound up with the politics of Jerusalem. For non-Jews, the connection was partly an accident of terminology. Diaspora

Jews were known to their neighbors as *ioudaioi* (in Greek) or *iudaei* (in Latin), words which could be understood either as "Jews" or as "Judaeans." The rights accorded to Herod's patron, the Hasmonaean high priest Hyrcanus, in 47 BCE by Julius Caesar included not only "rule over the Jewish nation" as ethnarch but also the right to be "protector of those Jews who are unjustly treated," by which Caesar must have meant to refer to Jews living in places not under Hyrcanus's rule. Caesar issued instructions that these rights were to be attested by a bronze tablet set up "at Sidon and Tyre and Ashkelon and in the temples, engraved in Latin and Greek characters," presumably for the benefit of the Jews living as minority communities in those cities.[27]

The title "ethnarch" (ruler of a nation) bestowed on Hyrcanus, seems to have been a novel Roman coinage, initiated either by Pompey or (more probably) by Caesar. The title was evidently intended specifically to permit the sort of intercessions by Hyrcanus on behalf of diaspora Jews which are recorded in Ephesus in Asia Minor soon after Caesar's death. In 43 the Roman governor of the province wrote to the city that "the envoy of Hyrcanus, son of Alexander, the high priest and ethnarch of the Jews, has explained to me that his co-religionists cannot undertake military service because they may not bear arms or march on the days of the Sabbath; nor can they obtain the native foods to which they are accustomed," and that they were therefore to be exempted from such service. It seems that the governor took the view that since the nation (*ethnos*) of the Jews was a nonterritorial entity spread far beyond the boundaries of Judaea, the ethnarch had authority to champion their cause wherever they lived.[28]

Herod thus had recent precedent to follow in his interventions on behalf of diaspora Jews. Our best evidence for such interventions derives from extensive accounts of the occasions on which Nicolaus acted as Herod's spokesman in Ionia (in western Turkey) during Herod's visit to Agrippa in Asia Minor in 14. Nicolaus, who was not shy in advertising his achievements, contrived to find room to include these occasions in both the 123rd and the 124th books of his *Universal History*. We are told that "a great multitude of Jews who lived in the cities" took advantage of Agrippa's presence in Ionia to complain that they were not allowed to observe their own laws. They said they were forced to appear in court on their holy days, deprived of the moneys they sent as offerings to Jerusalem, and compelled to participate in military service and civic duties, "although they had been exempted from these duties because the Romans had always permitted them to live in accordance with their own laws." When Herod induced Agrippa to listen to their pleas and assigned Nicolaus to speak on their behalf, the orator focused on the friendship between Agrippa and Herod:

> What act of goodwill toward your house has been left undone by him? What mark of good faith has he failed to give? What form of honour has he not thought of? In what emergency has he not shown foresight? . . . In reminding you . . . of our king, who is now present and sitting beside you, we ask for nothing special but only that you do not allow us [i.e., the Jews of Ionia] to be deprived by others of the rights that you yourselves have given us.

At the end of the speech, Agrippa is said to have specified that he was ready to grant the Jews whatever they might request on account of Herod's goodwill and friendship.[29]

But Herod showed little interest in promoting the welfare of diaspora Jews more generally, and he seems to have helped the Jews of Ionia more for self-glorification than out of a sense of solidarity or sympathy. There is no record that he made any effort to help the substantial Jewish populations of Alexandria or Cyrene, while by the end of his life the Jewish community in the city of Rome seems to have been positively hostile to him.

The delegation of fifty Jews from Judaea that petitioned Augustus after Herod's death for the dissolution of his kingdom on the grounds of Herod's rapacity was supported by more than eight thousand of the Jews in Rome.[30]

Ironically, if these hostile Jews in Rome were aware of the state of affairs in Judaea, it was in part because of Herod's success in turning Jerusalem into a destination for international pilgrimage. The notion that Jews, wherever they lived, should care about the regular performance of worship by the priests in the Jerusalem Temple was deeply ingrained in Jewish culture long before Herod. We have already seen from Cicero's defense of the Roman governor Flaccus in 59 that the Jews of Asia Minor collected funds for transmission to Jerusalem when Herod was still a teenager. But the vast sums expended by Herod as king on rebuilding the Temple sanctuary and its surroundings, which proved so effective in eliciting the enthusiastic admiration of non-Jewish tourists such as Marcus Vipsanius Agrippa, were designed to win the appreciation of diaspora Jews as much as of the Jewish subjects within his realm.

When Herod was a boy, few Jews from Egypt or Syria, let alone from more distant parts of the diaspora, had made the journey to Jerusalem to fulfill the commandment to appear before the Lord three times a year at the great pilgrimage festivals. Travel by sea ran the risk of capture by pirates until Pompey cleared them from the eastern Mediterranean in the early sixties. Journeys by land were slow and vulnerable to banditry, particularly in the border areas between fragmented kingdoms. Herod's great harbor at Caesarea, completed at the same time as his work on the Jerusalem Temple, and the pacification of the Mediterranean world under the unifying power of Rome, made pilgrimage from the Mediterranean diaspora far more attractive.[31]

How many diaspora Jews actually came on pilgrimage while Herod was alive, and how often they came, is unknown. The author of the Acts of the Apostles, probably a contemporary of Josephus writing toward the end of the first century CE, described a crowd in Jerusalem at the festival of Shavuot in around 30 CE, a generation after Herod's death, as "devout Jews from every nation under heaven . . . Parthians, Medes, Elamites, and residents of Mesopotamia, Judaea and Cappadocia, Pontus and Asia, Phrygia and Pamphylia, Egypt and the parts of Libya belonging to Cyrene, and visitors from Rome, both Jews and proselytes, Cretans and Arabs." It may have suited the author of Acts to exaggerate the variegated nationalities of this assembly, who found that, by a miracle, "when the disciples were filled with the Holy Spirit and began to speak in other languages . . . each one heard them speaking in the native language of each."[32]

For one group of international pilgrims at least, the Jews of Babylonia, Herod took steps in the last years of his reign to protect the pilgrimage route from brigandage. The Babylonian Jews traced their origins to the captives once deported to Mesopotamia after the destruction in 586 BCE of the Temple built by Solomon. The extent of continuity from these ancient roots is hard to establish, but in 40 BCE a great number of Jews were said to be in Babylon, "occupying the region as far as the Euphrates," at the time when the Hasmonaean high priest Hyrcanus was sent by the Parthians to live among them after the conquest of Jerusalem by Antigonus.[33]

Since these Mesopotamian Jews excitedly honored Hyrcanus as "their high priest and king," Herod's relationship with the community may have soured after he invited Hyrcanus to return to Judaea but then executed him on a charge of treason. Perhaps by that time Herod cared little about the attitude of Babylonian Jews. As Josephus complained, he had already broken tradition in taking the high priesthood away from Ananel, the Babylonian on whom he had conferred the position when he first gained control of Jerusalem, in order to bestow it on the young Hasmonaean Jonathan Aristobulus. We have seen that

Ananel was reappointed after Jonathan's death, but he was no longer in the post by the mid-twenties BCE (though whether he was dismissed or died is unknown). No other Babylonian priests were recruited to take his place during the rest of Herod's reign.[34]

Late in Herod's reign, in around 7, the king established a village "as large as a city" to house a troop of Babylonian Jewish mounted archers in a place he called Bathyra. They were to act as a military colony with a brief to keep the surrounding region free of brigandage in order to protect the Jews who came from Babylonia to sacrifice in Jerusalem. These archers and their commander Zamaris had already migrated from Babylon to a camp near Antioch, where they had been permitted to stay temporarily by the Roman governor of Syria. They were persuaded by Herod to settle instead in the wild country northeast of the Sea of Galilee with a promise that the land would be free of taxes and exempt from all the customary forms of tribute. Josephus, who himself knew the grandson of Zamaris, noted the success of this policy: "There came to him [Zamaris] many men—and from all parts—who were devoted to the ancestral customs of the Jews. And so this land became very populous . . . so long as Herod lived." But although the colony flourished, whether many Babylonian Jews benefited from the protection to pilgrims thus provided may be doubted, since Zamaris protected only a small section of the long overland route. In view of the time and expense incurred in travel through the northern reaches of the Fertile Crescent, few could have afforded to make the journey.[35]

Herod is said to have been friendly with the Babylonian priest Ananel long before he came to power in 37 (although we do not know where this friendship was struck up). But if he had many other contacts with the Jews of Mesopotamia, he may have felt it prudent during the twenties to tread carefully in his dealings with his Jewish compatriots across the border in Parthian territory at a time when Augustus was widely expected to embark on a major campaign to avenge the defeat of Crassus at Carrhae. Only after Augustus's diplomatic coup in 20, through which he recovered the legionary eagles lost by Crassus and provided for the return of Roman captives without having to go to war, was it safe to encourage the cross-border travel of the pilgrims protected by Zamaris and his troops.[36]

It is ironic that the aspect of Herod's Jewish identity which was to have the most implications for his relationship with his Roman patrons was his claim, after his emotional collapse following his execution of his second wife, Mariamme, in 29, that Jewish custom permitted him to cohabit simultaneously with multiple wives.

While Mariamme lived, the Hasmonaean princess seems to have been the sole focus of Herod's affections both for her political connections and because of her beauty. But in the decade after her death, Herod, now well into his forties, married at least three other women: his other wife named Mariamme (daughter of the high priest Simon son of Boethus, whose family came from Alexandria); Malthace (from Samaria); and Cleopatra (from Jerusalem). And three more marriages followed, although when they took place is not recorded, to women known only by their names: Pallas (who gave birth to a son who was named Phasael, presumably in memory of Herod's brother), Phaedra, and Elpis (who produced daughters, including one named Salome). Two additional wives were childless, and thus remain nameless in the lists Josephus provided for his readers to impress upon them that Herod's family was abnormally numerous. All these wives were fully integrated into Herod's household, where they jostled for influence and Herod's attention, and devised means to advance the interests of their children.[37]

Josephus was right to consider these marital arrangements bizarre. Herod did not need to marry in order to gratify his lust since like other male householders in Greek and Roman society, he could have made use of his numerous slaves for this purpose. Nonetheless the physical appearance of these wives seems to have been a primary motivation for their selection: in describing the arrogance of Glaphyra, one of Herod's daughters-in-law, Josephus specifically recorded that she mocked the low birth of his wives because they had all been chosen "for their beauty and not for their family." Certainly, appreciation for her beauty was said to have led to Herod's marriage to his second wife called Mariamme: according to Josephus, Herod married this Mariamme "at the promptings of his amorous desire . . . , for he had no qualms about living solely for his own pleasure." He had heard talk of her among the inhabitants of Jerusalem and "first became excited by what he had heard, and then, on seeing her, was greatly smitten by the girl's loveliness."[38]

Herod's daughter-in-law Glaphyra was the daughter of a king and may well have exaggerated the low birth of his wives. One can imagine political reasons for Herod's selection of some of his new brides, such as the two unnamed close relations (a niece and a cousin) by whom he had no offspring, for marriage to close kin was the pattern Herod imposed upon his own daughters. And there may also have been a political reason for Herod's choice of the Samaritan Malthace, to whom he was married around the time he was pouring money into the rebuilding of Samaria, the capital of the region, as the new city of Sebaste. But Glaphyra's taunt that all these wives were married solely for their beauty makes sense only if it was at least plausible.[39]

Marrying one young attractive wife after another was not unusual in the Roman world for a middle-aged man with power and money. What was extraordinary was Herod's choice to stay married to all of them at the same time. Both Romans and Greeks practiced serial polygamy, but this involved divorcing one partner before taking another. Herod could have done the same when taking his new wives, divorcing before remarrying and living with one wife at a time in the fashion standard among contemporary Romans and Greeks. Divorce of a wife by her husband was straightforward in Jewish law, and we have seen that when Herod had married the first Mariamme, he sent away his first wife, Doris.[40]

Herod's decision to maintain a court filled with simultaneous wives, all living together in one household and none specifically designated as his queen, was an innovation after the death of the first Mariamme. It was very strange. None of the Hasmonaean rulers who preceeded Herod had adopted polygamy. Nor did later generations of Herod's own family. Josephus recognized that Herod's domestic relations, which in 7 included "nine women living with King Herod," would strike some of his readers as strange, for he explicitly described polygamy as a characteristic of Jewish society "of which Herod gladly availed himself." But Josephus failed to add that in practice even bigamy was very rare in Herod's time, and that Herod's choice to cohabit with as many as nine wives, treating all their offspring as legitimate heirs, was without parallel in contemporary Jewish society. The choice seems to have been Herod's alone. His intention may have been to invite comparison with Macedonian royalty and Hellenistic dynasties, but if so, Josephus's statement about Herod's reliance on Jewish custom seems peculiar. More plausible might be emulation of the many wives of King David as recorded in the biblical book of Samuel. In any case, the decision was to have huge consequences in the intrigues surrounding the designation of an heir and the resulting tensions within his family which were to blight the last decade of Herod's life.[41]

5

A Family Tragedy

"In his family life, he was a paradigm of misfortune."[1] This lapidary judgment by Josephus was amply justified by the account of Herod's domestic miseries with which he regaled his readers. A long and detailed narrative of jealousy, suspicion, and plotting was embroidered with court gossip relayed by Nicolaus, who had been a mediator within the family for the last decade of Herod's life. Josephus's frequent assertions that Herod was the source of his own misfortunes enabled the historian to pontificate piously on divine judgment, the weaknesses of the king's character, and Herod's willingness to be swayed by unreasonable doubts sown in his mind by mischief makers. But at a basic level Josephus's ascription of blame was correct. Herod had been made king of Judaea not on account of his royal birth but because of his personal qualities. It was only because he himself fostered the political ambitions of his family that these came to overwhelm both his private and his public life during his last years.

* * *

Herod seems to have taken for granted that the best way to keep control of his kingdom was to rely on members of his family. Family solidarity must have seemed a prudent safeguard for Idumaean outsiders protecting their positions in the struggles for influence in the Hasmonaean court. The pattern had been set by his father, Antipater, when Herod was appointed to his first public role in 47 BCE along with his brother Phasael. After Antipater's death in 42, the two brothers continued to operate in tandem in support of Hyrcanus while Phasael was alive. We have seen that after Herod was appointed king of Judaea in his own right in 40, he turned first to his brother Joseph and then, in 35, to his uncle of the same name. Neither Joseph was conspicuously successful: Herod's brother was killed while making an unauthorized raid, and his uncle was executed on suspicion of adultery with Mariamme. But when Herod set off from his kingdom in spring 30 to seek confirmation of his rule from Octavian, it was again to a brother that he turned, handing over all his affairs to his youngest brother, Pheroras.

It is clear that Herod regarded this youngest brother with considerable affection. In 30 he left a request that if his negotiations with Octavian failed and he was imprisoned or killed, his friends in Judaea would do everything in their power to preserve the kingdom for Pheroras. They were also mandated to protect the interests of Alexander and Aristobulus, his sons by Mariamme, but this trust had little to do with the immediate government of the kingdom, since the boys were still young children at this date.[2]

Concern for the interests of Pheroras seems to have lasted throughout Herod's life, despite the tensions which arose from Pheroras's stubborn refusal to be manipulated into marital arrangements for which he had no enthusiasm. In the thirties BCE Herod had arranged for Pheroras to marry the sister of his own wife Mariamme as a clear sign that Pheroras was to be considered as royal as Herod himself through an independent connection with the Hasmonaean dynasty. When the plan was thwarted by the unexpected death of the princess designated as Pheroras's bride, Herod attempted to persuade his brother to accept a prestigious marriage to Salampsio, the eldest of Herod's own daughters. He expected Pheroras to welcome the match. Salampsio had Hasmonean heritage through her mother, and a union between uncle and niece was common among Jews—we have seen another example in the marriage of Salome to her uncle Joseph. The marriage link to the king was intended as a compliment, but Herod's plan failed again, despite the promise of a dowry of three hundred talents. Pheroras said he preferred the company of a slave concubine with whom he was deeply in love. Pheroras's devotion to this woman, whose name is not recorded, colored his relations with his brother for the rest of his life.[3]

The rejection of Salampsio was a palpable insult, not least because the notion that a love affair with a slave should preclude a political marriage would have struck most contemporaries as ridiculous. Herod was furious, but, remarkably, he continued to treat Pheroras as his closest colleague. In 20, at the height of his influence with Augustus, Herod even took advantage of the freedom of speech afforded him by the emperor to request successfully that his brother be granted rule over a tetrarchy in Peraea. Aware of the danger that his sons might be less charitable to Pheroras after his death, Herod turned over to him a hundred talents of his own money to ensure his continued independence.[4]

Herod's indulgence of this younger brother was extraordinary. Pheroras seems to have been able to get away with almost anything. Josephus described Herod, appropriately, as *philadelphotatos*, a very unusual Greek adjective which means "most brother-loving." The impression given is that Herod sought his brother's affection even when it was not reciprocated. Nor did he give up on the hope that he might entice Pheroras into a closer family union. Some years after Pheroras had turned down marriage with Salampsio, Herod offered his second daughter, Cyprus (named after their mother), as a bride. Pheroras apparently agreed, and the wedding to Cyprus was arranged. Pheroras took an oath to send away his concubine—evidently a condition for the marriage. But just before the wedding, he had a change of heart and reneged on the agreement, unable to abandon the woman he loved. Herod again forgave him through gritted teeth.[5]

Herod's relationship with his only sister, Salome, was no less fraught. As with Pheroras, resistance to Herod's plans for her marriage lay at the root of much of the tension between the siblings, but in her case, there was an added layer of frustration: it never seems to have occurred to Herod to place her in a position of political authority in her own right, so her only means of accruing influence was through intrigue within the court. Why she could not be allowed to exercise power independently is unclear, since Herod must have been well aware that women could rule effectively. The Hasmonaean queen Shelomzion—after whom Salome may indeed have been named, since she was born shortly after the queen's death and the names of the Hasmonaean dynasty were widely adopted across Jewish society during and after their rule—had ruled Judaea when Herod was a child. Herod had himself been much occupied in the early years of his rule in fending off the ambitions of Cleopatra of Egypt. But Romans did not customarily grant overt political roles to women—even Augustus's wife, Livia, was required to work behind the scenes in the imperial court. A request to Augustus to grant Salome a territory to rule at the same time as the grant of a tetrarchy to Pheroras would have been greeted with incredulity.

Instead of giving Salome power in her own right, Herod selected husbands for her with the expectation that they would become reliable political colleagues. The policy depended on Salome's compliance, which could not be guaranteed. We have seen that she fell out with her first husband, her uncle Joseph, accusing him in 35 of frequent adultery with Herod's beloved wife, Mariamme, and she seems to have been complicit in his execution by Herod.[6]

Salome's next marriage, to Herod's close friend Costobar, was equally disastrous. Costobar should have been a good match. A wealthy leader within Idumaean society, he could trace his ancestry back to priests of the Idumaean god Cos in the previous century, before the Idumaeans had converted to Judaism. Herod appointed him to govern Idumaea but lost faith in his friend in the late thirties when he picked up a rumor that Costobar harbored designs on ruling with greater independence. Costobar was said to have contacted Cleopatra with the suggestion that she might ask Antony to take Idumaea away from Herod's realm and add the region to her territory, with Costobar as governor. Presumably the rumor was not proven, since he was not accused in public of disloyalty, but Herod did not object when Salome dissolved the marriage a few years later by sending her husband a divorce document—"not in accordance with Jewish law," as Josephus correctly noted, since wives lacked the power to initiate divorce, but evidently with the required effect when the wife in question was the king's sister. Costobar was in any case soon accused of a serious act of treachery against the king. Around 27 Salome revealed to her brother that she had discovered that Costobar had hidden the Sons of Baba, the last remnants of the supporters of the Hasmonaean king Antigonus who had escaped Jerusalem after the siege ten years earlier, on his estates in Idumaea. Herod had Costobar put to death.[7]

Salome's status after 27 as a single mother with young children did not inhibit her considerable involvement in the political life of Herod's court. Her brother sometimes asked her to be present when he convened a council of friends to discuss urgent business. And her prolonged flirtation with the Nabataean Syllaeus was possible only because she could expect to meet him frequently when the family came together for dinner.[8]

Herod publicly advertised his devotion to members of his close family. Josephus noted the exceptional affection for his father which led Herod to found in his memory the city of Antipatris in the "most beautiful plain in his kingdom." Above Jericho, Herod built the fortress Cypros, dedicated to his mother. His older brother Phasael, by whose side he had first risen to prominence under their father's tutelage, was memorialized by the city of Phasaelis to the north of Jericho, as well as by the magnificent tower named Phasael which Herod erected in Jerusalem. For relatives at a slightly farther remove, Herod's family loyalty, which proved so stifling for Pheroras and Salome, provided opportunities for advancement. Herod's cousin Achiab, first encountered in Josephus's history as a commander in 28 placed in charge of the fortifications of Jerusalem along with other old friends of the king, was still close to Herod a quarter of a century later, when the king was on his deathbed. Herod's nephew Joseph, son of Herod's brother of the same name, was in command of a contingent of royal troops in Jerusalem which remained loyal to Rome in the disturbances after Herod's death.[9]

Herod made it clear to relatives that their membership within the extended family was a matter of great importance to him by taking upon himself the right to ensure appropriate marriages for his nephews and nieces as well as for his own children and his younger siblings (even if, as we have seen, both Pheroras and Salome felt entitled to resist his choices). Over the course of his reign, he negotiated at least ten marriages for members of the family. Many involved a match between uncle and niece or between cousins. But others established or strengthened marriage links to other influential families—most importantly, the remaining representatives of the Hasmonaean dynasty.[10]

Herod was not the only ruler in his time to depend so heavily on the political support of members of his family, but reliance on close relatives at the center of power was by no means standard in the Hellenistic courts of the Ptolemies and Seleucids or in the courts of the Hasmonaeans who preceded Herod as rulers of Judaea. The closest parallel in Herod's day was the regime of Augustus in Rome. It was Augustus's concern for his own heir that seems to have prompted the interference in Herod's succession plans which was to lead to tragedy.[11]

It was not obvious in 40, when Herod was selected as a ruler by the Roman Senate on the grounds of his personal qualities, that his installation implied continuity of rule within Herod's family for generations to come. The Senate routinely allocated rule over large areas of the empire to Roman governors without the expectation that these politicians would transmit the power entrusted to them to their children.

In 40 Herod's only son, Antipater, was still a child (about five years old) and must have seemed wholly inappropriate as a potential heir, not least because Herod had disowned his mother, Doris, on his betrothal to the Hasmonaean Mariamme. In view of the efforts Herod expended in his later years to ensure a suitable heir for his kingdom, it is clear that the issue eventually became one of great importance to him. But if Herod considered at all during these early years what would happen to his kingdom when he died, he probably assumed that his brother Pheroras, who had been left as his regent during his absence in 30, would take over.[12]

When in 23, seventeen years after he had been declared a king, the issue first arose of Herod publicly designating an heir to his kingdom, the person responsible seems to have been Augustus. The biographer Suetonius, who wrote a life of Augustus a century after his death, considered Augustus unusual in the special care he took to bring up the children of allied kings and educate them with his own children. It was probably thus at the instigation of Augustus that Herod in 23 sent his sons Alexander and Aristobulus to Rome for their education, allowing them to grow up away from the court in Jerusalem where their mother, grandmother, and great-grandfather had recently been executed. We are told that the emperor received the boys "with the greatest consideration," allowing them to stay in his own household. We are also told that he gave Herod the right to designate as his successor whichever of his offspring he wished. Clearly intended by Augustus as a compliment to Herod himself in return for his extravagant professions of loyalty, the grant of this right was to have dire consequences for the rest of Herod's reign.[13]

Augustus himself fell seriously ill in 23, and the issue of succession to his own power was on his mind. Despite the ostentatious restoration of the republic in 27, Augustus intended not only to hang on to power during his lifetime but also to found a dynasty. Family mattered: his reliance for more than two decades on the political support and military expertise of his close friend Agrippa notwithstanding, in 23 he effectively designated as his heir his nephew Marcellus, who was connected to him both as his sister Octavia's son and by marriage to his daughter Julia. When Marcellus died suddenly later in the same year, Augustus required Agrippa in 21 to divorce his current wife in order to marry Julia and provide her with sons. Gaius (born in 20) and his younger brother Lucius, Augustus's grandsons, were also adopted by the emperor as his own sons in 17 to be heirs to both his fortune and, by implication, his authority.

The later history of Augustus's succession plans, which he was in the early stages of formulating during the years that he imposed a similar model on his friend Herod, revealed the chilling calculation with which he was prepared to treat his own family. In 6 BCE, when Gaius was sixteen and Lucius thirteen, Augustus's intention to groom the youths as his successors was sufficiently blatant to drive his stepson Tiberius into voluntary retirement on Rhodes. Ten years later, foiled in these dynastic plans by the premature deaths of the two youths, Augustus reluctantly adopted Tiberius, thus denoting his stepson as his son, but he continued to seek an heir related to him by blood, adopting at the same time Agrippa Postumus, the younger brother of Gaius and Lucius, who was still a teenager. Agrippa Postumus later fell out of favor, however, and when Augustus died in 14 CE and Tiberius became emperor, he was murdered by a centurion. The order, so some believed, had come from Augustus. The rumor that Augustus had arranged for the disposal of his grandson as soon as he himself was dead was all too plausible. After all, he had acted throughout his political career on the assumption that only one man should wield supreme power in the Roman world.[14]

For Augustus, planning for succession to his power in Rome was complicated by a lack of biological sons and the need to rely on adoption, a traditional method for consolidating family relations within the Roman senatorial elite. Jewish society lacked a similar institution. But adoption was not an issue for Herod, who had a superfluity of children by his many wives, all of whom were considered legitimate. Augustus may have been surprised by Herod's exotic domestic arrangements when he granted him the right in 23 to appoint his own heir to his kingdom, but he would not have been disconcerted. We have seen that in many ways it was precisely their foreign and exotic status which provided client kings with their value as props to the imperial regime. Romans were accustomed to the notion that eastern royalty had idiosyncratic marriage customs, like the brother-sister unions in the Ptolemaic dynasty that were taboo for ordinary Romans. In any case, Herod's two young sons Alexander and Aristobulus, who were then installed in the imperial household, were the offspring of his monogamous marriage to the first Mariamme. Augustus presumably took for granted that the heir Herod would have in mind would be one of these two boys.[15]

In view of Augustus's reported interest in fostering ties between client kings, it is likely that he also engineered the marriage in 17 of one of these sons, Alexander, to the daughter of Archelaus of Cappadocia, which would link Herod's descendants with another major kingdom in the eastern Roman Empire. Archelaus had been installed as king of Cappadocia by Antony in 36, and he had been favored by Augustus in the twenties with additional territories in the neighboring regions of Cilicia and Armenia Minor. The central area of his kingdom lay on the Asia Minor plateau far to the north of Judaea. But he shared with Herod the incentive to show conspicuous loyalty to Augustus which came from having been granted his kingdom by Rome even though he was not connected to the previous royal line. He also shared with Herod a penchant for demonstrating publicly his devotion to Greek culture—in Archelaus's case, by writing a literary account of the territories conquered by Alexander the Great. He evidently considered his status to be on a par with Herod's. He was to intervene more than once with Herod on behalf of his son-in-law when the political imbroglios in Herod's court turned fetid, and we shall see that Herod treated him with considerable respect.[16]

In 17, Augustus's encouragement of the ambitions of Alexander and Aristobulus began to foment discord when Herod went to Rome to fetch his sons back to Judaea. Alexander was roughly nineteen—the same age Augustus himself had been when (as Octavian) he had first burst onto the stage of Roman politics in 44. Alexander was a year or so younger. Designated as Herod's heirs with the support of the emperor in whose household they had been living for the previous six years, they were bound to have a sense of their own importance. It was unsurprising that on their return to Jerusalem their relations with Pheroras and Salome, who could see the threat to their positions at the center of power in Herod's court, were fraught.

Nor is it hard to see why the boys resented their father:

Herod had ordered the deaths of their mother (Mariamme), uncle (Jonathan Aristobulus), grandmother (Alexandra), and great-grandfather (Hyrcanus). The wonder is that Herod should ever have expected their loyalty and affection. It did not ultimately help them that the emperor, presumably keen to see his own plans brought to fruition despite ostensibly having left Herod free to make his own choice, went to such efforts to reconcile the father to his sons when these tensions surfaced, nor that the family saga was enacted on a public stage under the gaze of the master of the Roman world.

In 17, Herod was in his later fifties, approaching an age when many in the Roman world would consider themselves too old for an active life. That Herod might retire and hand over power to his sons is first attested as a practical proposal in 12, when Augustus is said explicitly to have forbidden it, regardless of whatever Herod himself might wish. But the idea must have already occurred to many, including Alexander and Aristobulus themselves, five years earlier.

Herod's response was to insist on his continuing physical prowess and his superiority to his sons. When he walked next to his son Alexander, he expected the youth to stoop to avoid appearing taller than he. When the two of them went on hunting trips, Alexander felt compelled to shoot wide of the mark to ensure that his father was seen to excel. Competitiveness extended to sexual matters. When Herod gave presents to his daughter-in-law Glaphyra, he was seen by Alexander as a rival for her affections, a notion (probably scurrilous) apparently fostered by Pheroras to create trouble. Alexander in turn seduced three eunuchs of whom Herod was exceptionally fond. Confronted with their infidelity, which they admitted, they reported that Alexander was spreading a rumor that his father was disguising his advanced age by secretly dyeing his hair black.

Herod was in no mood to leave the limelight. On the contrary, at the age of sixty-two, he is said to have claimed in a speech to the general populace gathered in the Temple that old age was the time when a person was most experienced in ruling. He boasted that he was not given to the excessive lifestyle which could cut men off even in their youth. Nor did he lack "the other skills that enable one to govern a kingdom and rule one's sons."[17]

Herod's initial loss of confidence in Alexander and Aristobulus in the early years after he brought them home from Rome was founded on a sense that as the sons of a Hasmonaean princess and favored friends of the emperor, they were too self-important and failed to give him the respect he felt was his due. Furthermore, the young men attracted enthusiastic attention from the mass of the population because they looked like princes. Herod had arranged suitable royal marriages for them both: Alexander to Glaphyra of Cappadocia, as we have seen, and Aristobulus to his first cousin Berenice, daughter of Herod's sister Salome.

If the latter marriage was intended to disarm Salome, it did not succeed. Salome was all too aware of her own role in bringing about the demise of the boys' mother and the likelihood that they would seek revenge if one of them came to power after Herod's death. She plotted against them with as much energy as she had devoted to her opposition to their mother. Along with her brother Pheroras, she spread malicious but plausible rumors about Alexander and Aristobulus's resentment at being made to live in the same court as the man who had killed Mariamme. The young men responded with open hostility, which seemed to confirm the rumors.

Salome and Pheroras knew how to play on their brother's insecurity. When Herod returned to Judaea in 14 from the tour of Asia Minor in which he had so triumphantly consolidated his reputation as a close friend of Agrippa, they greeted him with the news that his sons were intending to blacken his name with Augustus by bringing a charge against him to the emperor for the execution of their mother.[18]

Such a reprise of the nightmare twenty years earlier, when Mariamme's mother, Alexandra, had charged him before Antony for the murder of Mariamme's brother Jonathan Aristobulus, had to be averted if Herod was to maintain the regard of Augustus on which his power ultimately depended. Deciding to protect himself by demonstrating to Alexander and Aristobulus that the succession was not to be taken for granted, in 14 Herod recalled from exile his eldest son, Antipater. Antipater had been born long before Herod became king, and he had no royal connections except through his father. Herod tried to bestow on him some Hasmonaean credibility by marrying him to a daughter of Antigonus, the Hasmonaean king and high priest whom he himself had ousted twenty years earlier and whose death he had engineered.

Antipater was in his early thirties. He had spent his entire adult life away from the court, and he was more or less unknown to the wider populace in Judaea. Herod evidently thought that this son, at least, would be sufficiently reliant on him, and sufficiently grateful for his recall, to represent his father's interests at all times. Herod's agreement, at Antipater's request, to take Antipater's mother, Doris, back into his marriage bed despite her advanced age and the competing attractions of his younger wives, was presumably intended to cement the relationship between father and son. We are not told whether Herod had remained fond of Doris despite their many years apart.[19]

Herod began to treat Antipater as the favored son, writing numerous letters to Augustus to recommend him. In 13 he sent Antipater to Rome in the company of Agrippa to become a friend of the emperor. Herod may even have felt a real bond with Antipater, who was, after all, his firstborn, the child of his youth, named after his beloved father. He does not seem to have taken sufficiently into account that Antipater, who had been banished from Jerusalem since early childhood, forbidden even to enter the city except to attend the pilgrim festivals, had his own reasons to resent his father. Nor did he take into account that Antipater's thirty years in exile from his father's court, which had been designed to prevent his overshadowing Mariamme's sons, had left a residue of rivalry and resentment of his younger half-brothers. In a series of letters sent from Rome, Antipater pretended to be protecting his father's interests by poisoning his mind against Alexander and Aristobulus as much as he could. By 12, Herod had become convinced that Alexander and Aristobulus were engaged in a conspiracy to murder him and seize power for themselves.[20]

Herod was an independent king, with the right to choose his own heir. He had dealt ruthlessly in previous years with others convicted of treason. But in this instance, instead of taking unilateral action, he set sail for Italy to accuse his sons before Augustus. He represented this behavior as a commendable commitment to justice: despite the wickedness of the two boys and their lack of gratitude for the kindly way he had treated them, "not even in such circumstances had he used his authority against them but he had brought them before Caesar, their common benefactor." He claimed to be presenting himself for judgment by Augustus on an equal footing with his sons.[21]

The ensuing trial is said to have reduced both boys to tears. They groaned pitifully, and Herod was also said to have been seized by "a genuine emotion." According to the speech attributed to Alexander by Josephus (who doubtless derived it from Nicolaus, who is likely to have participated in the trial), Alexander himself pointed out that Herod could have punished them on his own authority as king and as father. Bringing them before Augustus was therefore an indication that he wished for leniency.

Certainly, that was the result. Augustus reconciled Herod to both boys, and they returned to Judaea along with Antipater, who had to pretend to be pleased with the outcome.[22]

Granted again by Augustus the authority to dispose of his kingdom to "whichever of his sons he chose, or even to apportion it among them," Herod, accompanied by all three sons, addressed an assembly in the newly rebuilt Temple in Jerusalem to announce the settlement which had resulted from "Caesar's kindness to him." He called for unity, designating as the sons who were to reign after him "first Antipater and next his sons by Mariamme, Alexander and Aristobulus." All three sons were declared to be kings, and entitled to the succession, "this one by his age, the others by their noble birth." It sounded like a triumphant resolution, but in fact Herod's troubles were far from over. Augustus had explicitly said that he would not permit Herod to give up control of either his kingdom or his sons during his lifetime, and Herod could only beg his sons to live in harmony.[23]

The arrangement, foisted on Herod by Augustus, was a disaster. For the next five years, Antipater, with occasional connivance from Herod's siblings Pheroras and Salome, plotted against Alexander and Aristobulus, who in turn became increasingly disaffected. The court was a mass of intrigue in which Herod's siblings and wives, along with their sons and their sons' wives and relatives, spread rumors about plots and counterplots, stoking Herod's fear that his rule was under threat from all sides.

Relations between Herod and his siblings continued to be a complex mix of affection and outrage. Their mother, Cyprus, was not around to impose restraint—we hear nothing about her after 29 BCE. We are told that Herod "often lamented the wickedness of his own family and how badly he had been treated by those to whom he had been so good." He came to hate Pheroras and Salome as each blamed the other, but despite his fury with both of them, he continued to request gossip about Salome from Pheroras—who in turn continued to dine with his sister despite their mutual recriminations. Adding to the family tension, Glaphyra, Alexander's wife, made clear to all that as a descendant of the divine Greek hero Heracles on her father's side, and a descendant of the Persian king Darius on her mother's, she came from an altogether more exalted background than everyone else in court, not least Herod himself.[24]

Herod's method of dealing with his suspicion that Alexander was planning to murder him and seize power was to submit some of his son's friends to torture to establish the truth. He took their denials of the rumors about plots as evidence of their loyalty to Alexander and therefore of the truth of the charges. Sometime in the year 10, one of these friends finally cracked and asserted that Alexander had indeed plotted with his brother Aristobulus to ambush their father while they were out hunting and then flee to Rome to claim the kingdom from Augustus. Alexander was arrested and imprisoned, but Herod seems to have realized that the accusation, which presupposed that Augustus would hand over Judaea to his friend's self-confessed murderer, was not very plausible. He hunted for further evidence, but for a while came up with nothing more damning than a letter from Alexander to Aristobulus complaining about the excessive size of the annual allowance their half-brother Antipater was receiving from their father. Eventually one of the younger friends of Alexander, under torture, leveled more damaging accusations. Alexander, he said, sent messages to Rome accusing Herod of abandoning his allegiance to the Romans to seek an alliance with the Parthians. Alexander was alleged to have arranged for a poisonous drug to be prepared in Ashkelon and given to his father.[25]

No one could think that the powers in Rome would believe that Herod planned to transfer his allegiance from Rome to Parthia. The accusations were so bizarre that Alexander responded with a long, sarcastic screed, apparently "in four books," in which he told the world that there was no need to torture anyone or proceed farther since he could confirm that there had indeed been a plot against Herod. He claimed derisively that he had been able to take advantage of the help of Pheroras and "the most faithful of the king's friends" in the conspiracy and added, for good measure, that Salome had forced her way into his room one night and slept with him against his will. Everyone, he confirmed, was indeed keen to get rid of the king as quickly as possible. Such heavy sarcasm about the ridiculous accusations brought against him was dangerous. Herod was not behaving rationally. In a torment of anxiety, he threw many of Alexander's closest associates into prison. He trusted no one, and his "whole life became unbearable to him, so greatly was he disturbed. . . . In his imagination, he would often see his son advancing upon him or even standing over him with a drawn sword."[26]

Alexander's father-in-law, Archelaus, hurried from Cappadocia to Judaea to intervene. Defusing Herod's temper would require delicate diplomacy, which Archelaus conducted by first feigning indignation against Alexander and then, using Alexander's "four books" as evidence, shifting the blame away from Alexander and on to Pheroras and Salome. The obvious fact to which Archelaus could point was that Alexander had no need to plot against Herod; he had already been designated one of Herod's heirs. But calming Herod's temper required more than logical argument. King Archelaus treated Herod like a toddler, arguing so vehemently that his daughter Glaphyra should be divorced from Alexander now that Alexander's full wickedness had been revealed that Herod ended up pleading for leniency toward his son. It was Herod who insisted that the marriage should continue, stressing the value of the tie between him and the Cappadocian king. His fury assuaged and a full report sent to the emperor in Rome, Herod accompanied his royal guest on his return north as far as Antioch. There was a mutual exchange of valuable gifts—from Herod to Archelaus, seventy talents, a throne of gold set with precious stones, eunuchs, and a concubine—and Herod tried to bring himself to trust the sons whose hostility had been the stuff of nightmares.[27]

Herod's unwise engagement the following year in the Nabataean war—which, for a brief but desperate period, caused him to fall out of favor with the emperor—may well have been in part an attempt to demonstrate to his sons that he was still a force to be reckoned with. We have seen that Josephus's defensive account of the origins of the war, which must reflect the pleas to Augustus by Nicolaus that eventually succeeded in rehabilitating Herod with the emperor, portrays the Jewish king as an innocent victim of Nabataean skullduggery and his assault on Nabataean territory as primarily a police operation to suppress the cross-border banditry fomented by Syllaeus over a number of years. But Josephus does not explain why Herod did not seek to negotiate a solution to these issues with Roman help. It may be suspected that the king was not averse to grasping an opportunity to advertise to his subjects that he was still capable of vigorous military action. Instead of entrusting the campaign to a subordinate, for the first time in more than two decades Herod, now well into his sixties, led his army in person into Arabia. That we are told that Herod covered a seven days' march in three days at the start of the invasion of enemy territory is significant both for the impressive feat itself and for the fact that it was recorded as impressive.[28]

The Nabataean war also helped Herod bring Salome into line. For Salome, who was in her fifties, the prime attraction of Syllaeus had been his youth and good looks, even if Herod originally had more diplomatic reasons in his relations with the Nabataean kingdom for taking seriously the possibility that Syllaeus might marry his sister. Salome continued to hanker after Syllaeus when the marriage plans foundered, but evidently she could not marry without Herod's permission. Eventually she succumbed to pressure and, around the time of the Nabataean war, took as her third husband Herod's friend Alexas, about whose background little is known. Josephus reported that Salome's agreement to the marriage was on the advice of her friend Livia, the wife of Augustus, who urged that it would be prudent to avoid an open breach with her brother. The breach was successfully avoided, and Salome and Alexas were the relatives on whom Herod called during his last days.[29]

Herod's self-confidence, temporarily buoyed by his military victory in Nabataea, was dashed by Augustus's very public disapproval of his actions in waging war without permission from Rome. Herod could no longer assume that the emperor would automatically support him as a friend in a power struggle with his sons. His resolve to try to trust Alexander and Aristobulus was further undermined by the intrigues of the Spartan adventurer Eurycles, who insinuated himself into the confidence of both Antipater and Alexander and then ensured that Alexander's complaints about the maltreatment he had suffered at the hands of his father came to the king's ears. Trusting Eurycles, Alexander told him that he and his brother had been so alienated from their father by Antipater that Herod could no longer bear to speak to them at dinner parties and other gatherings. Eurycles reported these words to Herod. When Herod questioned two of his former bodyguards who rode out with Alexander and his friends about Eurycles' accusation, they reported under torture that Alexander had tried to persuade them to kill Herod and to make his death look like an accident.

This time the accusation was bolstered by the physical evidence of a hoard of gold hidden under a stable, presumably as payment for their role in the conspiracy. They testified that the chief hunter had given the king's spears to them and weapons to Alexander's servants on Alexander's orders. When a letter was found in Alexander's handwriting addressed to the commander of the garrison of the fort of Alexandrium near the river Jordan, apparently arranging for safe refuge "when with God's help we have achieved all that we set out to do," Alexander's guilt seemed proved. The son's protest that the letter had been written by Diophantus, one of Herod's secretaries, who was an expert in imitating handwriting—and who was later put to death for a crime of forgery—was not heeded.[30]

Herod brought the accusations before a wider public, requiring the men who had been tortured to repeat their testimony to a crowd in Jericho, but the crowd turned ugly, stoning the witnesses to death. Popular support was not easy to manipulate: the accused, Alexander and Aristobulus, were said to be in danger of a similar death at the hands of the mob. The crowd may have lost patience with the whole royal soap opera, which ignored the concerns of the wider population. Both young men were put under guard in isolation, and an accusation was laid against them before Augustus in Rome.[31]

Five years earlier Augustus had heard the accusations himself, but this time he advised Herod to convene a council in the new Roman colony of Berytus (modern Beirut) to sort out the problem on his own authority. He was to seek help from Saturninus, the governor of Syria, and other Romans. Augustus also advised Herod to summon to the council Archelaus of Cappadocia, whose intervention had proved so effective in protecting his son-in-law a few years earlier, but this advice, ominously for Alexander, Herod chose to ignore. It did not help that Alexander's wife, Glaphyra, was found to have been making plans of her own to escape with her husband from the poisonous atmosphere in Judaea by returning to Cappadocia and moving from there to Rome.[32]

Herod seemed bent on ensuring convictions. The council of 150 men heard Herod read aloud the offensive letters by his sons. The council agreed that such unfilial behavior should be punished. The two accused were not permitted to appear to plead their innocence. Saturninus, the senior Roman present, was accompanied in the council by three of his own sons and argued against the death penalty, but the majority disagreed. Herod sailed back south with his two sons in chains to the brand-new port of Caesarea, whose completion had recently been celebrated in magnificent style. Those who spoke up for the youths in face of the clear danger that the impending doom of Mariamme's sons would evoke popular unrest were themselves accused of conspiracy in a public assembly and beaten to death on the spot with cudgels and stones. Alexander and Aristobulus were taken to Sebaste and strangled on Herod's order. Their bodies were removed by night for burial in the fortress of Alexandrium, where Mariamme's father and most of their ancestors lay.[33]

Herod's new will still appointed his eldest son, Antipater, as his heir, but it also included one of the sons of the second Mariamme, named Herod after his father, who was designated to succeed if Antipater predeceased the king. The precaution was not without warrant: Antipater was about forty, which at this time constituted advanced middle age. The young Herod, by contrast, was only in his teens and probably unknown to Augustus—we are not told that he had ever been to Rome, and we shall see that Herod apparently found it easy to pass him over altogether when he drew up yet another new will, with different heirs, a year later.[34]

Antipater himself was all too aware of the opposition to his influence by his aunt Salome and those of Herod's subjects, especially within the army, who had supported Alexander and Aristobulus. Herod attempted to disarm discord among the remaining members of his family through a series of arranged betrothals, promising in marriage the young children of Alexander and Aristobulus to various close relatives and marrying Aristobulus's daughter to Antipater himself. The arrangements smacked of desperation and signally failed to engender the sense of family solidarity he intended.[35]

Herod himself finally fell out spectacularly with his brother

Pheroras over Pheroras's continuing devotion to his slave concubine, whom Herod considered a malign influence. Herod was furious to discover that when in 7 BCE Pheroras's concubine paid the fine incurred by a group of Pharisees who declined on grounds of conscience to take an oath of loyalty, these Pharisees had prophesied that the throne of Judaea would be taken by divine decree from Herod and his descendants and granted instead to her and Pheroras and any children they might have. Herod issued Pheroras with an ultimatum: choose between his brother and his mistress. On Pheroras's stubborn refusal to choose (which in effect constituted a decision for his concubine), Herod ordered him to retire to his own territory in Peraea. His brother responded huffily, leaving gladly and "swearing a mighty oath that he would not come back until he should hear of Herod's death." Pheroras evidently meant what he threatened. Even when the king was very sick and Pheroras was asked to return to receive confidential instructions in expectation of Herod's imminent death, he refused to break his oath.[36]

In the year 5, Pheroras himself fell ill, and Herod, yet again more forgiving, came unbidden to see him on what proved to be his deathbed. When he died, Herod had the body prepared for burial and brought to Jerusalem, where he provided a burial place and decreed solemn mourning. We do not know how much Herod's affection for his brother as revealed by his care over these obsequies was diminished by the story which emerged after his death that Pheroras had at one time conspired with Antipater to obtain poison from Egypt, through Nabataean intermediaries, to murder Herod, and that Pheroras had repented his fratricidal intentions only when Herod came to visit him on his deathbed.[37]

It is hard to know now whether there was any truth to these rumors. Accusations of poisoning were easy to make and difficult to disprove. Some even thought that Herod himself had poisoned Pheroras when he came for his final visit. The rumors about the plot against the king were sparked by claims from two of Pheroras's freedmen that Pheroras himself had been poisoned by his concubine at the dinner he had shared with her the day before he fell ill. She was said to have used a poisonous drug masked as an aphrodisiac. Torture of the slaves and freedwomen of Pheroras's concubine then elicited a host of further accusations relating to poison plots against Herod rather than his brother.[38]

The alleged plot against Herod had never been carried out, but what concerned him was the claim that Antipater had been involved. Antipater, who had been designated his heir, was a particular danger because he was out of reach in Rome. In 6 he had concluded from the fate of his younger half-brothers that the only place where he could be safe from his father's justified suspicion that everyone in the court in Jerusalem might be plotting over the succession was in the imperial court. He had elicited letters from his friends in Rome to advise Herod to send him to Augustus as quickly as possible. Herod had complied, dispatching Antipater with magnificent presents for the emperor as well as a copy of the most recent will, designating Antipater his sole heir, for which it seems Herod still felt a need for imperial approval.

Some of those in Pheroras's household who were tortured alleged that it was Antipater's absence in Rome, where he was unlikely to be suspected, that had encouraged Pheroras and his concubine to hatch their plot in league with him. These accusers added that Antipater's mother, Doris, had been behind the plan in an attempt to ensure that her son would inherit the kingdom from Herod as sole ruler. Pheroras's concubine confessed to her part in the plot and appeared to confirm her guilt by attempting unsuccessfully to kill herself by jumping from the palace roof. Subjected to further questioning with a promise that she and her household would avoid torture if she told the whole truth, she appeared to confirm her confession by producing the drug. She implicated in the conspiracy other members of Herod's close family, including the second Mariamme. Few people in antiquity considered evidence produced through torture unreliable, and the king was inclined to believe what he was told. The fear of poison was very real even near the end of his life: it was through poison, secretly administered at a banquet, that his beloved father had died nearly forty years earlier.[39]

Herod was old and tired and unsure who could be trusted, but he settled down to try to sort out this new family crisis. For the young Herod, the penalty for his mother's disloyalty seems to have been nothing worse than to be struck out of his father's will. Mariamme herself was divorced and sent away. It is striking that the charge of treason did not lead to her execution, as it had for her predecessor with the same name in 29, but her father, Simon, was deposed from the high priesthood he had held for close to twenty years. Dealing with Antipater, away in Rome, was trickier.[40]

The testimony of Pheroras's freedmen that Antipater had complained to Doris that "his father was dragging out his life too long and he himself was close to being an old man; even if the royal power came to him, he would still not be able to enjoy it" was all too plausible. Herod was convinced of the guilt of his eldest son and finally came to appreciate how Antipater had manipulated the downfall of his half-brothers. For Herod, this was a terrible revelation, coming too late to save the sons whose execution he had ordered two years earlier. Now Antipater could do nothing right. Letters sent from Rome to some of Herod's friends to accuse two other sons, Archelaus and Philip, of slandering their father as the murderer of Alexander and Aristobulus were now interpreted by Herod not as evidence of disloyalty by Archelaus and Philip but as part of a further plot by Antipater to rid himself of these half-brothers, in addition to the two whose deaths he had already engineered.[41]

Exacting retribution would have to wait until Antipater's

return home. Slaves carrying messages from Doris advising her son to stay in Rome and seek refuge with Augustus were intercepted. Even so, it took seven months before Antipater made his way back to Judaea, spurred to action finally by a carefully phrased letter from Herod which hinted that Doris was in trouble and needed help. Josephus noted that it was remarkable that no indication of the changed atmosphere in Judaea had reached Antipater in Rome over this long period. He attributed Antipater's ignorance to "the careful guarding of the roads and the general hatred of Antipater, for there was no-one who was found willing to endanger himself in order to provide for Antipater's safety." Antipater hesitated briefly in Cilicia (in southeast Turkey) on his journey home from Rome, concerned by Herod's message about his mother and what it might portend for his own fortunes. But he does not seem to have realized that he himself was to be put on trial until he arrived at the port of Caesarea, where the coldness of his reception made him aware of his danger.[42]

The trial was held before Varus, the new governor of Syria, who had come to Jerusalem at Herod's request. Herod and his relatives, including Salome, sat on the panel, but it was Varus who took control of the proceedings. Our knowledge of the course of the trial is undoubtedly skewed by the participation of Nicolaus as counsel for the prosecution, tasked with completing Herod's own speech when the king collapsed in tears. Once the accusations exacted from witnesses under torture about Antipater's plans to kill the king as well as his plots against his brothers had been laid out in detail, Varus attempted in vain to elicit a defense from Antipater. Antipater's guilt was finally demonstrated when Varus ordered that the drug Antipater was said to have prepared for his father be administered to a prisoner under sentence of death. When the prisoner died instantly, Varus rose and left the council, his task done, and departed for his headquarters in Antioch. Herod was left to deal with his son.[43]

Antipater was thrown into prison. Constrained by the ties

Antipater had established with the emperor and others in Rome, Herod refrained from inflicting further punishment. He was conspicuously lenient with Doris, whose penalty for scheming on behalf of her son was expulsion from the court (for the second time) and the loss of "all her finery." Herod appears to have been uncertain what to do with Antipater himself. He sent reports to Augustus about the uncovered plot and encouraged the emperor to take the charges seriously by adding to them new information about Antipater which showed that he had "corrupted the household of Caesar." Antipater was alleged to have conspired against his aunt Salome with the aid of a Jewish slave called Acme, who belonged to Livia. Herod considered sending Antipater to Rome for a further trial in front of Augustus (although it is hard to imagine what new information such a trial might have elicited) but worried that Antipater might escape on the journey. Instead he kept his son in chains in Judaea while awaiting instructions from the emperor.[44]

It would take time for such instructions to arrive, and Herod, old and increasingly frail, needed to make a new will. He chose one of his younger offspring, Antipas, the younger son of his Samaritan wife Malthace. We are told that Antipas's older brother Archelaus and his half-brother Philip were overlooked because Antipater had poisoned Herod's mind against them, but this may be special pleading by Nicolaus in favor of Archelaus, whose cause he represented to Augustus after Herod's death. Similarly, Nicolaus's reticence may explain the lack of information in our surviving sources about Malthace's part in the intrigues plaguing Herod's court in his last years. Antipas was brought up in Rome and presumably known to Augustus, if only distantly, but Herod had no chance to discuss with the emperor his selection of this particular son as his heir. The inclusion in the will of the huge sum of a thousand talents as a gift to Augustus may have been intended to serve as an inducement to uphold the will.[45]

By the time a response was received from Augustus to the

request for instructions about Antipater, Herod was mortally ill and facing a popular uprising sparked by religious enthusiasts, who destroyed the golden eagle he had erected as a votive offering above the main gate of the Temple in Jerusalem. Two teachers with reputations as exceptional interpreters of the ancestral laws and large numbers of young students took advantage of the news about Herod's incurable illness to incite their followers to destroy all the works built by the king in violation of Jewish law, in particular the eagle, even at the risk of martyrdom. When a rumor arrived in Jerusalem that the king had died, the plan was put into action in broad daylight at a time when the Temple was crowded. The young men climbed up to the roof of the Temple and, letting themselves down by rope, pulled the eagle off and chopped it up with axes. The Temple had a security force, and one of Herod's officers arrived rapidly on the scene with sufficient troops to arrest the two teachers and forty young men, some of them apparently bystanders. They were all taken in chains to Jericho.[46]

The Temple, which had been intended to preserve Herod's reputation for piety among future generations, became the catalyst for his Jewish subjects to attack him for the religious compromises he had made throughout his life. In the eyes of these dissidents, it was "because of his audacity in making these things in disregard of the Law's provisions that all these misfortunes, with which he [had] become familiar to a degree uncommon among mankind, had happened to him, in particular his illness." The king berated the prisoners at a meeting of Jewish leaders specially convened in the amphitheater, lying on a couch because he was too ill to stand, and shouting at them that he had adorned the Temple to the honor of God. The students who had let themselves down from the Temple roof were burned alive along with the two teachers. But Herod also blamed the high priest Matthias, presumably for failing to use the authority of his position to defend with sufficient robustness Herod's claim that the erection of the eagle had been an act of piety. Matthias had been appointed the previous year in place of Simon son of Boethus, when his daughter Mariamme had been revealed to be complicit in the plot to poison her husband. Matthias was now removed from office and replaced by Mariamme's brother Joazar. Since Joazar's father had served as high priest throughout the period of Herod's rebuilding works and had presumably condoned the erection of the eagle image, Herod might reasonably have hoped that he would prove a more loyal defender of his reputation.[47]

Josephus described in graphic detail the progress of Herod's final illness, which left him in agony:

> The fever that he had was a light one and did not so much indicate symptoms of inflammation to the touch as it produced internal damage. . . . There was also an ulceration of the bowels and intestinal pains that were particularly terrible, and a moist, transparent suppuration of the feet. And he suffered from an abdominal ailment, as well as from a gangrene of his privy parts that produced worms. His breathing was marked by extreme tension, and it was very unpleasant because of the disagreeable exhalation of his breath and his constant gasping. He also had convulsions in every limb that took on an unendurable severity.

His physicians recommended baths in the warm springs of Callirrhoe, near the northeast end of the Dead Sea, and the use of warm oil (presumably for anointing), but nothing worked. His mind had turned to arrangements for mourning after his death when a letter arrived from the envoys sent to Augustus to tell him that the slave Acme had been put to death for her part in abetting Antipater and that the emperor had decided that Herod, "as father and king," should use his own judgment about whether to exile Antipater or put him to death.[48]

Herod's decision to select the death penalty for his son was precipitated by the revelation that Antipater had been offering bribes to his jailor in expectation of imminent release after the death of his father. Antipater's hopes had been raised by the sound of lamentation in the palace, which he had wrongly assumed signaled Herod's death. It was in fact a response to a failed suicide attempt by the king, who had been prevented by his cousin Achiab from stabbing himself with a fruit knife to escape the pain of his illness. Antipater's misunderstanding proved fatal. Raising himself on his elbows, the sick king dispatched some of his bodyguards with orders for the immediate execution of his firstborn son.[49]

Josephus does not say what impelled Herod to make a final change to his will in his last days. Under the new arrangement, Archelaus, Malthace's other son, was to be king of Judaea in place of his younger brother Antipas, who was allotted instead a role as tetrarch of Galilee and part of Peraea. We are not told whether, in light of the long-standing hostility between Jews and Samaritans, Herod's Jewish subjects objected to a ruler with a Samaritan mother; either the maternal origins of a ruler were not seen as significant in this case, despite the importance of descent from the Hasmonaean Mariamme in the cases of Alexander and Aristobulus, or the evidence of dissent was suppressed by Nicolaus out of loyalty to Archelaus. Gaulanitis and other territories east and north of the Sea of Galilee were to be governed by their half-brother Philip, son of Cleopatra of Jerusalem.[50]

Antipas does not seem to have done anything to deserve demotion—if he had incurred Herod's displeasure, it would have been easy for the king to remove him from the new arrangements altogether. Herod might simply have changed his mind about the loyalty of his two other sons, once Antipater was no longer around to poison his view of them. But the king might also have calculated that a division of his kingdom was more likely to receive endorsement from Augustus than a transfer to the sole care of Antipas, who was only seventeen and lacking in political experience. It was true that Archelaus was not much older (about nineteen) and Philip a bit younger (about sixteen), but, like Antipas, they had been brought up in Rome, and had established contacts there who could lobby the emperor on their behalf. Giving them each a share in the realm might seem to a dying father the most effective way to ensure the harmonious transfer of power.[51]

Herod's last days were spent in terrible pain. His suffering might be construed as a just penalty for his impiety, but it is unlikely that Herod felt regret for his compromises with the Torah such as donations to pagan temples, which he argued had been necessary to ingratiate himself with his Roman friends, or that he indulged in introspection about the many victims of his rule—the bandits killed without trial in Galilee at the beginning of his career, the rival politicians liquidated at the start of his reign, the drowning of Jonathan Aristobulus, the suppression of demonstrators against the games he had initiated in Jerusalem and the eagle he had set up in the Temple, all those who had been tortured and executed on suspicion of treason. For Herod, these deaths were an inevitable result of statecraft, a political pragmatism that Mark Antony had recognized long ago when he insisted to Cleopatra that a king must have a free hand in such matters if he were truly to rule as a king. Perhaps Herod felt a twinge of conscience about his erstwhile friends who had suffered for collusion in conspiracies they had not led, such as the Pharisees caught up in the intrigues of his brother Pheroras. But Herod's main regret as he lay dying was for his family, to which he had devoted so much emotion and political capital throughout his life. His family tragedy was played out on a stage in the imperial court in Rome, where the domestic quarrels of the Judaean king were brought before the horrified gaze of a wide public, eliciting, it was alleged, the punning quip by Augustus that it was better to be Herod's pig (in Greek, *hus*) than his son (in Greek, *huios*).[52]

* * *

Herod died shortly before Passover in 4 BCE, five days after the execution of Antipater. He knew well that many of his Jewish subjects would greet news of his death with delight and is said to have taken steps to prevent public rejoicing. As he lay on his deathbed, he summoned notable Jews from all over the nation and had them corralled into the hippodrome in Jericho. Later stories circulated that these notables had been gathered together so that they could be slaughtered when he breathed his last, to ensure mass mourning to accompany his funeral. Whether this was Herod's motivation is unknown; the plan for a massacre, allegedly entrusted to Salome and her husband by "appealing to their family affection and their faith in God," was not carried out. When Herod died, Salome and Alexas are said to have balked at the savagery of the actions they had been enjoined to undertake. They sent the crowd home unharmed, claiming that the king had ordered them to do so. The story of the intended massacre may never have been more than a rumor which gained credibility from the ruthlessness with which Herod had imposed his will throughout his long reign, and the hatred of Jews who despised him as "a wanton king . . . a man rash and perverse," who for thirty-four years had killed both old and young, "showing mercy to none."[53]

The lack of widespread grief among his subjects did not prevent Herod's funeral from being a magnificent affair:

> Archelaus saw to it that his father's burial should be most splendid, and he brought out all his ornaments to accompany the procession for the deceased. Herod was borne upon a golden bier studded with precious stones of various kinds and with a cover of purple over it. The dead man too was wrapped in purple robes and wore a diadem on which a gold crown had been placed, and beside his right hand lay his sceptre. Round the bier were his sons and a host of his relatives, and after them came the army disposed according to the various nationalities and designations. They were arranged

> in the following order: first came the bodyguards, then the Thracians, and following them, whatever Germans he had, and next the Gauls. These men were all equipped for battle. Right behind them came the whole army as if marching to war, led by their company-commanders and lower officers, followed by five hundred servants carrying spices. And they went eight stades [about a mile] towards Herodium, for it was there that the burial took place.[54]

These arrangements had been carefully organized by Herod himself. He had prepared his tomb at Herodium in the palace he had built on a site selected to commemorate the victory over Antigonus and his Parthian allies that had enabled him to escape to Rome in the momentous year 40. Erected originally in the twenties in a remote site on the desert fringe near Bethlehem, Herodium was a remarkable engineering feat, as Josephus recorded:

> He built a fortress in the highlands facing Arabia and called it Herodium after himself, and gave the same name to the artificial breast-shaped hill about seven miles out of Jerusalem which he developed on a grander scale. Round the top of the hill he built a ring of circular towers, and filled the enclosed area with a sumptuous palace of a magnificence evident not only in the interior of its apartments but also in the riches lavished on the exterior—walls, copings, roofs. At huge expense he brought in an abundant water supply from a distance, and laid a flight of 200 steps of the whitest marble to form the approach.

Designed from the start as a memorial site for Herod himself, the palace seems always to have been intended as his eventual resting place. Over the years his plans for the tomb evolved. The original tomb structures, based on a burial cave, were dismantled and replaced by an elaborate Hellenistic style mausoleum placed on the northeastern slope, visible from the hills around Jerusalem.[55]

Herod's palace at Herodium, which also functioned as the site of Herod's tomb. Herod was buried in a white limestone mausoleum on the side of a huge artificial tumulus which dominated the surrounding landscape. The final design, created near the end of Herod's life and requiring an immense fill of dirt and stone on the summit of the hill to create its distinctive conical shape, was probably inspired by the circular design of the mausoleum of Augustus in Rome. (Photo: akg-images / Albatross / Duby Tal)

A few days after his burial it became clear that none of these arrangements would ensure that Herod's name would be revered by future generations. The crowds who gathered to mark his passing may have enjoyed the feast put on by Archelaus to mark the end of the seven days of mourning, but they took advantage of a mass assembly in the Temple to pour out their grievances. They demanded lighter taxes, the release of prisoners put in chains by Herod over many years, and the removal from office of the new high priest Joazar. Archelaus did his best to ward off this discontent by stalling. He asked the crowd for patience until his position as king had been confirmed by Augustus, but their anger boiled over during the Passover celebrations. Disorder was suppressed only by sending in the cavalry. The ensuing massacre left three thousand dead.[56]

Archelaus, as executor, had been charged by his father to carry his signet ring to Augustus, and he traveled to Rome, taking with him under seal the documents relating to the administration of the realm. On arrival he found his brother Antipas and his supporters, who included Salome and her son, who was also named Antipater. They had come to dispute Herod's final will, which had deprived Antipas of the succession he had briefly glimpsed as his. Malthace, the mother of both Archelaus and Antipas, was in Rome to support her younger son, but she died before she could witness the outcome of the protracted negotiations. In the meantime, the Greek cities subject to Herod sent embassies to petition for their freedom, and representatives of the Jews of Judaea, supported by the local Jewish community in Rome, petitioned to be subjected directly to Roman rule. They alleged that the king had reduced the nation to helpless poverty. Herod's attempt to ensure an orderly succession was in ruins.[57]

As the brothers argued in Rome, Judaea erupted. Unrest in Jerusalem reached a peak at Shavuot, seven weeks after the massacre at Passover which had followed Herod's funeral. In his autobiography, Nicolaus, who had himself sailed to Rome with

Archelaus to press his patron's case, described the turmoil as an uprising against Herod's children. Archelaus had left Philip in charge while he was away in Rome, instructing the commanders of Herod's fortresses and his treasury officials to keep Herod's property secure while they awaited the emperor's decision on the will. But these arrangements were thrown into disarray by Sabinus, imperial procurator for the province of Syria, who set out for Judaea on the news of Herod's death to take possession of the king's property on behalf of Augustus. An appeal by Archelaus to Varus, the governor of Syria, to restrain Sabinus from taking action while Herod's will was still being discussed in Rome was initially successful when the two Romans met in Caesarea. But as soon as Varus returned to Antioch, Sabinus took possession of the royal palace in Jerusalem, where he came under siege by the crowds of pilgrims from Galilee, Idumaea, Jericho, and Peraea who had gathered in the city for the festival. In the fierce battles which ensued, the porticoes of the newly rebuilt Temple were set alight.[58]

The whole of Herod's kingdom rapidly melted into chaos. In Jerusalem, the insurgent pilgrims were joined in the struggle against Sabinus by most of Herod's soldiers, although some of their former colleagues, including a force of cavalry and a troop of three thousand infantry from the city of Sebaste under the command of two Roman officers, gave support to the Romans. Elsewhere in Judaea, two thousand of Herod's veterans confronted the royal troops under Herod's cousin Achiab and forced him to retreat to the hills. Armed bands led by a shepherd named Athronges and his four brothers attacked both the Roman and the royal forces in search of plunder. In Galilee, a large group of Jews stormed the royal palace in Sepphoris and seized the weapons stored there. In Peraea, one of Herod's slaves, a tall, handsome man by the name of Simon, destroyed several royal residences, including the palace in Jericho, before he was captured and killed by the Sebaste infantry force, which had joined the Romans. The royal palace at Ammatha on the Jordan was burned down by another group of rebels.[59]

The Romans' solution to the turmoil was swift and brutal. Varus again marched south from Antioch, this time bringing with him a large army, including a considerable force of infantry and cavalry sent by the Nabataean king Aretas, who was said to have sided with the Romans out of hatred of Herod. The uprisings around the kingdom from Galilee to Judaea were suppressed with a degree of savagery enhanced by the troops of Aretas seeking revenge. By the time Varus's troops arrived outside Jerusalem, the Jewish insurgents had scattered and fled. Sabinus, who evidently recognized his culpability, quietly slipped out of the city. Those of the ringleaders who were captured were sent to Augustus in Rome; of these, the only ones to be punished were the relatives of Herod who had joined in the fighting, "because they had shown contempt for justice in fighting against their own kin." The "war of Varus" was recalled a century later by Josephus as one of the great upheavals in the history of Jerusalem, one that had created such havoc it threatened the integrity of the archives holding the records of priestly ancestry.[60]

The outbreak of such chaos following Herod's death demonstrated his failure to ensure a peaceful transmission of power, but it was also testimony to his success in suppressing the frustrations of his subjects for more than thirty years without recourse to massacres such as the one that marred the festival of Passover in Jerusalem so soon after he died. The suppression of the chaos by Varus was also testimony to the brutal truth that control of Judaea depended ultimately on the governor of Syria and his legions. Why should Rome entrust the country to a son of Herod when none of them seemed to have inherited their father's capacity to rule? For Herod's subjects, the rapid changes in his arrangements for the succession during the last decade of his life must have highlighted the arbitrariness of his choices and the lack of inherited authority held by any of his successors (apart, perhaps, from Alexander and Aristobulus, who could boast of their Hasmonaean heritage). To his fellow Jews, Herod had been plucked from insignificance by fiat of the Romans, and his sons had been selected as his successors by equally arbitrary fiats of his own. It was not accidental that some of the leaders of the uprisings presented themselves to their followers as kings, from Judas, the son of a bandit who had been captured by Herod four decades earlier, to the slave Simon in Galilee and the shepherd Athronges in Judaea. If Herod could make and unmake kings simply by announcing who should have the title, why should not Judas, Simon, or Athronges have similar ambitions?[61]

The decision of Augustus, sitting in council in Rome many miles away, to send Herod's three sons back to rule a region which was only just emerging from such turmoil is best explained if the person most determined to create a dynasty of rulers from Herod's offspring was Augustus himself. Among the friends convened to give him advice, the emperor gave first place at his side to his adopted son Gaius, who was the natural son of Herod's old friend Agrippa. Gaius was only sixteen, and this may have been the first occasion on which he taken such a role on a public stage, but Augustus was determined to demonstrate that he should be seen as his intended heir.

Nicolaus's detailed accounts of the speeches to the council, in which Nicolaus himself had a leading role, indicate that he was well aware of Augustus's hesitation to entrust a large and volatile kingdom to three teenagers on the basis of the last-minute wishes of a friend racked with pain on his deathbed. Herod had been selected as king because his proven qualities demonstrated his ability to rule; the selection of his sons, who had achieved nothing of note in their short lives, could claim no such justification. Reassuring other client kings that their choice of successor would be automatically recognized by Rome was presumably not the emperor's prime concern in his final decision, since the extended process of public consultation he followed before Herod's will was ratified demonstrated clearly that he did not feel bound by its terms. Nor can Augustus have been swayed by evidence of the personal competence of the rulers he was about to appoint: in the few weeks Archelaus had governed Judaea after his father died, there had been a massacre; the sixteen-year-old Philip had abandoned his role as regent at the urging of Varus to join his brothers in Rome in support of the claims of Archelaus as well as his own share of power; and Antipas, a year older, is not known to have had any administrative experience at all—the speeches in his favor at the imperial council, at least as reported by Josephus, were full of accusations against Archelaus but had nothing positive to say about his own qualifications.[62]

Thus when Augustus eventually dismissed the council and made up his mind on the disposition of Herod's kingdom, he followed Herod's wishes as laid down in his final will but took the precaution of appointing Archelaus not king but ethnarch, with a promise of the title of king in due course, "if he really proved able to act in that capacity." It would be hard to think of a more effective way of undermining the authority of a young ruler who had been enthusiastically acclaimed king by some of his subjects a few months earlier but now had also to rule over those who had made their opposition so clear by their embassy to Rome seeking an end to rule by a Jewish king. How could he face them all with self-confidence when his father had bestowed the royal title, at one time or another, on four of his brothers, then indicated publicly that it should also to be conferred on him, but the emperor had decreed that he was not worthy? In the event, Augustus never deemed Archelaus worthy to be called king: in the tenth year after his appointment as ethnarch, Archelaus was summoned to Rome to face charges of tyranny brought by a deputation of Jews and Samaritans and sent into exile in Gaul. A contemporary observer, the geographer Strabo, also reported that Antipas and Philip were the subject of accusations at the same time as Archelaus, but "by much obsequiousness, albeit with difficulty, obtained leave to return home, with a tetrarchy assigned to each." The fragility of Augustus's disposition of Herod's kingdom on the basis of Herod's final will, by which the realm was handed over to three of his sons simply because of their genetic descent, was evidently still patent decades later.[63]

It is all the more remarkable that Roman emperors were to continue for over a century to appoint Herod's descendants to rule over far-flung regions of the Near East on the basis of their birth. For Josephus, writing in the nineties CE, and a close acquaintance of Herod's great-grandson Agrippa II, the right of Herod's descendants to be thus favored was so obvious that the moral lesson to be learned from their fate was the eventual dying out of the line: the tale of Herod's descendants "affords a proof of the divine, showing how neither numbers nor any other worldly advantage can avail anything without acts of piety towards the divine; for within a century of Herod's decease it came about that all but a few of Herod's issue, and there were many, had perished." In order to demonstrate this point, Josephus provided his readers not just with a long list of Herod's children, their spouses and offspring, including those who ruled in Judaea and its environs over that century, but also the names of those appointed by Rome to rule in regions far from Judaea and unrelated to Jews. These included two kings of Armenia (both called Tigranes), descendants of Herod through Mariamme's son Alexander, who had "abandoned from birth the observance of the ways of the Jewish land and ranged themselves with the Greek tradition." But they also included a descendant of Mariamme's second son Aristobulus (called Aristobulus after his grandfather), who was appointed by Nero to govern Armenia Minor during the preparations for war against Parthia in the mid-fifties CE. This Aristobulus was sufficiently committed to Judaism to have interceded alongside his father and cousin with the emperor Claudius on behalf of the Jews of Jerusalem when they petitioned to be allowed to keep the robes of the high priest in the hands of the Temple authorities rather than leaving them in the custody of the Roman governor of Judaea.[64]

Just as Herod's descendants could choose how much to recognize their Jewish heritage, so too they could choose how much to advertise their connection to their royal ancestor. Herod himself gave his own name to two of his sons by different wives, and two of his grandsons, both born while he was alive, were also called Herod, but otherwise the name seems to have been used only rarely after his death and (unlike the name of Caesar in Rome) it did not become a dynastic title. Of his sons, Archelaus, as ethnarch of Judaea, and Antipas, as tetrarch of Galilee, both called themselves Herod on coins and inscriptions, but Herod's grandson Agrippa I, who was appointed by Claudius in 41 CE as king of Judaea to rule over a realm as extensive as his grandfather's, did not use the name. Agrippa may simply have wished to avoid confusion with his elder brother, Herod of Chalcis, but he may also have played down his line of descent from his grandfather, preferring to stress his legitimacy as a descendant of the Hasmonaean line through his grandmother Mariamme.[65]

A curious incident shortly after Herod's death showed that other Jews believed that only a descendant of one of Mariamme's sons Alexander and Aristobulus could be a legitimate king of Judaea. Just after Augustus had confirmed Archelaus as ethnarch and his brothers as tetrarchs, a young man claiming to be Herod's son Alexander, who had been executed by his father three years earlier, hoodwinked the Jews of Crete and Melos into giving him money to travel to Rome to claim the inheritance of the kingdom once promised him by Herod. The young man, who bore a strong physical resemblance to Alexander, asserted that neither he nor his brother Aristobulus had been put to death. On his arrival in Italy, the Jews of Puteoli and Rome acclaimed him, "regarding his extraordinary escape from death as an act of God, and giving him a joyful welcome because of their connection to him through his mother." The real Alexander had been away from Rome for eight years, but Augustus had known him well in earlier days and was not fooled. Unfortunately for the imposter it was noted that his body had been roughened by a lifetime of manual labor such as a genuine son of Herod would never have known. He was sentenced to the galleys. To the Jews who had so foolishly put their faith in him, his appeal lay in his claim of Hasmonaean ancestry. When the emperor tested his story by asking why, if his brother Aristobulus had also been saved from execution along with him, he had not accompanied the alleged Alexander to Rome to claim the rank to which he was entitled, the imposter explained that Aristobulus had been left behind on the island of Cyprus so that "if some misfortune should befall himself, the posterity of Mariamme should not be completely wiped out."[66]

For the historian Josephus, writing about Herod with the benefit of access to both the contemporary account of Nicolaus and the perspective of a century during which Herod's descendants had played a major role in Jewish and Roman history, the character and motivation of Herod himself was a notorious enigma:

> Now it has occurred to others to wonder at the inconsistency of Herod's natural tendencies. For when, on the one hand, we consider his munificence and the benefactions which he bestowed upon all men, it is impossible for anyone, even for those who have very little respect for him, to refuse to agree that he had a most beneficent nature. But when on the other hand, one looks at the punishments and the wrongs which he inflicted upon his subjects and his closest relatives, and when one notices how harsh and inexorable his character was, one

> is forced to regard him as bestial and lacking all feeling of moderation.

Josephus himself thought that both these tendencies had the same cause: Herod loved honors and displayed generosity whenever there was reason to hope it would enhance his present reputation or embellish his memory after his death, and he extorted funds from his subjects precisely because he wished to be uniquely honored. Just as he went out of his way to flatter Augustus and Agrippa and other friends more powerful than he, he expected his subjects to shower flattery on him: "What he believed to be the most excellent gift that he could give another he showed a desire to obtain similarly for himself." Unfortunately, as Josephus noted shrewdly, he was disappointed because "the Jewish nation is by law opposed to all such things and is accustomed to admire righteousness rather than glory."[67]

Herod was indeed an innovative and effective ruler. He rode out the storm of the Roman revolution with conspicuous success and transformed Judaea by integrating his kingdom into the Roman world, but he never received the adulation from his own people that he felt he deserved. It was not uncommon for rulers in the world into which Herod was born to be acclaimed as "the Great" in their lifetimes. The Seleucid king Antiochus III was accorded the title in recognition of his reestablishment of control over large areas of former Seleucid territory in the last quarter of the third century BCE. Shortly before Herod was born, the Roman general Pompey assumed the official cognomen Magnus ("the Great") after his victories in Sicily and Africa. Herod's own grandson Agrippa I was acclaimed on a series of inscriptions from Athens as "the great king" and "the great Marcus Julius Agrippa." But Herod himself seems never to have been called great while he was alive despite the magnificence and expense of the monuments which he hoped would elicit recognition of his glory. Only in comparison with the younger generations of the royal dynasty whose foundation, foisted on him by the Roman emperor, overshadowed both the last years of his rule and his posthumous reputation, was Herod ever described in antiquity, in Josephus's list of his many descendants, as "Herod the Great."[68]

EPILOGUE

From History to Myth

Herod's dedication to securing his posthumous reputation as a powerful king was successful, but it is ironic that for most of the past two thousand years he has been mostly known for an abuse of power which he did not commit.

The story of Herod's mass slaughter of innocent children was already current among Christians by the late first century CE, when it was incorporated into the narrative of the birth of Jesus preserved in the Gospel of Matthew. The basic story is both simple and horrific. Herod was frightened when the three Wise Men, alerted by astrological signs, came to Jerusalem from the East to pay homage to a child who had been born king of the Jews. When the Wise Men went off to Bethlehem to find the baby, Herod made arrangements to have him killed but was thwarted by their decision not to return to Jerusalem to tell him the child's precise location. In fury Herod killed all the children around Bethlehem age two or under, fulfilling the words of the prophet Jeremiah: "Rachel weeping for her children; she refused to be consoled, because they are no more."

Even if the chronological problem posed by Herod's death in 4 BCE is circumvented by positing that Jesus must have been born some years before the traditional date, the story is not likely to be true. It is not included in the other Gospels, nor is it mentioned elsewhere in the New Testament or in Josephus's rather full account of the end of Herod's reign. It also differs markedly from the birth narrative in the Gospel of Luke.

The story seems to have been constructed primarily out of a desire by the author of the Gospel of Matthew to build up a parallel typology comparing the infant Jesus to Moses. Joseph and Mary were said to have been instructed by an angel to flee to Egypt in a sort of reverse exodus. Herod was portrayed as a latter-day Pharaoh, who ordered the killing of Hebrew infants with even greater ruthlessness: Pharaoh in the Moses narrative in the book of Exodus wanted to kill the male children as soon as they were born, but Herod is said to have slaughtered all children up to the age of two. Herod's central role in the story seems to have derived from nothing more than his notoriety and the approximate coincidence of his death with the birth of Jesus. Herod's reputation for ruthlessness, the paranoia he exhibited in his last years about the succession to his kingdom, and his public execution of his sons gave the story a veneer of plausibility. It was all too easy to imagine Herod as the archetypical tyrant, anxious and insecure, suspicious of potential threats to his rule and willing to commit murder to maintain his power.[1]

The legend has been popular in the Christian imagination throughout the history of Christianity. It is commemorated in the Feast of the Holy Innocents, celebrated in the Catholic Church on December 28 and in other churches at around the same time of year. The story was included in the Passion Plays of Christians in medieval Europe, and it was depicted in numerous paintings. Sometimes Herod was imagined in consultation with his priests and magicians concerning the slaughter. At other times the artist focused on the agonizing death Herod must have suffered as appropriate punishment for his sins. In some English Mystery Plays, the king's wickedness was so overblown as to be comic, leading Shakespeare's Hamlet to urge the players in the court at Elsinore not to out-Herod Herod in their portrayal of the wickedness of a fictional king.

The caricature was reinforced by the use of the name Herod in the New Testament to refer to other wicked rulers descended from Herod, and many Christians may have failed to differentiate one wicked Herod from another. Herod's son Antipas, the tetrarch of Galilee who executed John the Baptist and (according to the Gospel of Luke) questioned Jesus at length in Jerusalem shortly before he was condemned by Pontius Pilate, is consistently called Herod in the Gospels, and in the Gospel of Mark he is even called (incorrectly) King Herod. Antipas is at least known to have used the name Herod, but we have seen that the same was not true of Herod's grandson Agrippa I, who persecuted Christian communities in Jerusalem a decade later. This did not prevent the author of the Acts of the Apostles referring to him also as King Herod. Evidently the name Herod was already conjuring up for Christians by the late first century CE an image of tyrannical abuse of power even when it did not refer to Herod the Great. In more recent times, the impact of Matthew's story on Christians can be dulled by familiarity. The sixteenth-century text of the Coventry Carol, a lullaby sung by mothers of infants doomed to death by Herod's monstrous order, was originally part of the cycle of Coventry Corpus Christi Plays, but it is now frequently sung as a carol at Christmas despite the horror it describes:

> Herod the king, in his raging,
> Charged he hath this day

His men of might in his own sight
All young children to slay.[2]

It is interesting, given the long history of antisemitism since the first century CE, that this early tradition about the wickedness of Herod did not become a specifically antisemitic trope. In the third century the Christian chronographer Sextus Julius Africanus claimed the authority of traditions, said to derive from the relatives of Jesus himself, to bolster his claim that Herod's father was the son of a temple slave in the temple of Apollo in Ashkelon, and by the seventh century, the Christian author of the *Chronicon Paschale* was claiming that the temple of Apollo in Ashkelon was built by Herod himself. In such Christian traditions, Herod was depicted as a wicked pagan rather than as a wicked Jew.[3]

The tradition about Herod and the massacre of the innocents in the Gospel of Matthew was much more popular among Christians throughout the Middle Ages than the accounts of Herod by Josephus, despite the wide availability of the writings of Josephus both in Greek and in Latin translation. Medieval Christian readers of Josephus's works seem to have focused for religious reasons more on the biblical narrative in the *Jewish Antiquities* and the account of the destruction of Jerusalem in the *Jewish War* than on the Herod material. It was only in the early modern period that some of the more lurid stories in Josephus's works about Herod began to claim their attention and capture the imagination of Christian playwrights and artists.

Once Christians began to appreciate the dramatic possibilities of Josephus's stories about the Jewish king, the doomed love affair between Herod and his Hasmonaean wife Mariamme spawned numerous dramatic treatments. These started in England with Elizabeth Carew's *Tragedy of Marian, the Faire Queen of Jewry* in 1613 (which was probably designed to be read rather than staged). The more popular *Herod and Antipater*, written by Gervase Markham and William Sampson at around the same time, reached a wider audience in the Red Bull playhouse with a tale of passion and violence focused on the murderous intrigues of Herod's son Antipater—whose characterization as a bastard, like Edmund in Shakespeare's *King Lear*, required the authors to take great liberties with the professed source of their drama in the writings of the "learned and famous" Josephus. An opera oratorio (*Herodes und Mariamne*) composed by Georg Philipp Telemann in the middle of the following century was less well received and does not seem to have been given a performance in his lifetime, perhaps because the presentation of Herod in the love story jarred with an audience accustomed to the traditional depiction of him as a villain. Voltaire's tragedy *Hérode et Mariamne* also encountered criticism on its first performance in 1724 for its characterization of Herod, although it received a more enthusiastic response from the audience when it was presented in revised form at the Comédie-Française in the following year.[4]

For many centuries the Christian traditions about Herod in the New Testament and in the histories of Josephus seem to have been unknown to Jews. So far as we know, separate Jewish traditions about Herod were scanty in the first millennium CE, but the Babylonian Talmud, compiled in the sixth century, recalled Herod as a slave of the Hasmonaeans who had killed his masters and put to death rabbinic sages who criticized him. He was said to have tried to make amends by building the Temple. The Temple itself was described as a marvel: "He who has not seen Herod's building has never seen a beautiful building in his life."[5]

Such lack of interest in Jewish history was characteristic of the early rabbinic tradition, when remarkably little seems to have been remembered about the late Second Temple period as a whole. Only a few of the stories in the writings of Josephus find echoes in the Talmud and other rabbinic sources of late antiquity. It was only at the end of the first millennium CE that these minimal traditions were supplemented for rabbinic Jews by the narrative of this period in *Sefer Yosippon.*[6]

The *Sefer Yosippon* was composed in Hebrew in southern Italy, probably in the tenth century. It tells the history of the Jewish people down to the destruction of Jerusalem in 70 CE. As well as Vergil and Livy and other non-Jewish sources, the compiler used the translation of Josephus's *Jewish Antiquities* from Greek into Latin which had been commissioned by the Christian scholar Cassiodorus around 576. He was therefore able to lay out for rabbinic Jews a much fuller narrative about Herod than they had previously known.

The story of Herod in *Sefer Yosippon* follows the structure and order of Josephus's account, but it is presented in a simplified, romantic form. There is no evidence that the author was aware of Christian traditions about Herod and the Massacre of the Innocents. Nor is there evidence that he felt constrained by the traditions in the Babylonian Talmud: his translation choice for one word in one passage may indicate that the author was aware of the depiction of Herod as a slave in the Babylonian Talmud, but such knowledge does not seem to have affected the rest of his account. In some episodes Herod is presented as a heroic Jewish leader—when the Senate in Rome pronounced him king, "They sounded the ram's horn and raised a cry and shouted, saying: 'Herod reigns in Judaea and in Jerusalem, the holy city!' " and when the Temple was in danger of being looted by Sosius's soldiers, "King Herod drew his sword and, standing before the Temple gate along with his lads, chased the Romans away from looking at the Holy of Holies." A number of passages refer to him as "God's beloved" or chosen by God in the eyes of others, and Herod was said to have died "a successful man" apart from his problems with his family. But we are also told that people said openly after his death that he had been "a burdensome and wicked man." He had been "crueler than Darius" and "more wicked than Artahshasta (Artaxerxes)."[7]

This account of Herod in the *Sefer Yosippon* was widely distributed among Jews, first in its original Hebrew; then, by the tenth or eleventh century, in Arabic; then, in the early modern period, in Latin, English, Polish, and Russian translations. The book was read in communities all over the Mediterranean world and in northern Europe. A Yiddish version, printed by Michael Adam in 1546 "for merchants who do not have time to study Torah," became a standard text for Ashkenazi Jews. When, a few years later, Azariah de' Rossi, the greatest Jewish scholar of the Italian Renaissance, became aware of the original text of Josephus's works in Latin translation and of how they differed from the *Sefer Yosippon*, he tried to combine what he designated "the Roman Yosippon" with "the Hebrew Yosippon" in his *The Light of the Eyes*, a learned foray into historical issues published in 1573–75. He had little to say specifically about Herod, but in his discussion of the sect of the Pharisees, he noted that "Herod of Ashkelon who was of Edomite origin" had "intermingled with the Jews in order to strengthen his rule over them" but "proceeded to put several thousands of Jews to death because he was not our brother," and in his discussion of the Essenes he referred to the prophecy of Menahem the Essene about Herod becoming king.[8]

It was in the nineteenth century that Herod's history as depicted by Josephus began belatedly to fascinate a Jewish public for its own sake. As Jews became increasingly integrated into wider European culture, they became aware of the portrayals of Herod's family dramas by Christians in plays and operas over the previous two centuries, and some Jews began to reevaluate their past in light of emancipation, enlightenment, and reform. The German rabbi Ludwig Philippson, who founded the influential *Allgemeine Zeitung des Judenthums*, wrote a novel in the 1860s with the title *Miriam die Hasmonaerin* which attributed the horrific circumstances of Herod's death to his grief at having killed the woman he loved. Jewish scholars such as Isaac Marcus Jost and Heinrich Graetz pioneered in Germany a new science of research into Jewish history in the first half of the century, and introduced enlightened Jewish readers to the writings of Josephus in their original form rather than paraphrased in *Sefer Yosippon*. Herod became an example of a powerful Jew who had negotiated successfully the uncomfortable line between subservience to the ruling power and service to his own people. Graetz himself depicted Herod as a semi-idolatrous tyrant, but his Galician contemporary, the philosopher Nachman Krochmal, praised the king for his suppression of the antagonisms that finally flared up after his death.[9]

Depictions of Herod served as surrogates for arguments about the current position of Jews in European society at a time of great social and cultural change. The play titled *Herodes: Dramatisches Gedicht in funf Akten*, published in 1887 by the Galician playwright Judah Loeb Landau when he was in his early twenties, seems to have been designed deliberately to attract attention by annoying his Jewish public through a depiction of Herod as an outstanding ruler who had saved Judaea from internal strife and Roman interference. Landau claimed that Herod's violent court intrigues were no different from those of other monarchies (including the Hasmonaeans) and that his reputation had been traduced by the notoriously unreliable testimony of Josephus. After its first performance in Lvov in 1890 the play met with satisfyingly furious reviews by, among others, Eliezer ben Yehudah, the driving force behind the revival of modern Hebrew.[10]

In the twentieth century, Jewish views about Herod were often affected by Zionist ideologies and responses to the Holocaust and the establishment of the State of Israel. Thus, in the Netherlands Abel Herzberg, an ardent Zionist who survived

World War II despite internment in Bergen-Belsen, wrote a play in 1955 which portrayed Herod as the usual tyrant, but when he published fictional memoirs of Herod some twenty years later, in 1974, he dealt in a much more nuanced way with Herod's emotions in his dealings with the Jewish people, presenting the political situation in Herod's time as a mirror of the complex relationship of the State of Israel to surrounding countries in Herzberg's own day.[11]

In the State of Israel itself, the historian Avraham Schalit, who had migrated in 1929 from Galicia to Palestine, in 1930 condemned Herod as a "reptile" for his acceptance of Roman rule (which Schalit compared to the iniquitous British Mandate). But by the time his monumental biography of Herod was published in 1960, he had come to appreciate Herod's accomplishments in furthering the interests of Jews through his astute avoidance of conflict. Schalit's biography remains by far the most thorough and detailed study of Herod's reign. Its positive portrayal of Herod evoked intense criticism within Israeli society when it first appeared, and it had little effect on the hostile depiction of the king in Israeli school textbooks of Jewish history. But after 1967 Schalit's work began to spark a debate among Israelis, comparing Herodian Realpolitik to the policies of successive governments since the victories of the Six-Day War.[12]

In 2013 an exhibition in the Israel Museum following the discovery by Ehud Netzer of what may have been Herod's tomb at Herodium drew large crowds and encouraged appreciation of Herod's impressive architectural monuments. The exhibition represented his reign as a glorious episode in Jewish history. But any implication that such statesmanlike achievements could outweigh the murderous violence which enabled them is in direct contrast to the conclusions of a best-selling "psychological biography" of Herod published by the Tel Aviv ancient historian Aryeh Kasher in 2007. Writing in collaboration with a psychiatrist, and presenting his version of Herod's life as a deliberate counter to Schalit's, Kasher claimed that Herod, the "persecuted persecutor," suffered from a paranoid personality disorder triggered by an inferiority complex and that his irrational behavior can be understood only through sophisticated psychological research.[13]

Diagnosis of Herod's complex personality after two millennia is not easy. He was a passionate man who wanted to be loved and admired. Ambition, arrogance, and audacity brought him to power, but in old age he was suspicious and thin-skinned. He was hurt whenever his devotion to his family was inadequately reciprocated, and he was angry when his subjects professed scorn for the achievements for which he strove so hard. Herod was not the last egotistical ruler whose domestic travails became a public spectacle which undermined his carefully fostered reputation. Hence the enduring fascination of his colorful life.[14]

APPENDIX

Josephus's Two Narratives

MOST OF THIS STORY of Herod's life has been based on Josephus's *Jewish Antiquities*, which was written to reveal to a non-Jewish readership the history of the Jews as a people from the beginning to his own day, with an emphasis on the divine intervention which had shaped that history.[1]

Josephus was an aristocratic Jerusalem priest, born in 37 CE, who could trace his lineage back to an ancestor who had been a Hasmonaean princess in the late second century BCE. He was deeply involved in the political life of Jerusalem in the years before the start of the Jewish revolt against Rome in 66. When war broke out, he was appointed by the government of the self-declared independent Jewish state to oversee the defense of Galilee against the expected Roman assault, but he was overcome by superior forces, and in the early months of 67 he was captured. According to his own account, he had made a suicide pact with the comrades with whom he was trapped in a cave, but when he found that only he and one other were left alive, he was divinely inspired to break the pact and surrender to the Romans. Hauled before the Roman general Vespasian and his son Titus, he was similarly inspired to prophesy to Vespasian in a private meeting that he would become emperor. At the time, the prophecy was highly implausible, and that he even made it may have been a fiction which it was in the interest of both Vespasian and Josephus to maintain. But when Vespasian made a successful bid for supreme power in 69, Josephus was rewarded by release from captivity. After the fall of Jerusalem in 70, he was given a new home in Rome in the house where Vespasian had lived before he became emperor.[2]

With a guaranteed income from land granted to him out of imperial munificence, Josephus could have retired into a life of pampered leisure, but instead he chose to write books about his Jewish heritage. His trustworthiness as a historian has been doubted by Jews since the early nineteenth century, primarily on the basis of his treacherous transfer of political allegiance from the rebels to Rome. Skeptics point also to discrepancies between the two accounts he gave of his own career as a general in Galilee, one incorporated into his history of the revolt and the other the main focus of the self-exculpatory autobiography he wrote toward the end of his life. But such doubts, even if they are partly justified for Josephus's narrative of the events in which he himself participated, should not affect evaluation of his history of the Jews in the time of Herod, who had died four decades before Josephus was born.[3]

Josephus completed the *Jewish Antiquities* in 93, but the decision to extend the history to twenty books seems to have been taken from the start of the project, ten years or more earlier. The number twenty was probably selected in imitation of the *Roman Antiquities* written by the Greek historian Dionysius of Halicarnassus earlier in the first century CE. Josephus wished to demonstrate to Greeks and Romans that the Jews had a proud history as long and impressive as theirs.[4]

The *Antiquities* begins with the creation of the world as portrayed in Genesis and essentially paraphrases the Bible for its first ten books, ending in the Persian period. But for the next ten books Josephus had much less source material—by book 19 he was reduced to narrating in detail the story of the assassination of the Roman emperor Caligula, an event that related to Jewish history only tangentially through the role of Herod's grandson Agrippa I, who engineered the succession of Claudius as the new emperor. Josephus's choice to tell the story of Herod in such great detail from the middle of book 14 to the end of book 17, allocating to a period of about fifty years an eighth of the total space devoted to Jewish history over some two thousand years, was prompted primarily by the availability of Nicolaus's history, on which he based his narrative.

The focus on Herod also permitted Josephus to expand on the major themes of the *Antiquities*, in particular the role of divine punishment for impiety, which he often, but not always, gives a specifically Jewish slant. Josephus's narrative in the *Antiquities* combines the public and private lives of Herod in approximately chronological order, showing how Herod's greed and cruelty affected his rule as much as his family dynamics, and depicting him as a remorseless tyrant who deserved to suffer in his final days.[5]

We are exceptionally fortunate to possess this extended narrative in the *Jewish Antiquities*, but it is an added bonus that we are able to compare that version of Herod's life to Josephus's earlier account in the *Jewish War*, a history composed in seven books to explain, primarily to Roman readers, the causes, course, and outcome of the war between the Jews and Rome from 66 to 70 in which, as we have seen, Josephus had himself played a distinctive role. The *Jewish War* was written in Rome in the seventies, soon after the Roman victory. Josephus chose to begin his analysis of the causes of the war with events two and a half centuries before its outbreak, writing about the attack on the Jerusalem Temple by Antiochus Epiphanes in the mid-second century BCE which had brought the Jews of Judaea into contact with Rome for the first time. The first of the seven books covers the period from the first intervention by Antiochus around 170 BCE to the death of Herod in 4 BCE. The first half of the second book deals with the history of Judaea over seventy years from the death of Herod to the outbreak of revolt in 66 CE. From the middle of the second book to the end of the sixth book Josephus focused on the four years of the war itself. The seventh book was devoted to the aftermath of the war, covering just three years.[6]

In light of his weighting of his history as a whole toward the most recent events, it is surprising to find that the story of Herod's rise, reign, and fall between 47 and 4 BCE constitutes almost two-thirds of the first book, with far more detailed treatment than that given the history of the Hasmonaean period for which Nicolaus's history also provided Josephus with his main source. The most plausible explanation is that the extended account of the reign of the Jewish king best known to his Roman readers presented an example of successful Jewish rule under Roman hegemony, fitting Josephus's insistence on the wisdom of alliance with Rome in his own day, in contrast to the breakdown of Roman hegemony which had led to the revolt of 66–70 CE, Josephus's main topic. Josephus in the *Jewish War* was thus primarily interested in Herod as a symbol of political cooperation with imperial rule. His depiction of the king as an ambitious and effective ruler who was a slave to his emotions is flat and distant. Josephus makes a clear separation between Herod's public career and his family life, shifting from one arena to the other at the discretion of the narrator and commenting in his own voice as author at the end of the story on the contrast between the king's public achievements and his disastrous domestic affairs.[7]

In neither of Josephus's accounts does Herod's character evolve over the course of his career. He is presented as already energetic, cunning, ambitious, shrewd, and hot-tempered as soon as he enters the public arena as a young man, without scruples or a moral, social, or religious code. He has the virtues of an aristocratic military leader blessed by good fortune in his martial skills and his victories in war, but he is subject to a tendency toward unreasoning passion, such as his wild frenzy after the death of Mariamme, which eventually led to his self-destruction. In telling the story, Josephus emphasized with admiration Herod's virtues and achievements but expected the reader, who would already have known at least the bare bones of the domestic disasters at the end of Herod's life, to appreciate the dramatic irony of Herod's apparent successes at the height of his reign.[8]

Most of the differences between the accounts of Herod's reign in Josephus's two versions can be explained by the difference in purpose of the two histories. The version in the *Jewish Antiquities* is much longer and more detailed than the earlier version. It is therefore unsurprising that some material treated at length in the later work has been omitted from the earlier, more succinct, narrative. Similarly, since history was expected to educate, Josephus's introduction of speeches, digressions, authorial asides, and other rhetorical devices into each narrative to emphasize specific aspects of Herod's career in light of his overall aim in each work would have struck his contemporary readers as standard practice in the writing of history. No ancient reader would have considered that the employment of rhetoric in this context posed any questions about truth or falsehood.[9]

Other explanations of the differences between the two accounts rest on Josephus's statement that he used assistants to help with his Greek style in the *Jewish War*, or his employment of additional sources for the narrative in the *Jewish Antiquities*, such as Herod's memoirs (to which, as we have seen, Josephus made just one reference, probably derived from Nicolaus) or a lost *History of King Herod* by a historian called Ptolemy which is known only from a passing mention about the relation of Jews to Idumaeans in a work on grammar written a century later. Some scholars have wondered whether Josephus's greater hostility to Herod in the *Jewish Antiquities* than in the *Jewish War* reflects greater use of anti-Herodian sources, either oral or written, in the later work, enabled perhaps by the decreased influence in Rome of Herod's great-grandson Agrippa II after his sister Berenice was dismissed from Rome by her lover Titus when Titus became emperor in 79 CE.[10]

Such explanations are often plausible in specific cases, but they are unnecessary in evaluating the narratives as a whole. Josephus was well aware that his readers might be able to compare his two accounts of Herod's reign, since he referred them in the preface to the *Jewish Antiquities* to his authorship of the *Jewish War*. Whether readers in antiquity did indeed read both accounts, we do not know, but Josephus would not have been worried if they did so. The two portraits of Herod do not contradict each other except in minor details and authorial judgments about the moral significance of the narrative. The discrepancies may in some cases go back to confusion in the source material from Nicolaus on which both portraits depended to a great degree and are best explained by the complexity of the story Josephus set out to tell.

We should be grateful to Josephus for having preserved for us so much of the contemporary evidence of Nicolaus about Herod. But in both narratives he wrote about the king not for his own sake but to make wider points, and neither narrative makes any real attempt to encourage readers to empathize with Herod himself. Josephus tells us a great deal about reactions to Herod by his subjects and his family, but his accounts of the king's own emotions are sketchy, and he did not try to explore how Herod's traumatic early upbringing and family relations shaped his complex personality. It is left to the modern biographer to try to fill in the gaps.

CHRONOLOGY

Date (BCE)	Judaea	Rome and the East
73	Birth of Herod	
67	Death of Shelomzion	
	Hyrcanus and Aristobulus at war	
	Herod left in Nabataea for safekeeping	
66		Pompey campaigns in eastern empire
65		Annexation of Syria as Roman province
63	Hyrcanus rules as Roman vassal	Capture of Jerusalem by Pompey
57–55	Aristobulus and sons attack Hyrcanus	
55–53		Crassus appointed governor of Syria

(Continued)

Date (BCE)	Judaea	Rome and the East
53		Death of Crassus in Parthian campaign
53–51		Cassius appointed governor of Syria (as quaestor)
51		Cleopatra becomes queen in Egypt
49	Aristobulus II and Alexander killed	Julius Caesar starts civil war against Pompey
48		Antipater helps Caesar in Egypt
47	Herod marries Doris	Julius Caesar in Syria
	Antipater made Roman citizen	Sextus Caesar governor of Syria
	Herod given command in Galilee	
	Herod on trial in Jerusalem	
44		Murder of Julius Caesar
43	Herod raises funds for Cassius	Cassius in Syria
	Antipater killed by Malichus	
	Death of Malichus	
		Antony, Octavian, and Lepidus appointed triumvirs
42	Herod betrothed to Mariamme, daughter of Alexandra, granddaughter of Hyrcanus	Deification of Julius Caesar
		Defeat of Cassius and Brutus at Philippi
41	Herod and Phasael made tetrarchs	Jewish embassy to Antony against Herod
40	Parthian invasion of Judaea	Antony and Octavian meet at Brundisium
	Death of Herod's brother Phasael	
	Parthians appoint Antigonus king	
	Herod escapes to Rome	Herod appointed king of Judaea by Senate
39–37	War between Herod and Antigonus	
38	Death of Herod's brother Joseph	Herod fights alongside Antony at Samosata

Date (BCE)	Judaea	Rome and the East
38–37		Sosius appointed governor of Syria
37	Herod besieges Jerusalem	Antony marries Cleopatra
	Herod marries Mariamme	
	Capture of Jerusalem by Herod	
36	Hyrcanus returns from Parthia	Antony grants territories to Cleopatra
		Antony's Parthian offensive
35	Drowning of Jonathan Aristobulus	
34	Execution of Herod's uncle Joseph	Herod summoned by Antony to Laodicea
	Cleopatra visits Herod in Jerusalem	Antony grants balsam groves to Cleopatra
32	War of Herod against Nabataeans	Antony and Octavian at war
31	Earthquake	
	Defeat of Nabataeans	Defeat of Antony and Cleopatra at Actium
30	Execution of Hyrcanus	Herod visits Octavian at Rhodes
	Octavian stops in Judaea on way to Egypt	Suicides of Antony and Cleopatra
		Herod visits Octavian in Egypt
	Octavian stops in Judaea on way north	
29	Execution of Mariamme	
28	Execution of Alexandra	
27	Execution of Costobar	Octavian is acclaimed as Augustus in Roman Senate
	Athletic games in Jerusalem	
	Conspiracy against Herod	
	Building of Sebaste is begun	
26–25		Campaign of Aelius Gallus into Arabia Felix

(*Continued*)

Date (BCE)	Judaea	Rome and the East
25–24	Famine and plague	
	Building of Jerusalem palace is begun	
23	Alexander and Aristobulus sent to Rome	Illness of Augustus
		Death of Marcellus
		Augustus gives Herod more territory
		Herod visits Agrippa in Mytilene
	Rebuilding of Temple planned	
22	Boethus appointed high priest	
	Building of Caesarea is begun	
21		Marriage of Agrippa and Julia
20	Zenodorus's territory to Herod	Augustus in Syria
	Pheroras appointed tetrarch in Peraea	Recovery of standards from Parthia
	Rebuilding of Temple starts	
17	Alexander and Aristobulus are proclaimed heirs	Augustus adopts Gaius and Lucius
		Herod goes to Rome to bring back his sons
		Celebration of Secular Games
	Alexander and Aristobulus return	
16	Alexander marries Glaphyra	Herod is with Agrippa in Mytilene
15	Agrippa visits Jerusalem	
14		Herod is with Agrippa in Pontus
	Antipater is back in Herod's court	
13	Doris is back in Herod's court	Herod is with Agrippa in Ionia
		Antipater is sent to Rome with Agrippa
12		Death of Agrippa
		Herod goes to Rome to accuse his sons

Date (BCE)	Judaea	Rome and the East
		Augustus reconciles Herod and his sons
10	Dedication of Caesarea	Saturninus appointed governor of Syria
	Alexander is imprisoned by Herod	
	Visit of Archelaus of Cappadocia	
9	Herod is at war with Nabataeans	Death of Drusus
8		Syllaeus in Rome accuses Herod
		Herod falls out of favor with Augustus
	Alexander and Aristobulus are accused and put in prison	Herod writes to Augustus to accuse his sons
7		Varus appointed governor of Syria
		Herod is back in favor with Augustus
		Herod is given free hand with his sons
		Trial at Berytus
	Alexander and Aristobulus are strangled	
6		Antipater goes to Rome
	Herod's will names Antipater as heir	
5	Death of Herod's brother Pheroras	Gaius Caesar assumes *toga virilis*
	Return of Antipater from Rome	
	Trial of Antipater in Judaea	Report sent by Herod to Augustus
	Antipas is named heir in Herod's new will	
4	Riots over the eagle on the Temple	
	Execution of Antipater	

(*Continued*)

Date (BCE)	Judaea	Rome and the East
	Herod's final will	
	Archelaus, Antipas, and Philip named heirs	
	Death of Herod	

Note: The dates of events in the wider Roman world in this period can generally be established with some precision from a combination of sources, but attempts to reconstruct the chronology of events in Judaea under Herod all have their problems, and many competing reconstructions have been proposed. Josephus often dated events in Herod's life to a specific year in Herod's reign, but calculation of the chronology is complicated by the use in antiquity of two different dates to mark the start of this reign: Josephus noted (*BJ* 1.665; *AJ* 17.191) that Herod's rule was sometimes calculated from the year when he was named king by the Senate in Rome (40 BCE) and sometimes from the date when he captured Jerusalem from Antigonus (probably 37 BCE). Further uncertainty arises from difficulties encountered in trying to make sense of the references by Josephus to the occurrence of sabbatical years. The chronology followed here is cautious and conservative, but it is indebted to a wealth of scholarly investigations, particularly by scholars concerned to identify the chronological background to the New Testament.

GENEALOGIES

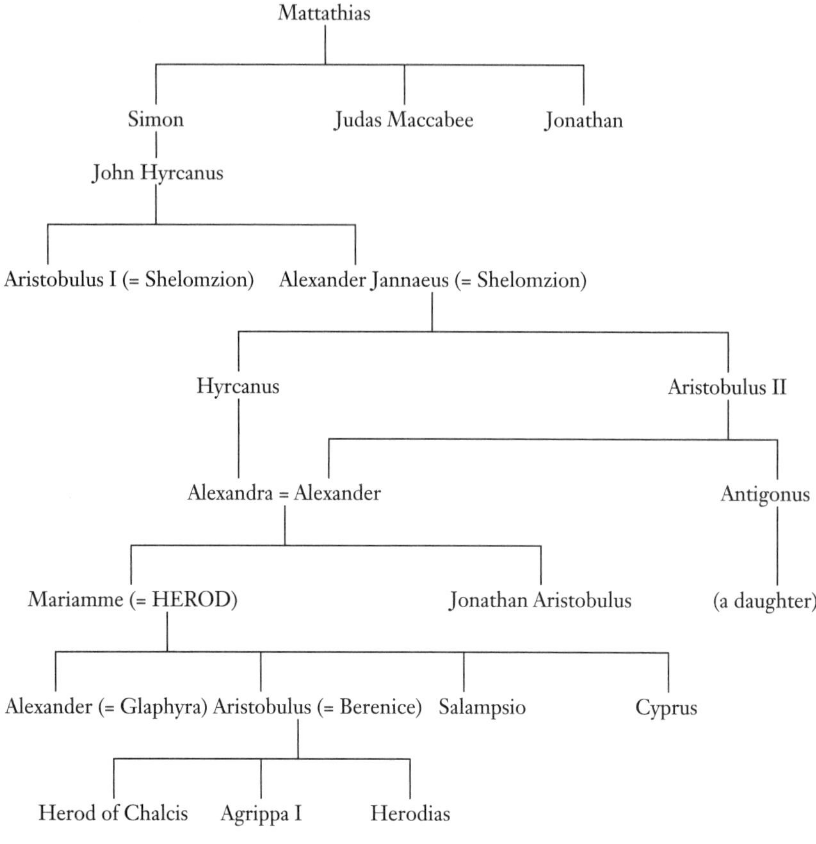

The Hasmonaean Line

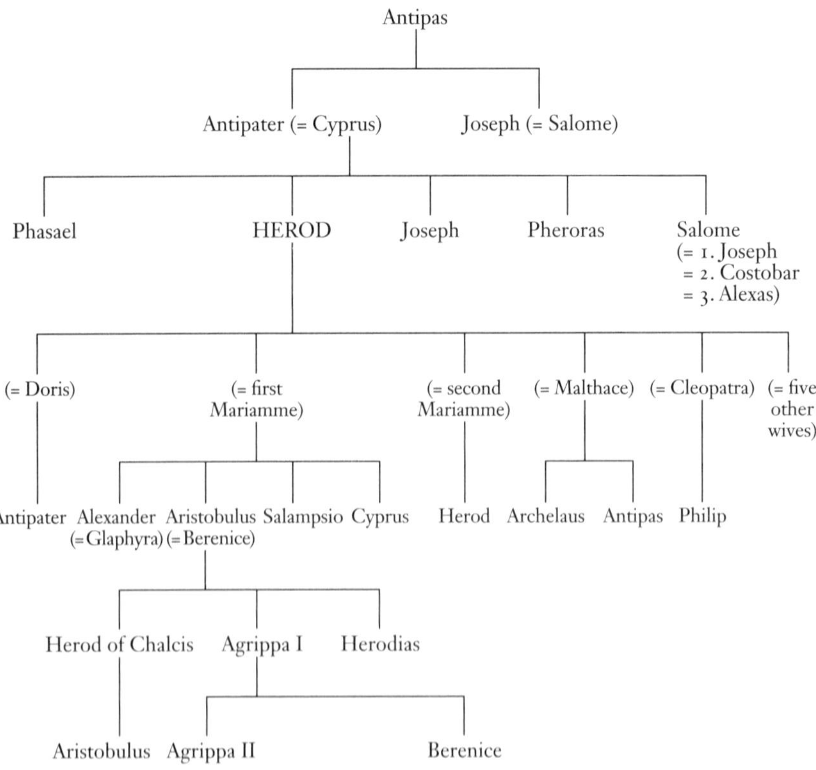

The Family of Herod

NOTES

Abbreviations

AJ	Josephus, *Jewish Antiquities*, in *Josephus*, trans. H. St. J. Thackeray et al., 9 vols., Loeb Classical Library 489 (Cambridge: Harvard University Press, 1926–65). Citations are to section numbers.
BJ	Josephus, *The Jewish War*, trans. Martin Hammond (Oxford: Oxford University Press, 2017). Citations are to section numbers.
GLAJJ	Menachem Stern, *Greek and Latin Authors on Jews and Judaism*, 3 vols. (Jerusalem: Israel Academy of Sciences and Humanities, 1974–84).
OGIS	Wilhelm Dittenberger, ed., *Orientis Graeci Inscriptiones Selectae*, 2 vols. (Leipzig: Hirzel, 1903–5).

Prologue

1. This account of Herod in Rome in 40 BCE comes from *AJ* 14.370–89. The shorter account in *BJ* 1.274–85 is similar. In

tracing the story of Herod's life I shall generally make use of Josephus's more detailed narrative in *AJ* for reasons discussed in the Appendix, but I shall provide references in the notes to parallel versions in *BJ* when they exist, and I shall draw attention to differences between the versions when they are significant for understanding Herod's actions or motivation.

2. *AJ* 14.385, cf. *BJ* 1.284.

3. A survey of Herod's building projects can be found in Duane W. Roller, *The Building Program of Herod the Great* (Berkeley: University of California Press, 1998).

4. On Nicolaus, see Ben Zion Wacholder, *Nicolaus of Damascus* (Berkeley: University of California Press, 1962); Mark Toher, "Nicolaus and Herod in the *Antiquitates Judaicae*," *Harvard Studies in Classical Philology* 101 (2003): 427–47; Toher, "Herod, Augustus, and Nicolaus of Damascus," in *Herod and Augustus*, ed. David M. Jacobson and Nikos Kokkinos (Leiden: Brill, 2009), 65–81; Kimberley Czajkowski and Benedikt Eckhardt, *Herod in History: Nicolaus of Damascus and the Augustan Context* (Oxford: Oxford University Press, 2021).

5. We can only guess at the contents of Herod's memoirs since their existence is known solely from a single reference by Josephus (*AJ* 15.74), for which Josephus, who does not himself seem to have had access to the memoirs, was probably transmitting a comment by Nicolaus.

6. *AJ* 16.184–85; *BJ* 1.665.

7. Although we know that some of Nicolaus's account of Herod's rule was composed after Herod's death, we do not know how much. The suggestion by Czajkowski and Eckhardt, in *Herod in History*, 7–9, that the material on Herod was added by Nicolaus during his retirement in Rome to an earlier version of his universal history is plausible but hypothetical.

Chapter 1. A World in Turmoil

1. The date of Herod's birth is deduced from his age ("about seventy") when he died (*AJ* 17.148). Herod's name was Greek in origin, as were the names of both his parents, but his siblings are

known by Semitic names. His parents may have followed the common practice of giving each of their children two names, one Greek and one Semitic, but no second name for Herod is known.

2. On the collapse of the Seleucid Empire, see Andrew Erskine, ed., *A Companion to the Hellenistic World* (Malden, Mass.: Blackwell, 2003); on the end of the Ptolemaic dynasty, see Alan K. Bowman, *Egypt After the Pharaohs, 332 B.C.–A.D. 642: From Alexander to the Arab Conquest* (London: British Museum, 1986).

3. See E. Badian, *Roman Imperialism in the Late Republic*, 2nd ed. (Oxford: Blackwell, 1968).

4. See David Braund, *Rome and the Friendly King: The Character of the Client Kingship* (New York: St. Martin's, 1984); Adam Kolman Marshak, *The Many Faces of Herod the Great* (Grand Rapids, Mich.: Eerdmans, 2015), 3–23.

5. On the revolt of the Maccabees and the Hasmonaean dynasty, see, Emil Schürer, *The History of the Jewish People in the Age of Jesus Christ (175 B.C.–A.D. 135)*, rev. and ed. G. Vermes et al., 3 vols. (Edinburgh: T. & T. Clark, 1973–87), 1:137–242; on Alexander Jannaeus, see *AJ* 13.320–406, cf. *BJ* 1.85–106; on the coins, see Ya'akov Meshorer, *A Treasury of Jewish Coins from the Persian Period to Bar Kokhba* (Jerusalem: Yad Ben-Zvi Press, and Nyack, N.Y.: Amphora, 2001).

6. On Antipas, see *AJ* 14.10. The narrative of Aristobulus's reign and the accession of Alexander Jannaeus is in *AJ* 13.301–23, cf. *BJ* 1.70–85; that this narrative may be legendary is suggested by the description of Aristobulus as "kindly and serviceable to the Jews" by the Greek historian Strabo, cited by Josephus at *AJ* 13.319. On the accession of Shelomzion, see *AJ* 13.407, cf. *BJ* 1.107–9. It is likely that Shelomzion was the widow of Aristobulus, but Josephus does not state this explicitly.

7. On Shelomzion, see *AJ* 13. 405–32, cf. *BJ* 1.110–19; Tal Ilan, *Jewish Women in Greco-Roman Palestine* (Tübingen: Mohr Siebeck, 1995); on her control of her son Aristobulus, see *AJ* 13.417, cf. *BJ* 1.109.

8. See *AJ* 14.4–18, cf. *BJ* 1.120–26.

9. See *AJ* 14.29–57, cf. *BJ* 1.127–40.

10. See *AJ* 14.69–70, cf. *BJ* 1. 141–54 (for the siege); *AJ* 14.73–74, cf. *BJ* 1.155–57 (for Pompey's settlement).

11. See *AJ* 14.90–91, cf. *BJ* 1.169 (for Hyrcanus stripped of secular power by Gabinius, governor of Syria).

12. See *AJ* 14. 101–2, cf. *BJ* 1.175–77 (on the role of Antipater).

13. On the career and death of Crassus, see B. A. Marshall, *Crassus: A Political Biography* (Amsterdam: Hakkert, 1976).

Chapter 2. Overcoming Obstacles

1. *AJ* 14.403.

2. See *AJ* 14.8 (Antipater an Idumaean); *BJ* 4.231–314 (Idumaeans during the revolt of 66–70 CE).

3. See *AJ* 14.8–10; quotation is from *AJ* 14.10.

4. Strabo, *Geography* 16.1.34, in *The Geography of Strabo*. trans. Horace L. Jones, 8 vols., vol. 7: *Books 15–16*, Loeb Classical Library 241 (Cambridge: Harvard University Press, 1930); *AJ* 13.257–58.

5. See Aryeh Kasher, *Jews, Idumaeans, and Ancient Arabs* (Tübingen: Mohr Siebeck, 1988); *AJ* 15.255 (Costobar); *BJ* 4.272, 274 (metropolis). The structures at Hebron and Mamre are identified as Herodian from the surviving masonry, particularly at Hebron; see D. W. Roller, *The Building Program of Herod the Great* (Berkeley: University of California Press, 1998), 162–64, 186–87. Josephus knew about these structures (see *BJ* 4.529–31, 533; *AJ* 1.196), but he did not ascribe them to Herod in his catalogue of Herod's building projects, probably because this catalogue, inherited from Nicolaus, focused on palaces and pagan buildings other than the Jerusalem Temple.

6. See *AJ* 14.121; *BJ* 1.181.

7. On the Nabataeans, see Nelson Glueck, *Deities and Dolphins: The Story of the Nabataeans* (London: Cassell, 1966).

8. See *AJ* 14.122, cf. *BJ* 1.181 (Antipater "entrusted his children" to the ruler of the Arabs when making war on Aristobulus); on the war against Aristobulus, see *AJ* 14.14–18, cf. *BJ* 1.124–26.

9. Herod's roots were evidently complex, but we should prob-

ably discount the rumor, first attested a century and a half after Herod's death, that his father's family originated not from Idumaea, Nabataea, or Judaea but from Ashkelon, an ancient city on the southern coast of Palestine; see, e.g., Justin Martyr, *Dialogus cum Tryphone* 52.3. For a vigorous attempt to defend the veracity of the tradition of Herod's origins in Ashkelon, see Nikos Kokkinos, *The Herodian Dynasty: Origins, Role in Society and Eclipse* (Sheffield: Sheffield Academic Press, 1998), 100–139.

10. See *AJ* 15. 373–78. Manaemus was an Essene, and the story is said to have encouraged Herod to show favor to the Essenes when he came to power (see Chapter 4).

11. Nicolaus, *On His Life*, cited in *GLAJJ* 1:249.

12. See *AJ* 13.408–9, cf. *BJ* 1.110–11 (influence of the Pharisees on Shelomzion); Nicolaus, *On His Life*, quoted in *GLAJJ* 1:248–49 (Nicolaus on Herod and history).

13. See *AJ* 15. 267–76 (athletic contest novel when introduced by Herod); *BJ* 1.429 (hunting and horsemanship); *BJ* 1.430 (javelin and bow); *AJ* 14.173 (hair carefully arranged in 47 BCE during trial); *AJ* 16.230–33 (hair dyed in old age); *BJ* 5.161–65 (Hippicus). On Herod's passion in his old age for a beautiful boy called Karos, see *AJ* 17.44.

14. See *BJ* 1.241, 432; *AJ* 14.300.

15. *Psalms of Solomon* 2:26–27, trans. Robert B. Wright, in *The Old Testament Pseudepigrapha*, ed. James H. Charlesworth, 2 vols. (New York: Doubleday, 1983–85).

16. See *BJ* 1. 200 (honors engraved on the Capitol); *AJ* 14.158 (Phasael and Herod).

17. See *AJ* 14.137, cf. *BJ* 1.194. If Antipater's sons, including Herod, had been included in the personal grant of citizenship by Caesar we would expect this to have been recorded by Josephus, so it is more likely that Herod himself received the status from the Senate when he was appointed king in 40 BCE. Later members of Herod's family were certainly citizens: a number of inscriptions refer to his grandson Agrippa I as Marcus Julius Agrippa (see, e.g., *OGIS* nos. 420 and 421). Agrippa's use of the name Julius must reflect a grant of citizenship either by Caesar or by Augustus, and although

the status might have been bestowed on him by Augustus as a personal favor, he is more likely to have inherited citizenship from his father, Herod's son Aristobulus.

18. See *BJ* 1.196 (accusation by Antigonus); *BJ* 1.197 (display of scars).

19. See *AJ* 14.158–60, cf. *BJ* 1.203–5.

20. On Herod as very young, see *BJ* 1.203 and *AJ* 14.158. Josephus's statement at *AJ* 14.158 that Herod was only fifteen at this time was almost certainly an erroneous deduction from the reference to Herod's youth in his source (presumably Nicolaus) or a misreading by Josephus or someone else of the number twenty-five in a manuscript copy of Nicolaus's history. Josephus himself stated elsewhere (*AJ* 17.148) that Herod was about seventy years old when he died (in 4 BCE), and we would expect our sources to remark on Herod's age when he was appointed king in 40 if he were only twenty-three. On Herod's insistence ten years later that the teenage Jonathan was too young to serve as a high priest, see *AJ* 15.34. At the end of Herod's life the sons he selected in desperation as his successors were all teenagers (see below, Chapter 5), but none was as young as fifteen. On the suppression of banditry and Herod's subsequent trial in Jerusalem, see *BJ* 1.204, 211; *AJ* 14.158–76.

21. See *AJ* 14.177–84, cf. *BJ* 1.212–15.

22. See *AJ* 14.180 (bribe); *AJ* 14.268, cf. *BJ* 1.216–17.

23. *The Deeds of the Divine Augustus* 7.1 in *Res Gestae Divi Augusti: Text, Translation, and Commentary*, ed. Alison E. Cooley (Cambridge: Cambridge University Press, 2009).

24. See *AJ* 14.119–21, cf. *BJ* 1.180–82 (Antipater and Cassius in 53–51 BCE); *BJ* 1.220 (Antipater "fearing the threats of Cassius").

25. See *BJ* 1.221; *AJ* 14.273 (Herod first to bring quota); *AJ* 14.280, cf. *BJ* 1.225 (army entrusted to Herod; promise to make Herod king).

26. See *AJ* 14.280–83 (assassination of Antipater, cf. *BJ* 1.226–27 on motivation); *AJ* 14.288–93, cf. *BJ* 1.233–35 (assassination of Malichus).

27. See *AJ* 14.298–99, cf. *BJ* 1.238 (disturbances in Galilee); 14.295–96, cf. *BJ* 1.236 (Herod's illness).

28. See *AJ* 14.84, cf. *BJ* 1.162 (Antony and Antipater in 57 BCE); *AJ* 14.326, cf. *BJ* 1.244 (Antony's friendship with Herod and Phasael in 41).

29. See *AJ* 14.302–3, cf. *BJ* 1.242 (delegation to Bithynia).

30. See *AJ* 14.324–25, cf. *BJ* 1.243–44 (delegation in Daphne); *AJ* 14.325 (Messalla); *AJ* 14.326 (Herod and Phasael appointed tetrarchs).

31. See *AJ* 14.330–50, cf. *BJ* 1.248–62 (Parthian attack); *AJ* 14.365–66, cf. *BJ* 1.269–70 (mutilation of Hyrcanus). On the death of Phasael, see *AJ* 14.367–79, cf. *BJ* 1.271–72; Julius Africanus in *Georgius Syncellus*, ed. W. Dindorf, 2. vols. (Bonn, 1829), 1:381 (on Phasael's death in battle).

32. See *BJ* 1. 265; *AJ* 14. 353–62.

33. *AJ* 14.370–73, 375. *BJ* 1.274–77 has a slightly different version of these events, including (at *BJ* 1.277) Herod's tart reply to the Arab messengers.

34. See *AJ* 14.375–78, cf. *BJ* 1.279–81.

35. *AJ* 14. 386–87. There is no parallel account in *BJ*.

36. See *AJ* 14.384; *BJ* 1.284.

37. See *AJ* 14.394–400, cf. *BJ* 1.290–94. Herod collected a large military force, winning over Galilee and capturing Joppa with Roman help, before advancing on Masada.

38. See *AJ* 14.413, cf. *BJ* 1.303 (Joseph in Idumaea); on Pheroras, see *AJ* 14.419 (provisions for Roman troops) and *BJ* 1.309 (provisions for Herod's troops); on Joseph left in charge, see *AJ* 14.438; *BJ* 1.323.

39. See *AJ* 14.439–47, cf. *BJ* 1.321–22 (Herod in Samosata); for events in Judaea, see *AJ* 14.448–50; *BJ* 1.323–25; in the account in *BJ*, the ransom is said to have been refused.

40. See *AJ* 14.421–30, cf. *BJ* 1.309–13 (capture of bandits in Galilee); *AJ* 14.456 (hit by javelin); *AJ* 14.455 (collapsing house; according to *BJ* 1.331, the banquet had just ended); *AJ* 14. 462–63 (escape in bathhouse, cf. *BJ* 1.340–41); *AJ* 16.464, cf. *BJ* 1.341 (Pappus's head).

41. See *AJ* 14.468–86, cf. *BJ* 1.345–58.

42. See *AJ* 14.484–86, cf. *BJ* 1.355–56 (control of plundering). The date of 37 BCE, derived from the explicit statement by Josephus at *AJ* 14.487, is probably correct, but it has been doubted on the basis of conflicting evidence in Cassius Dio, *Roman History* 49.22, in which the date is given as 38, and an apparent reference at *AJ* 14.475 to the sabbatical year, which might suggest 36; for discussion, see Bieke Mahieu, *Between Rome and Jerusalem: Herod the Great and His Sons in Their Struggle for Recognition* (Louvain: Peeters, 2012), 60–99.

43. See *AJ* 14.481, cf. *BJ* 1.353 (Antigonus's surrender to Sosius); *AJ* 14.488–90, cf. *BJ* 1.357 (Antigonus put to death).

44. See *AJ* 14.458; *BJ* 1.335.

45. See *AJ* 15.6, cf. *BJ* 1.358 (executions); *AJ* 14.175 (death of all the members of the court apart from the Pharisee Samaias).

46. See *AJ* 15.409: Herod gave the name to the fortress to honor Antony, "who was his friend and, at the same time, ruler of the Romans." The name was to continue in use for over a century, until the fortress was destroyed, along with the rest of the Temple, in 70 CE.

47. See *AJ* 14.300 (betrothal by 42 BCE). The reference at *BJ* 1.241 to a marriage in 42 must be an error, since the marriage in 37 is recorded at *BJ* 1.344.

48. See *AJ* 14.353, cf. *BJ* 1.264 (included in group sequestered on Masada).

49. See *AJ* 14.467 (marriage in Samaria; cf. *BJ* 1.344, on the wedding during the siege as evidence for Herod's contempt for the enemy); *AJ* 15.18–21 (return of Hyrcanus).

50. See *AJ* 14.365–66, cf. *BJ* 1.270 (Hyrcanus mutilated by Antigonus); *AJ* 15.22, 34 (Aristobulus passed over for the high priesthood); *AJ* 15. 23–24 (lobbying by Alexandra).

51. See *AJ* 15. 31–41 (appointment of Jonathan Aristobulus as high priest; cf. *AJ* 15.51 and *BJ* 1.437 on his age); *AJ* 15.52 (acclamation in Temple); *AJ* 15.53–56 (drowning); AJ 15.62–64 (Herod summoned to Antony).

52. See *AJ* 15.75–76 (Herod not punished by Antony); *AJ*

15.25–27, cf. *BJ* 1.439 (using Mariamme's beauty to win over Antony); *AJ* 15.82 (Herod's love for Mariamme).

53. See *AJ* 15. 65–67 (Herod's secret instructions); *AJ* 15.81–82 (rumors of Mariamme's affair with Joseph); *AJ* 15.87 (execution of Joseph); *AJ* 15.85 (protestation by Mariamme). The narrative of these events in *BJ* 1.441–44 is muddled.

54. See Plutarch, *Life of Antony* 26, 30; *AJ* 14.375–76 (Herod detained by Cleopatra in 40 BCE).

55. See *AJ* 15. 27–29 (portrait of Jonathan); *AJ* 15.48 (Alexandra encouraged to escape to Egypt); *AJ* 15.32 (Herod's suspicions).

56. See *AJ* 15.65 (Cleopatra turning Antony against Herod); *AJ* 15.76 (instructions not to meddle).

57. See *AJ* 15.92, cf. *BJ* 1.359–60 (Cleopatra's request for Judaea and Arabia); *AJ* 15.94–95, cf. *BJ* 1.361 (Judaean, Nabataean and coastal territories).

58. See *AJ* 15.96, cf. *BJ* 1.362 (balsam groves); *AJ* 15.132 (Nabataea).

59. See *AJ* 15.96–103.

60. See Plutarch, *Life of Antony* 61.3; *AJ* 15.109 (auxiliary force); *AJ* 15.189 (money and wheat).

61. See *AJ* 15.110 (campaign against Malchus); *AJ* 15.116 (intervention by Cleopatra's general); *AJ* 15.122 (earthquake); *AJ* 15.124 (envoys); *AJ* 15.122, 145 (army unscathed in earthquake); *AJ* 15. 147–60 (fighting). Parallel account in *BJ* 1.366–85.

62. See *BJ* 1.283 (Octavian in 40 BCE); *AJ* 15.162 (desperate situation).

63. *BJ* 1.386 (victory incomplete); see *AJ* 15.184 (kingdom entrusted to Pheroras).

64. *BJ* 1.387–90 (longer account in *AJ* 15. 187–93).

65. *AJ* 15.195–200, cf. *BJ* 1.393–97.

66. See Plutarch, *Life of Antony* 72.3 (Alexas).

67. See *AJ* 15. 217–18, cf. *BJ* 1.396–97.

68. See *AJ* 15.161–78. There is no parallel narrative in *BJ*.

69. See *AJ* 15.220 (Mariamme hated by Cyprus and Salome); *AJ* 15.185–86 (Herod's instructions); *AJ* 15. 204–6 (instructions revealed to Mariamme); *AJ* 15. 222–28. It is surprising that Herod

should have left the same inflammatory secret instructions a second time, and it is possible that the instructions were given only once and this second account reflects confusion either by Josephus or by his source. In favor of accepting the story as it is transmitted is the explicit statement at *AJ* 15.204 that the revelation of the secret was brought about by Mariamme's recollection of the previous occasion, but this may be a literary invention.

70. *AJ* 15. 229–36. The detailed account of Mariamme's execution in *AJ* is more plausible than the confused version in *BJ* 1.441–44

71. *AJ* 15. 237–39.

72. See *AJ* 15. 240–46.

73. See *AJ* 15.247–51 (Alexandra); *AJ* 15.260–66 (Sons of Baba). Josephus's assertion at *AJ* 15.266 that Herod sought free rein to act unlawfully depicts him a stereotypical tyrant, cf. Jan Willem van Henten, "Constructing Herod as a Tyrant: Assessing Josephus' Parallel Passages," in *Flavius Josephus: Interpretation and History*, ed. Jack Pastor, Pnina Stern, and Menahem Mor (Leiden: Brill, 2011), 193–216. In fact, of the family of Hyrcanus, apart from Herod's own sons by Mariamme, a daughter of Antigonus survived to marry Herod's eldest son Antipater in 14 BCE as a representative of the Hasmonaean line (*AJ* 17.92). A reference at *AJ* 14.488 to Herod's fear in 37 BCE that the Romans might in principle want the sons of Antigonus to rule after him by virtue of their lineage might seem to imply that such sons existed, but nothing is known about their fate.

74. On Augustus's system of promoting provincial rulers, see Tal A. Ish-Shalom, "Provincial Monarchs as an Eastern *Arcanum Imperii:* 'Client Kingship,' the Augustan Revolution and the Flavians," *Journal of Roman Studies* 111 (2021): 153–77.

Chapter 3. A Roman Kingdom

1. See D. W. Roller, *The Building Program of Herod the Great* (Berkeley: University of California Press, 1998); *AJ* 15.299–312 (drought and famine); the date of the rebuilding of the Temple in Jerusalem given in *AJ* 15.380 ("eighteenth year of his reign") ap-

pears to be contradicted by *BJ* 1.401 ("fifteenth year"), but the earlier date may refer to the start of planning for the project.

2. See *AJ* 15.354 (20 BCE); *AJ* 16.6 (17 BCE); *AJ* 16.87–135, cf. *BJ* 1.452–54 (12 BCE). The apparent implication by Josephus at *AJ* 16. 270–71 that Herod went to Rome again in 10 BCE is probably a mistake.

3. See *AJ* 16.128 (three hundred talents); *AJ* 17.190 (bequest by Herod); *AJ* 17.322–23, cf. *BJ* 2.98–100 (gifts by Augustus).

4. See *AJ* 15.343 (Pollio); on Messalla, see Elimar Klebs, Paul de Rohden, and Hermann Dessau, eds., *Prosopographia Imperii Romani Saeculi I, II, III*, 3 vols. (Berlin: Georg Reimer, 1897–98), 3:363–68; on Agrippa, see Meyer Reinhold, *Marcus Agrippa: A Biography* (Geneva, N.Y.: W. F. Humphrey Press, 1933); J.-M. Roddaz, *Marcus Agrippa* (Rome: École française de Rome, 1984).

5. M. Grunewald, "Ein neues Fragment der Laudatio Funebris des Augustus auf Agrippa," *Zeitschrift für Paprologie und Epigraphik* 52 (1983): 61–62 (translation mine).

6. See *AJ* 15.350 (meeting in Mitylene); *AJ* 15.361, cf. *BJ* 1.400 (claim about friendship); *AJ* 15.318 (halls in palace in Jerusalem; cf. *BJ* 1. 402 for the names).

7. See *AJ* 16.13–14.

8. See *AJ* 16.16 (with Agrippa in Asia Minor); *AJ* 16.23 (return overland); *BJ* 16.61 (embrace); *AJ* 16.86 (Antipater brought to Mitylene).

9. The new name for Anthedon was less long lasting, since Josephus was unclear whether it should be Agrippias or Agrippeum (see *AJ* 13.357; *BJ* 1.87), and by the second century CE the geographer Ptolemy had reverted to the old name Anthedon (Ptolemy, *Geography* 5.16.2); for the name on the gate of the Temple, see *BJ* 1.416; for arguments that the naming of Herod's grandson Marcus Julius Agrippa took place in late 11 BCE, after Agrippa's death, see Nikos Kokkinos, *The Herodian Dynasty: Origins, Role in Society and Eclipse* (Sheffield: Sheffield Academic Press, 1998), 271–72.

10. See *AJ* 15.342 (Alexander and Aristobulus to Rome); *AJ* 16.76–86 (Antipater to Rome); *AJ* 17.20–21 (Herod's younger sons to Rome); *AJ* 17.10 (Salome and Livia); Strabo, *Geography* 16.2–46.

Salome's daughter Berenice, who was married to Herod's son Aristobulus, became a close friend of Antonia, wife of Augustus's stepson Drusus. Drusus was a powerful presence in the imperial court, particularly between the death of Agrippa in 12 BCE and his own premature death in 9 BCE, and Antonia herself was an important figure in Roman society as the daughter of Mark Antony. Berenice almost certainly forged this friendship with Antonia in Rome, since Agrippa I, her son by Aristobulus, is known to have lived in Rome as a child starting in 6 BCE or earlier.

11. See *The Deeds of the Divine Augustus* 4, in *Res Gestae Divi Augusti: Text, Translation, and Commentary*, ed. Alison E. Cooley (Cambridge: Cambridge University Press, 2009); *AJ* 18.240–46, cf. *BJ* 2.181–82 (petition for royal title); *AJ* 18.252 (exile to Lugdunum in Gaul; *BJ* 2.183 gives Spain as the place of exile).

12. See Suetonius, *Augustus* 60.

13. *AJ* 16.141.

14. See *AJ* 15.215–17, cf. *BJ* 1.396–97; 15.343–45, cf. *BJ* 1.398; 15.354, 360, cf. *BJ* 1.400.

15. See *AJ* 14.75–76, cf. *BJ* 1.155–56 (Hyrcanus stripped of some territory by Pompey); *AJ* 14.90–91, cf. *BJ* 1.169 (stripped of all secular authority by Gabinius, governor of Syria); *AJ* 14.202–10 (restoration by Caesar).

16. See Appian, *Civil Wars* 5.319; *BJ* 1.213 (Herod governor of Samaria in 47 BCE).

17. See *AJ* 15.351 (complaint to Agrippa); *AJ* 15.354 (complaint to Augustus); *AJ* 17.320 (granted independence); Nicolaus, *On His Life* in *GLAJJ* 1:254. On the coins of Gadara, see Andrew M. Burnett et al., eds. *Roman Provincial Coinage* (London: British Museum Press, 1992–).

18. *BJ* 1.422–25.

19. *BJ* 1.427; *OGIS* nos. 414, 427.

20. See Appian, *Civil War* 5.75.319.

21. See *AJ* 15.159; for the debates on the meaning and significance of the Greek term *prostates*, translated here as "leader," see *Flavius Josephus: Translation and Commentary*, vol. 7b: *Judean Antiquities 15*, ed. Steve Mason, trans. Jan Willem van Henten

(Leiden: Brill, 2014), 107, n. 925; *OGIS* no. 415 (Greek inscription recording the dedication; the statue does not survive); on Augustus in 7 BCE, see *AJ* 16.353–55.

22. See *AJ* 16.279 (loan); *AJ* 15.351–53 (tension over territory); *AJ* 16.220 (character of Obodas).

23. *AJ* 16.224–25.

24. See *AJ* 16.275 (Syllaeus fomenting trouble); *AJ* 16.280 (permission from Saturninus); *AJ* 16.289 (fury of Augustus).

25. See *AJ* 16.286–92 (Syllaeus in Rome); *AJ* 16.290 (Herod as a subject); *AJ* 16.294 (despair and fear); *AJ* 16.335–55 (second embassy).

26. See Strabo, *Geography* 16.4.23; *AJ* 15.317 (Arabian campaign).

27. On the campaign, see *AJ* 16.16–27; Cassius Dio, *Roman History* 54.24.5; on Herod, Archelaus, and Glaphyra, see *AJ* 16.11, 23, and Chapter 5, below.

28. *BJ* 5.177–81; the term "Herodian doves" for captive pigeons, found in the Mishnah (*m Shabbat* 24:3), probably reflects Herod's introduction to Judaea of the Roman fashion of pigeon breeding.

29. See Ehud Netzer, *The Architecture of Herod, the Great Builder*, 2nd ed. (Grand Rapids, Mich.: Baker Academic, 2008); Silvia Rozenberg, "Interior Decoration in Herod's Palaces," in *Herod the Great: The King's Final Journey*, ed. Silvia Rozenberg and David Mevorah (Jerusalem: Israel Museum, 2013), 166–223.

30. On Roman dining, see Katherine M. D. Dunbabin, *The Roman Banquet: Images of Conviviality* (Cambridge: Cambridge University Press, 2003); *AJ* 16.222–23; A. Ecker, "Dining with Herod," in Rozenberg and Mevorah, *Herod the Great*, 66–79. On the foodstuffs imported to Masada, see Hannah M. Cotton and Joseph Geiger, "The Economic Importance of Herod's Masada: The Evidence of the Jar Inscriptions," in *Judaea and the Graeco-Roman World in the Time of Herod in the Light of Archaeological Evidence*, ed. Klaus Fittschen and Gideon Foerster (Göttingen: Vandenhoeck & Ruprecht, 1996), 163–70.

31. On Herod's court, see Samuel Rocca, *Herod's Judaea: A*

Mediterranean State in the Classical World (Tübingen: Mohr Siebeck, 2008), 65–127.

32. See Nicolaus, *On His Life*, cited in *GLAJJ* 1:248–49; on Herod's memoirs, see *AJ* 15.174. Among the Romans in Herod's court was a man called Gemellus (a Latin name) who was expelled from the court during a crisis toward the end of Herod's life; he is said to have been Herod's long-term friend, to have helped Herod's family through embassies and councils, to have provided Herod's son Alexander with a place to stay when he went to Rome for his education, and to be too distinguished for Herod to do more than dismiss him when he fell out of favor (*AJ* 16.242–43).

33. See *AJ* 14.377 (40 BCE); *AJ* 16.191 (overseer of finances); *BJ* 1.473 ("most honoured"); *AJ* 16.25 (out of favor); *AJ* 17.195 (seal and will). Rocca, *Herod's Judaea*, 85, suggests that Ptolemy was a Hellenized Jew, which is possible.

34. On Eurycles, see G. W. Bowersock, "Eurycles of Sparta," *Journal of Roman Studies* 51 (1961): 112–18; *AJ* 15.301–10; *BJ* 1.513 (Eurycles' arrival in Judaea); *BJ* 1.515 (Herod's regard for Sparta).

35. *AJ* 15.267–75 (Jerusalem); *AJ* 16.136–40, cf. *BJ* 1.415 (Caesarea).

36. *AJ* 15.296–98, cf. *BJ* 1.403.

37. See *AJ* 15.331–41, cf. *BJ* 1.408–15; on the temple, see *AJ* 15.339; on the statue, see *BJ* 1.414.

38. Monika Bernett, *Der Kaiserkult in Judäa unter den Herodien und Römern* (Tübingen: Mohr Siebeck, 2007); on these temples, see Roller, *Building Program*, 210–12 (Sebaste), 190–92 (Paneion); *AJ* 15.363–64 (Paneion).

39. See David M. Jacobson, "The Jerusalem Temple of Herod the Great" in *The World of the Herods*, ed. Nikos Kokkinos (Stuttgart: Franz Steiner, 2007), 145–76.

40. Philo, *The Embassy to Gaius*, 157, 317, trans. Francis H. Colson, Loeb Classical Library 379 (Cambridge: Harvard University Press, 1962); on Agrippa, see *AJ* 16.14; Philo, *Embassy to Gaius*, 295–96.

41. See *BJ* 1.416 (Agrippa's name on the gate); *AJ* 17.151 (erection of eagle); *AJ* 17.163 (eagle destruction as sacrilege). Jon-

athan Bourgel, "Herod's Golden Eagle on the Temple Gate: A Reconsideration," *Journal of Jewish Studies* 72 (2021): 23–44, highlights the legendary elements in Josephus's narrative of this episode, but the legendary motifs do not constitute sufficient reason to doubt the basic historicity of Josephus's account.

42. See Cassius Dio, *Roman History* 56.42.3 (eagle from Augustus's pyre); on the eagle image on the Belvedere altar in ca. 9 BCE, see Bridget A. Buxton, "A New Reading of the Belvedere Altar," *American Journal of Archaeology* 118 (2014): 91–111; on the date of the construction of the mausoleum, see Suetonius, *Augustus* 100. Despite the frequent depiction of eagles in later Jewish art and the wide variety of interpretations of Judaism in Herod's time, the eagle image is not likely to have been promoted by Herod as a distinctively Jewish religious symbol.

43. *AJ* 15.387; on Augustus's religious program see *The Deeds of the Divine Augustus* 19–21.

44. See *AJ* 15.380 (payment for Temple rebuilding); *AJ* 15.306 (chopping up gold and silver).

45. See *AJ* 16.153–55 (finances); *AJ* 16.179–83 (tomb of David).

46. On Herod's finances in general, see Emilio Gabba, "The Finances of King Herod," in *Greece and Rome in Eretz Israel: Collected Essays*, ed. A. Kasher, U. Rappaport, and G. Fuks (Jerusalem: Yad Izhak Ben-Zvi Publications/The Israel Exploration Society, 1990), 160–68; *AJ* 17.204–5 (demands after Herod's death); *AJ* 17.307 (confiscations).

47. See *AJ* 15.96, cf. *BJ* 1.361 (balsam groves); *AJ* 16.291 (interest on loans and rental from land from Nabataeans); *BJ* 1.428 (tax concessions); *AJ* 16.128 (Cyprus copper mines); on Herod's appointment in Syria in 20 BCE, see *BJ* 1.399 ("procurator of all Syria") and *AJ* 15.360 ("associate of procurators").

48. On Herod and tourism, see Martin Goodman, "The Pilgrimage Economy of Jerusalem in the Second Temple Period," in Martin Goodman, *Judaism in the Roman World: Collected Essays* (Leiden: Brill, 2007), 59–67; on the bequest to Augustus, see *AJ* 17.190.

Chapter 4. Ruling as a Jew

1. See Strabo, *Geography* 2.46; *AJ* 14.9 (Nicolaus); Shaye J. D. Cohen, *The Beginnings of Jewishness: Boundaries, Varieties, Uncertainties* (Berkeley: University of California Press, 1999), 13–24 (chapter titled "Was Herod Jewish?").

2. On changing attitudes toward Jews and Judaism in the Roman world, see Martin Goodman, *Rome and Jerusalem: The Clash of Ancient Civilizations* (London: Allen Lane, 2007).

3. Persius, *Satire* 5.180–84, in *Juvenal and Persius*, trans. G. G. Ramsay, Loeb Classical Library 91 (London: Heineman, 1918). Suggestions that Persius, who was writing in Rome some decades after Herod's death, was referring not to the Sabbath but to Herod's birthday or the anniversary of his accession to power in Judaea are implausible, but it is possible that he had in mind one of Herod's descendants rather than Herod himself.

4. See Silvia Rozenberg, "Interior Decoration in Herod's Palaces," in *Herod the Great: The King's Final Journey*, ed. Silvia Rozenberg and David Mevorah (Jerusalem: Israel Museum, 2013), 166–223.

5. On Judaism in this period, see Martin Goodman, *A History of Judaism* (London: Allen Lane, 2017), 91–221.

6. Jodi Magness, "Herod the Great's Self-Representation Through his Tomb at Herodium," *Journal of Ancient Judaism* 10 (2019): 258–87, argues, based on the location of Herodium, that Herod wished to be seen as a Davidic messiah, but the evidence is thin. On the possible religious significance of the baths in Herod's palaces, see Eyal Regev, *The Social Archaeology of Late Second Temple Judaism* (New York: Routledge, 2022), chap. 7.

7. *AJ* 15.377–79.

8. Strabo, *Geography* 16.2.46.

9. See *AJ* 14.386–87 (Jonathan as more likely to be backed by Rome than Herod).

10. See *AJ* 15.34 (Jonathan too young); *AJ* 15.53–56, cf. *BJ* 1.437 (drowning).

11. See *AJ* 15.56 (Ananel reappointed); *AJ* 15.40 (end of high priesthood held for life); *AJ* 15.22, 39 (Ananel from diaspora fam-

ily); *AJ* 15.322 (Simon son of Boethus). For a list of high priests, see James VanderKam, *From Joshua to Caiaphas: High Priests After the Exile* (Minneapolis: Fortress, 2004).

12. *AJ* 15.383, 385 (speech at start of project); *AJ* 17.162 (speech at end of Herod's life).

13. *AJ* 15.392–402, 410–20.

14. See *AJ* 15.390 (priests trained as construction workers); *AJ* 15.421 (inner sanctuary completed); *AJ* 15.442–43 (sacrifice to coincide with celebration of Herod's accession).

15. See *AJ* 15.424 (secret passage); *AJ* 15.411–16 (Royal Portico).

16. See *AJ* 15.403 (vestments kept in Antonia); *BJ* 5. 231–36 (vestments of the high priest).

17. See *AJ* 17.151, cf. *BJ* 1.650 (eagle image "contrary to the law"); Donald Tzvi Ariel and Jean-Philippe Fontanille, *The Coins of Herod: A Modern Analysis and Die Classification* (Leiden: Brill, 2012), 102.

18. See *AJ* 15.277–79 (trophies); *AJ* 15.329–30 (Herod's claim that he breaks Jewish law outside Jewish territory only on Roman command).

19. See *AJ* 16.182 (memorial at David's tomb); *AJ* 15.385 (comparison to Solomon); *AJ* 16.179–81 (on Herod seeking treasure from David's tomb).

20. On Hasmonaean rulers as aligned either to Pharisees or to Sadducees, see *AJ* 13.288–98 (on John Hyrcanus, who ruled as high priest from 134 to 104 BCE); *AJ* 13.401–4 (on Alexander Jannaeus and on Shelomzion); cf. also Hanan Eshel, *The Dead Sea Scrolls and the Hasmonaean State* (Grand Rapids, Mich.: Eerdmans, 2008); on Manaemus, see *AJ* 15. 372–79; on Pollio, see *AJ* 15.3–4, 370; on Samaias, see *AJ* 14.172–76.

21. See *AJ* 15.368–72, 17.42 (oaths); *AJ* 17.41 (Pharisees helped the king but hostile to him).

22. See *AJ* 15.280–90.

23. *AJ* 15.366–67.

24. See *AJ* 17.198 (bodyguard). Josephus (*AJ* 16.1–5) singled out as one cause of his unpopularity Herod's imposition of a law

requiring convicted housebreakers to be sold into slavery abroad, but responses to this legal innovation may have been mixed, since it seems to have been presented as part of an effective effort to clamp down on crime.

25. See *BJ* 1.282 ("king of Jews").

26. See Philo, *Embassy to Gaius*, 281–82; Cicero, *On Behalf of Flaccus* 22.66–69.

27. *BJ* 2.398 (speech by Agrippa II); *AJ* 14.196–97 (rights of Hyrcanus).

28. *AJ* 14.222–27 (Ephesus). Nadav Sharon, "The Title 'Ethnarch' in Second Temple Period Judea," *Journal for the Study of Judaism* 41 (2010): 472–93, argues that the title was first employed by the Romans and reflects a distinctively Roman perception of the Jews as a people not confined to Judaea.

29. See *AJ* 12.127 (Nicolaus's history); *AJ* 16.27–28 (Jews in Ionia); *AJ* 16.51, 57 (Nicolaus's speech); *AJ* 16.60 (Agrippa's response).

30. See *AJ* 17.300, cf. *BJ* 1.80 (hostility of Jews in Rome).

31. See Martin Goodman, "The Pilgrimage Economy of Jerusalem in the Second Temple Period," in Martin Goodman, *Judaism in the Roman World: Collected Essays* (Leiden: Brill, 2007), 59–67.

32. Acts 2:4–11.

33. *AJ* 15.14–15, cf. *BJ* 1.273.

34. See *AJ* 15.15 (high priest and king); *AJ* 15.39 (Ananel from Babylonia); *AJ* 15.39, 56 (Ananel deposed and reappointed).

35. *AJ* 17.23–28 (Zamaris); on Josephus and the grandson of Zamaris, see Josephus, *Life* 46–51, 59–61, 177–84, 407–9.

36. See *AJ* 15.40 (Ananel as friend of Herod long before 37 BCE).

37. See *BJ* 1.562–63; *AJ* 17. 19–22. The order and dates of these marriages is not recorded, and the varying suggestions by scholars depend on their assumptions about how Herod might have behaved. For a tabular presentation of recent proposals, see Peter Richardson and Amy Marie Fisher, *Herod: King of the Jews and Friend of the Romans* (London: Routledge, 2018), 384.

38. See *BJ* 1.477 (mocking by Glaphyra); *AJ* 15.319–22 (attraction to the second Mariamme). Most of what we are told about Herod's sexual preferences relates to his marriages, but Josephus also referred in passing to Herod's gift to a friend of a slave concubine called Pannychis (*BJ* 1.511), to his passion in his old age for a pretty boy called Karos, probably also a slave (*AJ* 17.44), and to his fondness for the beautiful eunuchs he kept in his household and his fury when they were seduced by his son Alexander (*AJ* 16.230–31).

39. See *AJ* 15.296–98, cf. *BJ* 1.403 (building of Sebaste).

40. See *BJ* 1.432 (Doris dismissed by Herod when he came to power).

41. *AJ* 17.19 (nine women); on polygamy permitted for Jews, see *BJ* 1.477; *AJ* 17.14; *Mishnah Ketubot* 10.1; Justin Martyr, *Dialogue with Trypho* 134; *P. Yadin* 26 (husband of a Jewish woman named Babata had another wife also living with him and not divorced); Nikos Kokkinos, *The Herodian Dynasty: Origins, Role in Society, and Eclipse* (Sheffield: Sheffield Academic Press, 1998), 143–44. Kokkinos notes (211) that the betrothal arranged by Herod in 7 of his son and heir Antipater to Antipater's niece Mariamme (see *AJ* 17.18) would have been bigamous if it had been consummated (which is unlikely, since Mariamme was still a child), but that this apparent encouragement of bigamy by someone in his family apart from himself is exceptional. On polygamy in Macedonian and Hellenistic dynasties, see Daniel Ogden, *Polygamy, Prostitutes and Death: The Hellenistic Dynasties*, 2nd ed. (Swansea: Classical Press of Wales, 2010). On King David's wives, see 2 Samuel 5:13.

Chapter 5. A Family Tragedy

1. *BJ* 1.665.

2. See *AJ* 15.184 (Pheroras in control of affairs); *AJ* 15.186 (preserve kingdom for Pheroras).

3. See *BJ* 1.483 (Hasmonaean bride); on Salampsio, see *BJ* 1.483–84 and *AJ* 16.194–95. On the social status of Pheroras's concubine, see below, n. 36.

4. See *AJ* 15.362, cf. *BJ* 1.483 (tetrarchy in Transjordan).

5. See *BJ* 1.485 (most brother-loving); *AJ* 16.196–99 (aborted wedding to Cyprus).

6. See *AJ* 15.81, cf. *BJ* 1.443 (accusation of adultery); *AJ* 15.87 (execution of Joseph).

7. See *AJ* 15.253–54 (ancestry of Costobar); *AJ* 15.257 (governor of Idumaea); *AJ* 15.258 (Costobar and Cleopatra); *AJ* 15.259 (divorce); *AJ* 15.260–66 (Sons of Baba); *AJ* 15.252 (death of Costobar).

8. See *AJ* 17.93 (Herod's council in 4 BCE); *AJ* 16.220, 223 (dinner).

9. See *BJ* 1.417 (Antipatris and Cypros); *BJ* 1.418 (Phasael); on Achiab, see *AJ* 15.250, 17.184.

10. *BJ* 1.483, 565–66; *AJ* 15.254; 16.11; 17.14, 22; K. C. Hanson, "The Herodians and Mediterranean Kinship," *Biblical Theology Bulletin* 19 (1989): 75–84, 142–51.

11. On the complex issues involved in the inheritance of power in the imperial family in the early Julio-Claudian period, see Alisdair G. G. Gibson, ed., *The Julio-Claudian Succession: Reality and Perception of the "Augustan Model"* (Leiden: Brill, 2013); Olivier Hekster, *Emperors and Ancestors: Roman Rulers and the Constraints of Tradition* (Oxford: Oxford University Press, 2015); Alison E. Cooley, "From the Augustan Principate to the Invention of the Age of Augustus," *Journal of Roman Studies* 109 (2019): 71–87.

12. See *AJ* 15.184, 186.

13. See *AJ* 15.343.

14. On the death of Agrippa Postumus, see Tacitus, *Annals* 1.6; Tacitus doubted that Augustus was responsible on the grounds that the emperor had never been callous enough to kill any of his relations, but Suetonius (*Augustus* 65) thought it possible that Augustus had considered executing his daughter Julia when she was sent into exile for adultery, and reported that he ordered infanticide by exposure of a baby born to his granddaughter, the younger Julia, when she also was in exile.

15. On brother-sister unions in Egypt, see Sabine R. Huebner, "'Brother-Sister' Marriage in Roman Egypt: A Curiosity of Hu-

mankind or a Widespread Family Strategy?" *Journal of Roman Studies* 97 (2007): 21–49.

16. On Archelaus of Cappadocia, see Richard D. Sullivan, *Near Eastern Royalty and Rome, 100–30 BC* (Toronto: University of Toronto Press, 1990), 182–85.

17. See *AJ* 16.129, 134 (no retirement); *AJ* 16.248 (competing with Alexander); *AJ* 16.206–7 (rumors about Glaphyra); *AJ* 16.230–33 (eunuchs on dyed hair); on speech in Temple, see *BJ* 1.462 and *AJ* 16.134.

18. See *AJ* 16.6–11 (Salome), 66–77 (Salome and Pheroras). The parallel account in *BJ* 1.447 does not give names for the plotters who were said to have accused Herod's sons.

19. See *AJ* 16.78–81, cf. *BJ* 1.448 (recall of Antipater); *AJ* 17.92 (Antipater's wife); *BJ* 1.451 (recall of Doris).

20. See *AJ* 16.86 (Antipater to Rome); *AJ* 16.89 (letters).

21. See *AJ* 16. 90–99. The quotation is from *AJ* 16.98.

22. See *AJ* 16. 100–126, cf. *BJ* 1. 452–54.

23. See *AJ* 16.132–35; *BJ* 1.457–65 (with Herod's speech).

24. See *AJ* 16.208–18, cf. *BJ* 1.487 (mutual recriminations of Pheroras and Salome); *AJ* 16.220–23 (gossip and dining); *AJ* 16.190–93; *BJ* 1.476 (Glaphyra's background).

25. See *AJ* 16.244–53, cf. *BJ* 1.495–97.

26. *AJ* 16.256–60, cf. *BJ* 1.498.

27. See *AJ* 16.261–70. *BJ* 1.499–512 provides a more detailed account.

28. *AJ* 16. 282–85 (Herod's campaign in Nabataea, with reference to his impressive forced march at 16.283).

29. See *AJ* 17.9–10, cf. *BJ* 1.566 (marriage to Alexas); *AJ* 17.175, cf. *BJ* 1. 660 (Herod's last days).

30. See *AJ* 16.300–310, cf. *BJ* 1.513–31 (Eurycles); *AJ* 16.314–16, cf. *BJ* 1.527–28 (bodyguards); *AJ* 16.317–19, cf. *BJ* 1.529 (forged letter).

31. See *AJ* 16. 320–21, 323, cf. *BJ* 1.535.

32. See *AJ* 16.356–60, cf. *BJ* 1.536–38 (council); *AJ* 16.331–32 (Glaphyra's plan to escape).

33. See *AJ* 16.361–72, cf. *BJ* 1.539–43; on lynching, see *AJ* 16.393–94, cf. *BJ* 1.550; on the death of Alexander and Aristobulus, see *AJ* 16.394, cf. *BJ* 1.551.

34. See *AJ* 17.53, cf. *BJ* 1.573 (will); *AJ* 17.78 (passing over of the young Herod).

35. See *AJ* 17.2 (army); *AJ* 17.9, 12–18, cf. *BJ* 1.556–58 (betrothals)

36. See *AJ* 17.42–50 (Pheroras's mistress and Herod's ultimatum); *AJ* 17.58 (oath). The eventual social status of Pheroras's concubine is obscure; in Josephus's references to her at the end of Pheroras's life and after his death, she is termed his wife, and her mother and sister are reported to have been involved in the intrigues in Pheroras's court; Josephus also reports that they had slaves and freedwomen of their own (*AJ* 17.63–64). It is possible that Josephus's ascription of servile origins to the concubine was a slur reflecting Herod's hostility to her and the abuse of her political opponents, including Nicolaus, who evidently considered her a malign influence, but it is more likely that she had been Pheroras's slave but had been freed by him along with some of her relatives. Cf. *BJ* 1.568, 571–72, 578–79.

37. See *AJ* 17.59, cf. *BJ* 1.580–81 (Pheroras's death and burial); *AJ* 17.74–75 (Pheroras on his deathbed).

38. See *BJ* 1.581 (rumor that Herod killed Pheroras); *AJ* 17.61–63 (accusations that Pheroras was poisoned); *AJ* 17.63–67 (plot against Herod). Cf. *BJ* 1.582–607, a parallel narrative to *AJ* 17.61–82.

39. See *AJ* 17.52 (Antipater to Rome); *AJ* 17.69 (plot to poison Herod while Antipater in Rome); *AJ* 17.71 (attempted suicide of Pheroras's concubine); *AJ* 17.72, 77 (confession); *AJ* 17.78 (implication of Mariamme).

40. See *AJ* 17.78 (divorce of Mariamme and deposition of Simon from high priesthood).

41. See *AJ* 17.60–82, with Antipater's complaint at *AJ* 17.66.

42. See *AJ* 17.80–92; *BJ* 1.604–16.

43. See *AJ* 17.93–132.

44. See *AJ* 17.133; *AJ* 17.68 (punishment of Doris); *AJ* 17.134–42 (Acme conspiracy); *AJ* 17.144–45 (Antipater kept in chains).

45. See *AJ* 17.20 (Antipas brought up in Rome); *AJ* 17.146, cf. *BJ* 1.646 (new will).

46. See *AJ* 17.146, 148, cf. *BJ* 1.647 (Herod's illness); *AJ* 17.149–60, cf. *BJ* 1.648–55 (eagle incident).

47. See *AJ* 17.150, cf. *BJ* 1.656 (impiety said to have led to illness); *AJ* 17.161–67, cf. *BJ* 1.655 (punishment of perpetrators).

48. See *AJ* 17.168–69, cf. *BJ* 1.656 (Herod's symptoms); *AJ* 17.171–72, cf. *BJ* 1.657 (medical interventions); *AJ* 17.182, cf. *BJ* 1.661 (letter from envoys sent to Augustus).

49. See *AJ* 17.183–87, cf. *BJ* 1.662–64.

50. See *AJ* 17.188–89, cf. *BJ* 1.668. The account in *AJ* wrongly describes Philip as a full brother of Archelaus.

51. See *AJ* 17.20–21 (Archelaus and Philip both brought up in Rome).

52. See *AJ* 15.76 (Antony's retort to Cleopatra). It is uncertain whether the citation in Latin of Augustus's quip, originally made in Greek, by Macrobius (*Saturnalia* 2.4.11) in the fifth century CE, was genuinely based on a source from the time of Augustus or a later invention.

53. See *AJ* 17.174–79, 193, cf. *BJ* 1.659–60, 666 (massacre); the quotations are from *Testament of Moses* 6.2–4, trans. John Priest, in *The Old Testament Pseudepigrapha*, ed. James H. Charlesworth, 2 vols. (New York: Doubleday, 1983–85), an apocryphal text about the assumption of Moses into heaven of which this section, preserved in a Latin translation first identified in the nineteenth century, seems to have been composed in the generation immediately after Herod's death.

54. *AJ* 17.190, 196–99, cf. *BJ* 1. 670–73, where the procession is said to have accompanied the body all the way to Herodium.

55. *BJ* 1.265, 419–20; Ehud Netzer, *The Palaces of the Hasmonaeans and Herodians* (Jerusalem: Yad Ben-Zvi Press and the Israel Exploration Society, 2001), 98–116.

56. See *AJ* 17.200–218, cf. *BJ* 2.1–13.

57. See *BJ* 1.669 (Archelaus with signet ring to Rome); *AJ* 17.219–49, 299–323, cf. *BJ* 2.20–38 (disputes in Rome); *AJ* 17.250, cf. *BJ* 2.39 (death of Malthace).

58. See Nicolaus, *On His Life*, cited in *GLAJJ* 1:254; *AJ* 17.219 (Philip in charge); *AJ* 17.221–23, 252–64, cf. *BJ* 2.16–19, 41–51 (Sabinus).

59. See *AJ* 17.265–85, cf. *BJ* 2.52–65.

60. See *AJ* 17.286–94; *AJ* 17.298 (punishment of Herod's relatives); Josephus, *Against Apion* 1.34 ("war of Varus").

61. See *AJ* 17.271, cf. *BJ* 2.56 (Judas); *AJ* 17.273–74, cf. *BJ* 2.57–59 (Simon); *AJ* 17.278, cf. *BJ* 2.60–61 (Athronges). The aspirations of these leaders are sometimes described as messianic (see, e.g., Martin Hengel, *The Zealots: Investigations into the Jewish Freedom Movement in the Period from Herod I Until 70 A.D.*, trans. David Smith [Edinburgh: T. & T. Clark, 1977]), but this characterization is not found in any ancient source.

62. See *AJ* 17.229, cf. *BJ* 2.25 (Gaius in council; cf. *The Deeds of the Divine Augustus* 14 in *Res Gestae Divi Augusti: Text, Translation, and Commentary*, ed. Alison E. Cooley [Cambridge: Cambridge University Press, 2009], on Gaius and Lucius appointed consuls at fifteen, to hold office five years later); *AJ* 17.301–16, cf. *BJ* 2.84–92 (speeches).

63. See *AJ* 17.317–20, cf. *BJ* 2.93–97 (disposition of kingdom); *AJ* 17.200, cf. *BJ* 2.1–2 (acclamations); *AJ* 17.314, cf. *BJ* 2.91 (opposition); *AJ* 17.342–44, cf. *BJ* 2.111 (Archelaus to exile). Strabo, *Geography*, 16.2.46, in *The Geography of Strabo*, trans. Horace L. Jones, 8 vols., vol. 7: *Books 15–16*, Loeb Classical Library 241 (Cambridge: Harvard University Press, 1930).

64. See *AJ* 18.127–42.

65. On Herod's descendants in general, see Nikos Kokkinos, *The Herodian Dynasty: Origins, Role in Society and Eclipse* (Sheffield: Sheffield Academic Press, 1998); on Antipas, see Harold W. Hoehner, *Herod Antipas* (Cambridge: Cambridge University Press, 1972); on Agrippa I, see Daniel R. Schwartz, *Agrippa I: The Last King of Judaea* (Tübingen: Mohr Siebeck, 1990).

66. *AJ* 17.324–38, cf. *BJ* 2.101–10.

67. *AJ* 16.150–58.

68. See *OGIS* nos. 418, 419, 421, 422 (Agrippa I). On "Herod the Great," see *AJ* 18.130, 133, 136.

Epilogue

1. See Matthew 2:1–16 (NRSV). On the literary background of Matthew's story of Herod's policy of infanticide, see W. D. Davies and D. C. Allison, *A Critical and Exegetical Commentary on the Gospel According to Saint Matthew*, 3 vols. (Edinburgh: T. & T. Clark, 1988), 1:264–65; Exodus 1:15–22 (Pharaoh story).

2. See William Shakespeare, *Hamlet* 3.2 (out-Herod Herod); Matthew 14; Luke 3:19–20, 9:9 (Antipas called Herod in story of death of John the Baptist); Luke 23:7–12 (Antipas called Herod in meeting with Jesus); Mark 6:14–29 (Antipas called King Herod); Acts 12:1–2 (Agrippa I called King Herod); Pamela M. King and Clifford Davidson, eds., *The Coventry Corpus Christi Plays* (Kalamazoo: Medieval Institute Publications, Western Michigan University, 2000).

3. See Julius Africanus, *Letter to Aristides*, cited in Eusebius, *Ecclesiastical History* 1.7.2–16; *Chronicon Paschale*, ed. Ludwig A. Dindorf, 2 vols. (Bonn: E. Weber, 1832), 1:351, 358.

4. See Peter Auger, "Playing Josephus on the English Stage," *International Journal of the Classical Tradition* 23 (2016): 326–32; Ernst Baltrusch, *Herodes: König im Heiligen Land: eine Biographie* (Munich: Beck, 2012), 354–79; Marvin Carlson, *Voltaire and the Theatre of the Eighteenth Century* (Westport, Conn.: Greenwood, 1998), 16–17.

5. *Babylonian Talmud, Baba Bathra* 3b–4a.

6. See Tal Ilan and Vered Noam, *Josephus and the Rabbis* (Jerusalem: Yad Ben-Zvi, 2017).

7. Steven B. Bowman, trans., *Sepher Yosippon: A Tenth-Century History of Ancient Israel* (Detroit: Wayne State University Press, 2023), 180, n. 8 (translation of *privatus* by *eved* noted by the translator), 178 (Senate in Rome), 184 (defense of Temple gate), 183 (God's beloved), 230 (king whom God has chosen), 240 (successful), 240–41 (burdensome and wicked; cruel).

8. On Jewish uses of *Sefer Yosippon*, see Martin Goodman, *Josephus's "The Jewish War": A Biography* (Princeton: Princeton University Press, 2019), 31–35; Azariah de' Rossi, *The Light of the Eyes*,

trans. Joanna Weinberg (New Haven: Yale University Press, 2001), 102 (Pharisees), 108 (Menahem).

9. See Yaacov Shavit, "Herod: From Monster to Nearly a National Hero?" in *"Let the Wise Listen and Add to Their Learning" (Prov. 1:5): Festschrift for Günter Stemberger on the Occasion of His 75th Birthday*, ed. Constanza Cordoni and Gerhard Langer (Berlin: De Gruyter, 2016), 683–701.

10. See Shavit, "Herod," 693–94.

11. See Jan Willem van Henten, "Abel J. Herzberg's *The Memoirs of King Herod:* The Interaction Between a Tragic Tyrant and His Subjects," in *Strength to Strength: Essays in Appreciation of Shaye J. D. Cohen*, ed. Michael L. Satlow (Providence: Brown University Press, 2018), 631–50.

12. On Schalit, see Daniel R. Schwartz, "From Masada to Jotapata: On Josephus in Twentieth-Century Hebrew Scholarship," in *A Companion to Josephus*, ed. Honora Howell Chapman and Zuleika Rodgers (Chichester, UK: Wiley Blackwell, 2016), 419–39; Schwartz, "Herod the Great: A Matter of Perspective," in *Herod the Great: The King's Final Journey*, ed. Silvia Rozenberg and David Mevorah (Jerusalem: Israel Museum, 2013), 42–43.

13. Aryeh Kasher and Eliezer Witztum, *King Herod: A Persecuted Persecutor; A Case Study in Psychohistory and Psychobiography* (Berlin, 2007).

14. I am grateful to Sami Kamal for pointing out to me how often Herod was described as frustrated in his search for reciprocal affection.

Appendix

1. On the *Antiquities*, see the introduction by Steve Mason to Louis H. Feldman, *Judean Antiquities 1–4*, vol. 3 of *Flavius Josephus: Translation and Commentary*, ed. Steve Mason (Leiden: Brill, 1999); Martin Goodman, "Introduction," in Josephus, *The Life of Herod: From the Jewish Antiquities of Josephus*, trans. John Gregory (London: Everyman 1998), xiii–xxi.

2. See Tessa Rajak, *Josephus: The Historian and His Society*, 2nd ed. (London: Duckworth, 2002).

3. On doubts about Josephus's trustworthiness as a historian beginning in the nineteenth century, see Andrea Schatz, ed., *Josephus in Modern Jewish Culture* (Leiden: Brill, 2019), and Martin Goodman, *Josephus's "The Jewish War": A Biography* (Princeton: Princeton University Press, 2019); on the discrepancies between Josephus's two accounts of his own career, see Shaye J. D. Cohen, *Josephus in Galilee and Rome: His Vita and Development as a Historian* (Leiden: Brill, 1979).

4. See *AJ* 20.267 (date of completion).

5. See Tamar Landau, *Out-Heroding Herod: Josephus, Rhetoric, and the Herod Narratives* (Leiden: Brill, 2006), 115–85.

6. See Martin Goodman, "Introduction," in *Josephus, The Jewish War*, trans. Martin Hammond (Oxford: Oxford University Press, 2017), xiii–xxxvii.

7. See Landau, *Out-Heroding Herod*, 69–113.

8. See Landau, *Out-Heroding Herod*, 187–202.

9. See Arnaldo Momigliano, "Historicism Revisited," in Arnaldo Momigliano, *Essays in Ancient and Modern Historiography* (Oxford: Blackwell, 1977), 366–67.

10. On Josephus's use of assistants (Joseph, *Ap.* 1. 50) as a major explanation for variant accounts, see Henry St. J. Thackeray, *Josephus, the Man and the Historian* (New York: Jewish Institute of Religion Press, 1929), with critique in R. J. H. Shutt, *Studies in Josephus* (London: SPCK, 1961); on Herod's memoirs, see *AJ* 15.174; on the *History of King Herod* by Ptolemy, see Ammonius, *On the Differences of Synonymous Expressions* , no. 243, in *GLAJJ* 1:356; on Josephus's historical narrative as affected by political changes from 70 to 100 CE, see Seth Schwartz, *Josephus and Judean Politics* (Leiden: Brill, 1990).

FURTHER READING

The magisterial biography of Herod by Abraham Schalit, published in Hebrew in 1960, was translated into German in the 1960s (as *Koenig Herodes: Der Mann und sein Werk* [1969; 2nd ed., with foreword by Daniel R. Schwartz, Berlin and New York: De Gruyter, 2001]). This huge volume (675 pages of text and more than 100 pages of additional material in the second German edition) was the product of great erudition and a lifetime of study of Herod as a successful king, but it is rather dry, and it has not been translated into English.

Very different is the lively biography by Peter Richardson and Amy Marie Fisher (*Herod: King of the Jews and Friend of the Romans* [London: Routledge, 2018]), a much revised second edition of Peter Richardson's book originally published in Columbia, South Carolina, in 1996, which provides a full narrative, with detailed discussions pitched for the most part at a level accessible for general readers. For French readers, Mireille Hadas-Lebel, *Hérode* (Paris: Fayard, 2017), incorporates recent discoveries into a clear and straightforward discussion; for German readers, the biography by Ernst Baltrusch (*Herodes: Koenig im heiligen Land, eine Biographie* [Munich: Beck, 2012]) focuses particularly on Herod in the context of the Hellenistic and Roman world. The thorough study by Adam Kolman Marshak (*The Many Faces of Herod the Great* [Grand Rapids, Mich.: Eerdmans, 2015]) has a similar perspective.

A detailed discussion of many aspects of Herod's world can be found in Samuel Rocca, *Herod's Judaea: A Mediterranean State in the Classical World* (Tübingen: Mohr Siebeck, 2008). The standard history of Jews in this period remains the first volume of the revised English version of Emil Schürer's classic history, published nearly fifty years ago (*The History of the Jewish People in the Age of Jesus Christ*, rev. and ed. Geza Vermes and Fergus Millar, 3 vols. [Edinburgh: T. & T. Clark, 1973–87]).

ACKNOWLEDGMENTS

I AM GRATEFUL to Anita Shapira and Steven Zipperstein for inviting me to write on Herod for Yale University Press's Jewish Lives series. It has been an enjoyable and interesting project which has encouraged me to look much more closely at a period of Jewish history that I have taught to students for over forty years. I am much indebted to many of these students for their queries and suggestions, which have encouraged me to reevaluate the history during this period, as also to my own teachers, Fergus Millar and Geza Vermes.

Writing on this book began in March 2020, and the first draft was produced under the unusual conditions imposed by the coronavirus pandemic, which began in the United Kingdom the previous month. One fortunate effect of the restrictions on movement which kept us both at home during much of the rest of 2020 was that I was able to discuss the book with my wife, Sarah, at an early stage. Her comments on drafts both then and at later stages have had a decisive effect on the final form of the text.

It is a pleasure to thank once again Neelum Ali for heroically typing out the early drafts of the text and notes from my handwriting; Alison Wilkins for producing the maps, family trees, and chronological chart; Cecilia Mackay for sourcing the illustrations; and Susan Laity for her expert and perceptive copyediting.

Kim Czajkowski and Tessa Rajak generously read through an earlier draft of the book and alerted me to omissions and errors of judgment. Any that remain are my responsibility alone.

INDEX

Jewish Lives is a prizewinning series of interpretative biography designed to explore the many facets of Jewish identity. Individual volumes illuminate the imprint of Jewish figures upon literature, religion, philosophy, politics, cultural and economic life, and the arts and sciences. Subjects are paired with authors to elicit lively, deeply informed books that explore the range and depth of the Jewish experience from antiquity to the present.

Jewish Lives is a partnership of Yale University Press and the Leon D. Black Foundation. Ileene Smith is editorial director. Anita Shapira and Steven J. Zipperstein are series editors.

PUBLISHED TITLES INCLUDE:

Rabbi Akiva: Sage of the Talmud, by Barry W. Holtz
Ben-Gurion: Father of Modern Israel, by Anita Shapira
Judah Benjamin: Counselor to the Confederacy, by James Traub
Bernard Berenson: A Life in the Picture Trade, by Rachel Cohen
Irving Berlin: New York Genius, by James Kaplan
Sarah: The Life of Sarah Bernhardt, by Robert Gottlieb
Leonard Bernstein: An American Musician, by Allen Shawn
Hayim Nahman Bialik: Poet of Hebrew, by Avner Holtzman
Léon Blum: Prime Minister, Socialist, Zionist, by Pierre Birnbaum
Louis D. Brandeis: American Prophet, by Jeffrey Rosen
Mel Brooks: Disobedient Jew, by Jeremy Dauber
Martin Buber: A Life of Faith and Dissent, by Paul Mendes-Flohr
David: The Divided Heart, by David Wolpe
Moshe Dayan: Israel's Controversial Hero, by Mordechai Bar-On
Disraeli: The Novel Politician, by David Cesarani
Alfred Dreyfus: The Man at the Center of the Affair, by Maurice Samuels
Einstein: His Space and Times, by Steven Gimbel
Becoming Elijah: Prophet of Transformation, by Daniel Matt
Becoming Freud: The Making of a Psychoanalyst, by Adam Phillips
Betty Friedan: Magnificent Disrupter, by Rachel Shteir
Emma Goldman: Revolution as a Way of Life, by Vivian Gornick
Hank Greenberg: The Hero Who Didn't Want to Be One, by Mark Kurlansky

Peggy Guggenheim: The Shock of the Modern, by Francine Prose
Ben Hecht: Fighting Words, Moving Pictures, by Adina Hoffman
Heinrich Heine: Writing the Revolution, by George Prochnik
Lillian Hellman: An Imperious Life, by Dorothy Gallagher
Herod the Great: Jewish King in a Roman World, by Martin Goodman
Theodor Herzl: The Charismatic Leader, by Derek Penslar
Abraham Joshua Heschel: A Life of Radical Amazement, by Julian Zelizer
Houdini: The Elusive American, by Adam Begley
Jabotinsky: A Life, by Hillel Halkin
Jacob: Unexpected Patriarch, by Yair Zakovitch
Franz Kafka: The Poet of Shame and Guilt, by Saul Friedländer
Rav Kook: Mystic in a Time of Revolution, by Yehudah Mirsky
Stanley Kubrick: American Filmmaker, by David Mikics
Stan Lee: A Life in Comics, by Liel Leibovitz
Primo Levi: The Matter of a Life, by Berel Lang
Maimonides: Faith in Reason, by Alberto Manguel
Groucho Marx: The Comedy of Existence, by Lee Siegel
Karl Marx: Philosophy and Revolution, by Shlomo Avineri
Golda Meir: Israel's Matriarch, by Deborah E. Lipstadt
Menasseh ben Israel: Rabbi of Amsterdam, by Steven Nadler
Moses Mendelssohn: Sage of Modernity, by Shmuel Feiner
Harvey Milk: His Lives and Death, by Lillian Faderman
Arthur Miller: American Witness, by John Lahr
Moses: A Human Life, by Avivah Gottlieb Zornberg
Amos Oz: Writer, Activist, Icon, by Robert Alter
Proust: The Search, by Benjamin Taylor
Yitzhak Rabin: Soldier, Leader, Statesman, by Itamar Rabinovich
Walther Rathenau: Weimar's Fallen Statesman, by Shulamit Volkov
Man Ray: The Artist and His Shadows, by Arthur Lubow

Sidney Reilly: Master Spy, by Benny Morris
Admiral Hyman Rickover: Engineer of Power, by Marc Wortman
Jerome Robbins: A Life in Dance, by Wendy Lesser
Julius Rosenwald: Repairing the World, by Hasia R. Diner
Mark Rothko: Toward the Light in the Chapel, by Annie Cohen-Solal
Ruth: A Migrant's Tale, by Ilana Pardes
Gershom Scholem: Master of the Kabbalah, by David Biale
Bugsy Siegel: The Dark Side of the American Dream,
by Michael Shnayerson
Solomon: The Lure of Wisdom, by Steven Weitzman
Steven Spielberg: A Life in Films, by Molly Haskell
Spinoza: Freedom's Messiah, by Ian Buruma
Alfred Stieglitz: Taking Pictures, Making Painters, by Phyllis Rose
Barbra Streisand: Redefining Beauty, Femininity, and Power,
by Neal Gabler
Henrietta Szold: Hadassah and the Zionist Dream,
by Francine Klagsbrun
Leon Trotsky: A Revolutionary's Life, by Joshua Rubenstein
Warner Bros: The Making of an American Movie Studio,
by David Thomson
Elie Wiesel: Confronting the Silence, by Joseph Berger

FORTHCOMING TITLES INCLUDE:

Abraham, by Anthony Julius
Hannah Arendt, by Masha Gessen
The Ba'al Shem Tov, by Ariel Mayse
Walter Benjamin, by Peter Gordon
Franz Boas, by Noga Arikha
Bob Dylan, by Sasha Frere-Jones
Anne Frank, by Ruth Franklin
George Gershwin, by Gary Giddins

Ruth Bader Ginsburg, by Jeffrey Rosen
Jesus, by Jack Miles
Josephus, by Daniel Boyarin
Louis Kahn, by Gini Alhadeff
Mordecai Kaplan, by Jenna Weissman Joselit
Carole King, by Jane Eisner
Fiorello La Guardia, by Brenda Wineapple
Mahler, by Leon Botstein
Norman Mailer, by David Bromwich
Louis B. Mayer and Irving Thalberg, by Kenneth Turan
Robert Oppenheimer, by David Rieff
Ayn Rand, by Alexandra Popoff
Rebecca, by Judith Shulevitz
Philip Roth, by Steven J. Zipperstein
Edmond de Rothschild, by James McAuley
Jonas Salk, by David Margolick
Rebbe Schneerson, by Ezra Glinter
Stephen Sondheim, by Daniel Okrent
Susan Sontag, by Benjamin Taylor
Gertrude Stein, by Lauren Elkin
Billy Wilder, by Noah Isenberg
Ludwig Wittgenstein, by Anthony Gottlieb